DOWNSIZING

BOOKS BY

BENJAMIN ROBERT SILL, JR.

Inflation – Worse than Vampires, Zombies or the Plague

Inequality- Must There be Blood in the Streets

Government Economics Gone Wild

Downsizing- Efficiency or Greed?

Observations

DOWNSIZING

Efficiency or Greed?

Professor Benjamin Robert Sill, Jr. retired

To my beloved wife, Yasmin, and my wonderful
children, Brittany and Parker

ABSTRACT

Research on downsizing is done because it is a critical issue with diametrically opposed viewpoints and, as yet, an unresolved question as to its ability to succeed. Or more to the point, succeed for whom. Most researchers do their best to objectively observe the positive versus negative effects on the several effected parties; the corporation, those employees left behind and those made redundant. To a lesser degree there is an effect on the community and the nation's economic well-being itself. In order to deal with any strong viewpoint it is important to secure a solid background in the facts and so this paper reviews the research on these topics and discusses them as to their theoretical implications. More importantly, however, this book concedes a number of contrary viewpoints examined by the research, in order to move forward in a strategic direction rather than fight a battle not in keeping with the ultimate objective of the paper. This is calculated to allow more time to solve what is seen as a perceived dilemma of monumental proportions and spend more time suggesting solutions.

Who's to say we are not allowed to fight or dispute the assumption that "Survival of the fittest is an untouchable given?" Of course Mother Nature can't be toyed with. That is not to say we can't attempt to improve on the situation.

ACKNOWLEDGMENTS

Dr. Tom Verney, Dr. Tony Winters and Dr. Steve Holoviak at Shippensburg University, and, Dr. Karen Frey and Dr. Charles Walton at Gettysburg College, for their kindness, input and support. My DBA teammates for their support, my students for their youthful energies and survey results, my children, Brittany and Parker, for giving me the incentive to want to leave them with a sense of pride and the urge to succeed; and last but most importantly, my loving wife Yasmin, without whose love, devotion, encouragement and optimistic outlook, this effort would not have been possible and I would have become a shell of a man long, long ago.

TABLE OF CONTENTS

CHAPTER 1 INTRODUCTION

Statement of the Problem

There appears to be a strong possibility of the negative macro effects of downsizing offsetting any positive individual effects. That of course, assumes there is any positive micro effect. To continue on our current path of destruction would seem to be leading us to economic ruin- fewer decent well-paying jobs and little manufacturing industry from which to produce in case of the need to protect ourselves. The economic and business community assumes that downsizing is a necessary evil at best; nevertheless, good citizens never stop searching for other avenues to explore and solutions to economic downturns. The only thing in question here might be the time it takes for this to happen.

The spread between the wealthy and the poor is increasingly more like that in a third world country. Graft and corruption in government and business must surely be at an all-time high. Huge disparities exist between the salaries of those at the top and those in the trenches. Has it always been this way? It doesn't matter. That's why we read Charles Dickens; to learn from the past and our mistakes. The spread between Japan's highest paid personnel and the lowest was "only" a factor of 7 or 8 thirty years ago when ours was 20. Today ours in around 350. Are we sure that we can't balance the budget by simply capping our talent industries at a reasonable figure (say $300,000 a year) and apply the rest to the deficit. Yeah, it would probably take a long time- like a year or two.

Yet we continue to be irresponsible and get away with it. Even as the dollar lost 75% of its value against the Japanese Yen and German Mark over the last twenty five years. Figures state our living standard kept rising and unemployment remained trivial by comparison to the past. The question is, was the increase evenly distributed and are the unemployment figures accurate? Statistics issued by the Economic Policy Institute in a paper entitled "The State of Working America 1994-95" do not agree with the above statement concerning rising living standards (Mishel & Bernstein, 1994). There are a number of unaccounted for White Anglo-Saxon Protestant Males over 40 who may not feel it's trivial. In the last 12 years, white males with no more than high school educations have actually lost over 17% of their annual income. In our quest to right the injustices forced upon the black ghetto children we have overlooked the white underclass. The report also challenges the belief that the college educated are immune from wage stagnation. Although not as badly as the group above, the real wages of the college educated group have declined nearly 3%. (Mishel & Bernstein) In England there are able bodied men who have never worked a day in their lives. That may sound great but living a hopeless, unemployed existence takes its toll. Then the sickening lack of hope, depression and total disregard for life makes every day a drudgery not fit for upright man. It's time we learned from those who have gone before us. We should be concerned because it may be our plight as well. It is also time to do something for those individuals. That something is to provide education and meaningful employment for them. To be sure, technology is how we have improved our production over the last 20-30 years, not any increased labor effort. Also, there will be individuals who cannot be trained on the new technology. That does not mean they are to be cast aside or thrown away. I cannot believe that is the direction society is headed, but to date we have not utilized the spare time created by technology in ways to benefit all of us. It appears that technology has made some of us work that much harder while others of us have been put out of work. Education alone will not solve our problems either. To be fair, we should also mention those under-employed in the Barrios of Mexico, Venezuela and the newly freed of Eastern Europe. There are lessons here as well, for we can observe the new class of brash capitalists with their cellular telephones, sleek Mercedes and disregard for their fellow man. Greed and corruption is more naked there but I doubt there's much difference in the corporate boardrooms of America. Let's face it, take away the sugar coating and the basic premise of Capitalism is principled in greed and avarice. Competition means destroying your enemy. Capitalism takes time to implement and then more time to weed out the carpetbaggers. Communism at least gave people security. It still appears that a little of both would be in order if we are to give incentive yet care for those unable to cope. To observe examples of this, one needs only to go east to China and South Korea. China makes no excuses for its measured and scrutinized modernization under semi-capitalistic guidelines. South Korea though, has fooled the world for thirty years, throughout their economic miracle of growing 1,500% and having per capita income grow eightfold since 1960. (International Monetary Fund, 2014)Most westerners are unaware that during that time banks were nationalized, detailed 5 year plans were numerous, and legal systems were lubricated by coerced bribes, extralegal payments and reciprocal favors. Theirs has not been an egalitarian society. In many ways its high leverage, cheap government credits, micro-managing technocrats, office corps ministries and incestuous (International Monetary Fund)governmental/corporation/trading company relationship was a poor man's version of the Japanese model. The difference is, the Japanese model worked wonders- at least for a while. Only now is Japan going through a restructuring. But even if some changes have to be made, they both have had a long prosperous upswing during a time when the United States and its system has experienced a rough road. In a recent article in the Washington Post we learn that, once again, the Japanese, facing almost the same problems economically as the United States, have come up with a humanitarian solution. Instead of dumping fired middle managers on the street they "farm them out" to wherever they are needed and make up any wage difference. There is also no longer guaranteed advancement in position or income. But the gentle means of incorporating this strategy is to give an upcoming manager ten years to prove herself/himself after which, if they don't succeed they will be relegated to another path with a slight reduction in pay. Although I like this methodology I admit it has not had time to be proven viable.

Milton Friedman declared over forty years ago in his youth that we are depression proof because we cannot have a major deflation until we have major inflation on a scale far, far greater than that which we had in the 1970's (Friedman, 1971). It's still bothersome that those who indicate we are not going to come crashing down in flames seem to say only that we will continue to be consumed in a slow moving cancerous way. It looks like a lot of downside exposure and very little upside possibilities. We are barely out of the last recession (many are still in it) and the brakes are being applied. For all of the Fed's tweaking and fine-tuning of the economy we still do not seem to know what it takes to have sustained growth without accelerating inflation.

It is a little hard to sympathize with Management's plight with multi-million dollar salaries and bonuses- as opposed to the 55 year old who gets fired or laid off after working for the company all his/her life only to be let go without a pension or severance. Yes, managers are mean, not even efficient, over paid and the work environment is uneasy. However, workers are also overpaid (some), lazy, talk too much on the phone, pensions are too onerous, (my 403B contribution was 10%) and the quality of work is poor. Remember, Capitalism is a Predatory Market environment by definition. There seems to be a tradeoff between productivity and happiness.

What have we improved? Technology-so what? Automobile transmissions are now electric- how are they better- less expensive-no, last longer-no, more expensive to repair-yes, work better-how? Do we have more leisure-no, we work harder, 2 people in a family now work, and the divorce rate is up. We seem to be going the wrong way regarding the poor and their standards. We need to cut out overtime and give to others- makes for no family life anyway for those who have to do the work.

The days of Grandpa's well paid manufacturing union job are gone. In its place are low paying fast food or service jobs, many without benefits and not full time.

Downsizing defined

One of the main culprits for this phenomenon is

downsizing. Defined many different ways and sugar-coated to suit the purpose, the simple matter is, you get sacked. You lost your job. Whether it was done because the company was no longer competitive or simply because a CEO wanted to look good short term doesn't really matter to the person let go.

My objective in writing this book is to cure this festering misconception. Failing that, I will at least attempt to condense the information, outline the fallacies and put forth suggestions for a better system.

Motivation for this book is wanting to see my children experience a better life and have a more level playing field than we have currently. Considering human nature being what it is, that's is a near impossible task. But, it must be tried.

In attempting to understand the reasoning behind downsizing, we try to learn from the past whenever possible. Mortimer Lipsky's biography of Alfred Nobel (1966) may shed some light. Like dynamite, downsizing seems to be, on the surface, some sort of business, if not strictly technical, improvement. But its very nature is destructive. Lipsky quoted Nobel as saying "this is the greatest problem confronting mankind -the problem of survival or extinction". (Lipsky, 1966) No doubt any destructive force; that is, dynamite, the Atomic bomb, etc., is a problem. The reason for dwelling on Nobel and peace so much is that there is a strong tie between his wishes to destroy others and his quest for economic well-being. Having people just survive without dignity, without peace and with unrest is a major subset of that problem. The quest for peace was Nobel's stated purpose and ended up causing destruction on a great level. The quest for a more efficient and leaner company through Downsizing may end up causing more heartache. Just as the high explosives (Dynamite) that Nobel had hoped would eliminate conflict did not work, the results of downsizing seem to have not only not solved the problem but created a new monster. There is some hope for modest men to hold out a low opinion of government and man and yet still contribute to society and perhaps even save them from their own destructiveness as Nobel thought.

Nobel felt his invention (dynamite) would make people hesitate to begin a war if they thought it would mean mass destruction for both sides. He was obviously wrong. The Atomic bomb was thought to have that same affect. Nobel in 1895 was quoted by M.E. Schneider Bonnet as having said "My hope was that the terrible effect of dynamite would keep men from war. But now I see to my utter dismay that my life's work amounts to nothing. High explosives will not deter men from war. Nobody will profit from my invention except manufacturers of the war materials, some generals, some diplomats and the arms merchants. Mankind on the whole will be the loser." (Lipsky, 1966)

Peace and prosperity do not bode well on an empty stomach and to get the stomach full one must have a job.

Assumptions

The following Assumptions have been make:
that any sample group used is representative, that downsizing will continue for at least 10-20 years, that no equaling out of foreign demand and foreign competition will occur in next 20 years, and that there will be no suitable solution to the problem if allowed to take its natural course.

When a company falls on difficult times, one of the things that seems to happen is they reduce their staff and workers. The remaining workers must find ways to continue to do a good job or risk that their job would be eliminated as well. Wall Street and the media normally congratulate the CEO for making this type of "tough decision", and the board of directors gives upper corporate management big bonuses. Even though that entire system has huge flaws, it seems like we should hold our government accountable and dump some of them in the same manner.

Therefore: why not consider ways to level the playing field? We could start by reducing the House of Representatives from the current 435 members to 218 members. Then reduce Senate members from 100 to 50(one per State) and finally, reduce their remaining staff by 25%. This could be accomplished over 8 years (two steps/two elections). Yearly gains would include: Around $50 million for elimination of base pay for congress. These number only get better as the years go on. $500 million for elimination of their staff. Over $100 million for the reduction in remaining staff by 25%. $7,500,000,000 reduction in pork barrel earmarks each year. (Those members whose jobs are gone. Current estimates for total government pork earmarks are at $15 Billion/yr.). The remaining representatives would need to work smarter and improve inefficiencies. It might even be in their best interests to work together for the good of our country! (Walther, 2009)

We may also expect that smaller committees might lead to a more efficient resolution of issues as well. It might even be easier to keep track of what your representative in government is doing. Regarding efficiency, Congress has more tools available to do

their jobs than it had back in 1911 when the current
number of representatives was established.
(Telephones, computers, cell phones to name a few).
Supporting these suggestions is the fact that Congress
does not hesitate to head home for extended weekends,
holidays and recesses, when what the nation needs is a
real fix for economic problems. Also, an incalculable
amount of time is spent on the campaign trail. These
facts alone support a reduction in senators and
congress.

      Yes, this is just a drop in the bucket and likely
won't be implemented. But there is always hope and
every little bit helps. Plus it sets an example for others
to follow.

      This book does some addressing of inequities in
the workplace in a capitalistic system (in corporate
America) with suggested solutions. Evidence suggests
that these inequities are intertwined closely with
downsizing. The book attempts to reconcile the profit
motive with the advancement of human dignity in an
effort to have both at the same time. Efforts will be
made to consider ways that the technological advances
to date can assist humane efforts catch up. Today's
technology should be providing far more help in
gaining knowledge and implementing improvements to
prevent downsizing or enhance the quality of life for
those downsized. Constructing inflexible downsizing
programs is usually painful because of vested interests
of those at the top; therefore there should be more
flexible options. Certainly we are better off than we
were 800 years ago when no one could read and lived
in mud huts; and equally so compared to the world of
Charles Dickens one hundred years ago. However, the
comparison begins to take on a different tone when

comparing to only forty or so years ago. The current situation begs the question "what is the purpose of technology if not to improve the social well-being of mankind as a whole, not just those at the top. As always, the dilemma is to evolve from being naive as to what would be nice, to what can be done.

From a short term perspective we should focus on ways to maintain a corporation's competitive edge and yet provide alternatives to downsizing existing work forces. Although everyone has unsubstantiated opinions as to why this problem (downsizing) exists, it is important to remain unbiased as the research is pursued. Many issues or problems are unknown at this time and it is important to be flexible as change may occur as knowledge and understanding of the problem is furthered.

Scope

The purpose of any dissertation is; to gain an understanding of something (why organizations downsize and the adverse effects on employees), develop a skill, understand key strategies, analyze needs, of employees who are downsized or employers who are downsizing, influence/persuade (employers to consider alternatives to downsizing), identify benefits (to corporations if they do not downsize), review solutions and test approaches chosen.

It may be a stretch but HR Development may be one of those few wedges between reasonable worker pay, benefits and working conditions, and total management running wild.

Initially came the gathering of theories of respected writers, economists, college professors and consultants, which I then interpreted and analyzed. Finally, I drew conclusions and hopefully offer suggestions for solutions to the problems I have researched.

One must be certain to ask very early on: if the proposal can be accomplished, is the scope correct, is the methodology feasible, can data be collected and is the population receptive to investigation. In broad brush answer at this point I can say yes, I have considered these questions. I have high goals which haven't been reached to date and may never be accomplished but civilized people have been working on the improvement of mankind for centuries, so a little longer won't hurt. Even an incomplete theory analysis of this nature, if given to any new contribution of knowledge will be considered successful.

In addition to the trite phrase "those who can, do; those who can't, teach", scholars are always in trouble due to the fact that businesses don't want to hear about taking care of their people- unless there is something in it for them. In spite of the revolving door between Wall Street and the government, scholars are often times politically unpopular as well. Socrates was condemned to drink hemlock because he did not give sufficient respect to the then current Athenian divinities. Galileo was forced to recant his beliefs that the earth revolved around the sun. An interesting portion of the research for this book was to analyze whether or not any corrective effort needs to be global; is it necessary that many, if not all, nations participate in any effort to achieve truly full and fulfilling employment? Otherwise the United States (or any nation) must operate in isolation, which has many a naysayer as to its feasibility. This book must question and analyze from different sources in different countries in order to see the complete picture and determine the overlapping subsets that will work in each.

Both data collection schemes are used because Secondary Research is faster than Primary and less expensive, even though the data may be obsolete or incorrect. That's acceptable because part of my purpose it to determine if they are incorrect prior to offering corrections.

Initial understanding of what has already occurred requires that I interpret and understand those theories before moving ahead. I may even provide new theoretical contributions.

Previous efforts to somehow control and redistribute wealth have always worked well in theory and fallen apart in practice. Thus, an analysis of the reasons are paramount.

To obtain breadth of knowledge, every effort was made to acquire and integrate theory based knowledge by reading originals, not the opinions of others. I defined the knowledge area and its seminal thinkers, their basic assumptions, evidence, reasons, conclusions, and implications. I compared them to each other and then blended them together. In reading the work of others I adhered to certain standards, such as: how well did they handle the research question as to its relevance and limitations. Did their methodology seem appropriate? No matter what I just said above regarding opinions of others, human nature being what it is, there is a lot of that going around. Therefore, I evaluated the methodology and the conceptual framework. I looked for weaknesses and oversights in the theories and tried to put into personal value systems and culture context in some cases.

The final stage was to apply what I learned by preparing recommendations and designing a workable system focusing on curing some of the unhappiness downsizing has caused while still allowing corporation to remain competitive.

Downsizing and unemployment are certainly not new. So, how come it has been allowed to continue? Is it really necessary for civilizations to rip each other apart?

Aim

The aim of any book on this subject should be to investigate the implications of downsizing; to acquire knowledge as to the success or failure if downsizing has occurred already- in order to feel secure that the technique works for all concerned, or develop suggested solutions if perceived that it did not. If downsizing has not been implemented in the organization yet, then there should be a framework for innovation that will render the effort needless.

The objective of this dissertation is the enhancement of knowledge and understanding of the implications of downsizing for all parties as well as potential solutions for those implications. Specific competences within the knowledge framework to be developed are: information gathering, understanding, conceptualizing and analyzing. This in order to provide a complete service to any future clients, prescribe treatments or assist them in an ongoing manner and to research existing knowledge base for course or lecture material on downsizing in order to teach awareness of the problem or consult.

My goals and objectives will be accomplished by investigating and analyzing the effects of downsizing in organizations. All of this knowledge will assist my consultancy in its effort to analyze how corporations deal with downsizing and the implications for individuals and organizations in maintaining a competitive advantage. The knowledge gained, because it comes from addressing a specific and as yet unsolved problem, and because I have not addressed the problem previously, is newly contributed and not replicating previous knowledge gained. I must analyze what the corporations, employees still working, and employees made redundant, want/need. I need to gain an understanding of a corporation's perceived necessity for downsizing in order to determine what it is they really wish to do-get rid of people or improve their bottom line. With the newly acquired knowledge in hand I can then suggest to them new key strategic alternatives to downsizing I have developed, or existing alternatives that may accomplish their goal better without having to downsize. Finally the results must be put in a form that will appeal to all parties concerned.

Contribution will occur by developing consulting skills through the design and developing of appropriate and relevant materials, such as books written, working manuals and any lecture notes developed. All of this will question, investigate and analyze a corporation to determine causes for potential downsizing, then seek ways to avoid downsizing by offering alternative solutions.

Clients, Guinea pigs or worthy opponents will be corporations now downsizing, or who believe they may have to, who are seeking a better method, and are willing to utilize my services as a consultant. There may be an attempt to introduce my work into academic curriculum also, and to groups of out of work executives. I may even volunteer some of my services "Pro Bono" in order to move the process along.

My aim is also to develop knowledge and awareness in others through the implementation of innovative teaching techniques as well as the written word I have generated on downsizing, perhaps combining it with the other critical issues such as inflation and inequality. I would like to develop international experience in teaching and lecturing so as to broaden my dissemination of knowledge, using unique and invigorating techniques to convince up and coming economists to help correct the problems we have today.

I expect many of my goals to go unanswered. Those common threads here again woven of "human nature needs a lot of help, the rich get richer and greed is good" have been around for thousands of years so I am not naive enough to expect instant results. Plus being older, having no podium and few contacts isn't going to help the cause. There is the strong likelihood that most of the proper solutions determined here will fall on deaf ears anyway All I can do is try through any vehicle to use my information gained on downsizing to affect some change.

The reasons for research are clear. Like Maslow, one looks to address needs on a number of different levels. Perhaps to set an example for one's children as a proponent of higher education and find solutions to what are perceived as critical problems regarding our current business climate as it pertains to the loss of jobs and family life as we know it in the United States and Western Europe. The subject needs further research and solutions need to be found to increase the socioeconomic well-being of our society. As to the latter, we need to add value to the workplace in the form of profits and human experience, motivate employers to seek solutions other than downsizing and make it easy to implement those options. Ideally the intent is to construct early-on preventative measures.

A solid educational base from which to build a consultancy is necessary. The objective is to acquire knowledge on how to use technology to help and not merely replace human beings or sacrifice our human emotional needs and dignity. The approach to be taken might be a literature search, interviews, or consulting assignments. The alternatives being suggested by the Plan may also help in long term goals to serve better those who have already been made redundant by getting then rehired due to implementation of strategic alternatives; putting them right back into the corporation as a consultant with their newly acquired consulting techniques or simply training them in more salable skills with which to go forward. This module may be distributed to reemployment agencies as well.

Relevance

The importance of this book is that since 1960 or so the United States -and some other developed countries- have experienced a decline in the standard of living of its middle class. If left unchecked, the slide will be finite, we just don't know how long it will take to self-destruct. A re-thinking of our values and business structuring might be in order if we are to continue as a viable society.

Research of any decent kind should bring forth questions. Following are some of those:

What are the key issues and concerns surrounding downsizing and for whom? How to pay the bills, health care, self-image. These are addressed only in order to determine how best to create a better system.

What is or should be the role of government on employment practices?

How can government, corporations and employees better work together?

Is there an opportunity for executive type outplacement firms to work with hourly workers?

Is Lifetime "Full employment" a myth? Research and project the number of workers who will be permanent full time in so many years.

What can management do to prevent downsizing and why should they?

How can they better manage the rightsizing initiative?

How can companies have a more humanistic approach to rightsizing? Should they?

What is the role or responsibility of the company in the career of its employees, or what should it be?

What is the role of the employee for managing his/her career?

Most everyone agrees that Strategy and planning are an absolute must if you must downsize. We just need more. In fact, the hope is that if more is done the downsizing may be avoided.

Supposedly a good nonfiction economics book is focused and non-biased. You haven't read any financial newsletters then. Judging impartially is quite a skill- unavailable to most of us. Either the facts uncovered, basic leanings, or a thirst for knowledge prevents it.

How can downsizing be made to either go away or be much less harmful to those made redundant?

In order to better understand the actions of corporate executives and perhaps why our government does what it does to support them, it would be useful to have a basic understanding of the economics involved. It would probably be helpful to have a working knowledge of theories such as Keynesian and Monetarists economics.

CHAPTER 2 LITERATURE REVIEW

Historical

The discipline under investigation is downsizing and the purpose is to examine previous knowledge acquired in order to arrive at a narrower scope.

Since the dawn of time there has always been some form of retooling and readjustment to meet then current situations-cave men etc. In many ways, society has been the beneficiary of significant improvement over the last ten thousand years. That the last 40 or 50 years have contributed their fair share is in doubt. Downsizing has occurred in almost all U.S. industries. Almost 40 million jobs have been eliminated from 1982 through 2003. In December 1999, Eastman Kodak laid off 1,150 employees (Brister, 2000), a move that was part of an overall downsizing project to decrease global staffing by 20,000 (Elkin, 1998). Looking back from 2013 that doesn't appear to have been the smartest move for Kodak based on the fact that they are a shell of a company today. Though certainly not their only misstep, the Downsizing move was obviously not the move they should have made. During 2001 to 2002, various companies resorted to mass layoffs, including Boeing Company. Boeing was formed from the merger of British Aerospace with Marconi Electronic Systems, which also eliminated jobs. Isuzu Motors, IBM , VF Corporation, and Sears, all eliminated thousands of positions (Florian, 2001); and American Airlines, American Eagle, and TWA slashed

19,000 jobs collectively (Glynn, 2002). By the end of 2001, Fortune 500 companies reported cumulative layoffs of 1,040,466 positions. By April 2002, more layoffs were reported, adding 255,260 lost jobs to the already staggering numbers (Florian). During most of the twentieth century, U.S. firms were focused primarily on growth. From the 1950s to the 1980s, the large multi-divisional organization was a common design (Heenan, 1989). The expression is: "Those who fail to observe history are doomed to repeat it." Or, the definition of insanity is "doing the same thing over and over again, hoping for a different result." (Mathews & Duran., 1999) examined the impact of downsizing on a single hospital, which underwent five separate staff reductions between 1994 and 1998. The purpose behind each reduction was to decrease costs, and each reduction targeted different staffing levels (e.g., upper management, middle management, product line staff, etc.). The study found that although costs decreased, the decrease did not meet the expected rate. Furthermore, Mathews and Duran observed that productivity increased following the early staff cuts of 1994 and 1995, but productivity was unaffected following latter cuts. (Mathews & Duran.)The outcomes experienced by this hospital may or may not be experienced by other facilities.

Numerous studies admit that limited empirical data exists and there is no clear cut evidence to vindicate the practice, suggesting that the issue has not been resolved adequately and leaving the door open for further research on the validity of the technique. To refocus attention toward the anticipated goal, downsizing is often called different names such as productivity improvement, right sizing, cost reduction (Cash, 1993), growth in reverse (Cascio W. , 1995), restructuring, or re-engineering, to name a few (see Cameron 1994 for an exhaustive list). Downsizing is defined as a reduction in personnel through position elimination (Cascio W. , 1993)

Relevance

The economic and business community assumes that downsizing is a necessary evil at best; nevertheless, good citizens never stop searching for other avenues to explore and solutions to economic downturns.

Anyone with the least bit of compassion would or should be motivated to learn as much as they can regarding such unhappiness brought about for so many people. How would Churchill say it? "Never have so few wrought so much misery on so many".

It is probably fair to state that much of the information and determinations arrived at by researchers are capricious, self-serving, biased and egregious. That because they are often harmful to the average person. On occasion the results are probably due to methodological differences. That's being generous to a fault. It does however, require us to examine these different methodologies. Although misinformation and misinterpretation could be due to bad/selective memory, it is likely that significant research is nothing more than biased guessing. Not only has that but, in some circumstances, people tended to conform to the opinions of others. This is true for both the downsizing process and for the research process.

Nevertheless, no matter what the flaws in the research process, since this phenomena is so wide spread and affects so many workers and families, the relevance is unquestionable.

This book examines the various players in this melodrama- the corporate vultures, the downsized and those left behind. Since focus is always an issue the scope will narrow ultimately to those left go- the real sufferers.

The scope of the book begins in a broad enough manner to ensure relevant material is covered and narrows gradually in order to focus and do a credible job on one of the particular aspects of the technique. All of the publications reviewed are peer reviewed academic journals. They have been critically analyzed to determine if they are unbiased and relevant to a narrower segment suitable for dissertation. Some are not relevant but are included only as a backdrop to the overall scenario. Some are biased.

Problems

This problem of using downsizing as a means of eliminating workers is immense, effecting millions of people and the challenges are overwhelming. As always, baby steps begin any process. To solve problems you need to understand the problem as well as the significance of the problem – in order to form a strategy. (Maybe you can merely see possible ways to resolve problems by observing other people's approaches.) The recent rather steep recession is reason enough to justify further research on downsizing. The paper reviews the development of research in downsizing and discusses a few key papers by describing its methods and key findings, then identifies weaknesses in the method and/or limitations in the findings. Finally I discuss how the next researchers might try to address these problems.

Downsizing has been a managerial practice for the past three decades. One ostensible reason to do so is to make an organizational entity more competitive compared to its rivals (Kets de Vries & Balazs, 1997). While some empirical evidence suggests that downsizing announcements have resulted in positive short-term stock market reactions (Cascio W. F., 2002), the ability of downsizing to generate positive, sustained financial and organizational improvements remains questionable (Gandolfi F. , 2008).

Definition

(Cameron K. , 1994) defines Downsizing as "a set of activities, undertaken on the part of the management of an organization and designed to improve organizational efficiency, productivity, and/or competitiveness" (p 192). (Cascio W. , 1993) claims that downsizing is essentially "the planned eliminations of positions or jobs" (p 95). In other words, the purpose of downsizing is not to increase organizational performance, but to cut workforce levels. Downsizing is not to be equated with employee layoffs, which is solely concerned with the individual; rather, downsizing is a broad concept covering micro, organizational, industry, and global levels (Pinsonneault & Kraemer, 2002). Employee layoffs are an operational mechanism used to implement a downsizing endeavor (Cameron, Freeman, & Mishra, Organizational downsizing, 1993), while downsizing *per se* can be seen as a strategic intent, also known as rightsizing (Hitt, Freeman, & And Harrison, 2001)

A precise conceptual understanding is required to distinguish downsizing from organizational decline and other related concepts, and to adopt a cumulative approach to the study of downsizing. Four attributes of downsizing were identified by different authors: First, downsizing is an intentional set of activities that strongly implies organizational action (Cameron K. , 1994). No kidding. Why bother to make such an obvious statement. Second, downsizing frequently involves a reduction in the number of employees (Cascio W. F., 2002). Really? Frequently? When wouldn't it entail that? Third, downsizing concentrates on improving the efficiency of a firm in order to contain or decrease costs, to enhance revenues, or to increase competitiveness (Gandolfi F. , 2008). Fourth, downsizing inevitably influences work processes and leads to work redesign (Cameron K. , 1994). Downsizing represents a reactive/defensive, or proactive/ anticipatory, strategy that inexorably impacts an organization's size, costs, work processes, shape, and culture (Cameron K. , 1994). While a single definition of downsizing does not exist, it is clear that downsizing reduces the size of a firm, frequently resulting in job losses and retrenchments (Gandolfi F. , 2006). The key issues are whether to implement downsizing, how to implement it, and its effects on the entity.

Should we or should we not implement downsizing? Downsizing is a multifaceted phenomenon. Conceptualizing the reasons for it is problematic and complex. While various driving forces have been identified, no single cause can account for the pervasiveness of the phenomenon. (Luthans & Sommer, 1999) They postulate that global competition, technological innovation, increased customer influence, macroeconomic factors, and pressures from rival firms constitute the main driving forces. There is an acknowledgment that the adoption of downsizing can be linked to corporate mismanagement and strategic errors (Kets de Vries & Balazs, 1997)

If we do so, how do we implement downsizing? Studies concerned with how an organization implements downsizing are frequently based on a theoretical model of downsizing approaches or a discussion of "best practice" (Cascio W. F., 2002). Cameron et al (1993) identified three forms of downsizing. The three have been referred to as the downsizing implementation strategies – workforce reduction, organization design, and systemic strategies. The workforce reduction strategy concentrates on the elimination of headcount through activities such as layoffs, retrenchments, and buyout packages. The organization redesign strategy focuses on eliminating work, including abolishing functions, groups, divisions, and products, rather than reducing the number of employees (Luthans & Sommer, 1999) The systemic strategy focuses on changing the firm's intrinsic culture and the attitudes and values of its workforce, and is considered a way of life (Gandolfi & Oster, 2009).

In the past, downsizing was generally a last resort and was a result of strategic planning. This paper provides a review of literature on the topic written from the early 1980's through 2016. In some cases earlier references are found within the reviewed papers. Findings are generally inconsistent, with strong opinions on both sides, sometimes biased and often inconclusive. As is generally the case with human beings, it appears to depend on which side of the practice you are on and whether the effects are positive or negative for you. There does appear, however, to be a significant body of evidence that there is no long term financial gain to be had by the practice; this being one of the most damning arguments advanced by the opponents of the practice since this would seem to have been the primary purpose for the practice. The trend has only been exacerbated since 1995 and the continued use of downsizing as a strategy makes it worthy of a study.

Downsizing may actually help some corporations. But at what cost to others? Looks more like the overall destruction of human lives during a sometimes extended (20 years) period in order to justify the end result of profits for the company. The pendulum is swinging ever so slightly against the practice of downsizing now that the economy is doing poorly. That slight swing is barely perceptible. Just more cheap talk. It makes it easier to claim the existing techniques are perhaps the culprits causing the downturn in the economy. In other words, just when things are getting a little tough, you lose your job. How can that help the overall economy? If you are of the belief that we are a consumer oriented economy and need to spend out way out of trouble, then why take away your spending vehicles? Again, further research is needed on whether or not there is merit to that kind of logic.

A unique subset of this downsizing phenomenon centers on the process when corporations merge. (Bazzoli, LoSasso, Arnould, & Shalowitz, 2002) examined mergers occurring between 1989 and 1996. The results of this study showed that substantial reductions in part-time and full-time staff occurred after a merger. The further research would have to study what benefits accrue to whom and at whose expense? Does the one offset the other? Economic data as of 2013 indicate that fewer and fewer people control more and more of the money (Bureau of Labor Statistics, U.S. Department of Labor, 2015)

Extended mass layoffs

Bruce Bergman's article by that name starts out stating

that New York City has the largest metropolitan workforce in the nation. That's a safe assumption. For the largest metropolitan area in our country, what else would you expect? (Bergman, 2008)That alone would be reason enough for it to not be transferrable information.

According to the BLS (Federal Bureau of Labor Statistics), the layoff activity in New York City was "somewhat elevated in the years that followed the 2001 recession; a rising level of job cuts due to contractual turnover among growth industries helped transform the mass layoff experience in the metropolitan area." This entire line of information is so specific as to be utterly worthless. Due to the 911 disaster, which hopefully was a one off event, any information derived during the time period between 2001 and around 2006 should be rendered not relevant to generalizing for academic purposes. (Bergman, 2008)

If this is an example of the work produced by some, or many, of our academics, I can understand the animosity and total lack of respect for our profession. Bear in mind, this is only one of many that I question for its usefulness. This was approximately a 25 page paper that I can sum up in about 3 pages. Seriously, these people need to get a job! Preferably at a canning factory somewhere.

It is likely that after 911 people were afraid of the City, so fewer contracts were let, therefore, fewer jobs were available. The author goes on to say that "Viewed over the longer period of 11 years for which comparable data are available, extended mass layoff actions caused hundreds of thousands of New York area employees to be involuntarily separated from their workplaces. (Bergman, 2008) This is a convoluted way of saying "Fired". Plus, isn't that statement self-evident? A question that arises, then, is, was the New York area different in terms of layoffs, or did it not differ qualitatively from the Nation in that regard? BLS data indicated that it did deviate. While the nation began improving after 2001, NY did not. (Bergman) So, was there any reason for the deviation other than the terrorist attacks? It might be helpful in order to prevent future layoffs to know the previous reasons for them. Permanent work-site closures resulting in internal company restructuring, e.g. all events involving financial difficulty, bankruptcy, ownership change, and reorganization might be addressed in a different fashion than more temporary reasons like slack work or completion of a contract. Seasonal layoffs accounted for 39 percent of the extended layoff actions in the New York metropolitan area during the 11-year period. So what? Incidentally, why do we always have to seasonally adjust? If it's down, it's down. Period. If people aren't working, they aren't working. Do you think they feel any better because it's a tough season to get a job? "Involuntarily separated". What the hay? Say fired- that's what you mean. If you're intellectually challenged, you're stupid! What should be of concern would the fact that these layoffs more than doubled over a 10 year period. And that from 2006-2011, the recession was a jobless one, or nearly so. That's a real worry. Of interest but not earth shaking, would be the comparison of contract completion versus major job cuts. Permanent work-site closings in New York City were a factor 45% of the time that layoffs occurred. (Bergman) Fairly significant. Historically, economic downturns result in layoffs. What is far more worrying is that the New York experience indicates that layoffs might still increase in good times as well. Why? Well, because of the global competitiveness and availability of less expensive labor elsewhere. Theoretically, where there are more cheap workers, there should also be more consumers for everyone's product. Somehow that either isn't the case, or there is a long lag between the two. As an aside, a bright spot for New York City was the construction trade, which was the recipient of numerous contracts in lower Manhattan after the terrorist attacks. The opposite is true during most recessions everywhere, however, because downturns affect real estate heavily and therefore, construction suffers. This does not reflect an industry in decline, however. Construction is both seasonal and subject to recessions disproportionately. (Bergman)

Manufacturing accounted for a dwindling, but significant, share of national and New York City employment. (Bergman, 2008). Despite evidence that manufacturing is coming back to the United States, there are a lot of empty buildings around. We are simply not a great manufacturing power anymore. Lessons not learned from World War II. Specifically as to New York City, when you bother to think of it at all, it is not thought of as a manufacturing hub, but one of white collar workers, e.g. marketing, advertising, and finance. Part of that is due to the higher price of doing business in New York City. Even these industries are finding it expedient to establish a presence elsewhere for cost reasons. The type of manufacturing had a lot to do with all decreases. Apparel and machinery are no longer produced in any large quantity and neither are chemical and food products. Apparel manufacturing continued to be one of the metropolitan area's primary industries, while maintaining international prominence, even with declining employment. Seems like the two would not go together but that's because the management may be in the city but the work is being done in China or elsewhere. It should also be noted that much of the outsourcing of manufacturing from New York City had already taken place decades ago. Transportation and warehousing is another section of interest. Not so much any difference between New York City and the rest of the nation but is it reducing at all? It would seem that neither is an industry that can be outsourced so both should continue to be necessary and maintain their employment numbers.

The problem with leisure and hospitality, if any, is that it is a parasite industry. Parasitic in the respect that without some other basic industry that provides food, shelter or clothing, it would not exist. Much more research should be done on whether this is a problem and, if so, what to do about it. The counter prevailing theory is that more people have discretionary income and can travel more. One trip to Paris or Rome will verify that this appears true. Yet the basics theory of food, clothing and shelter says it can't be sustained without a host support system. New York City naturally, as a destination city, would have good numbers in these fields in good times and bad. The only drawback to my theory is that figures show the sectors to be only 2% of total employment. I guess it's not Paris or Rome. In the study, indications were that layoffs accounted for 7.5% of totals, which leaves me wondering and questioning.

The communications and information industry plays a larger and larger role in our everyday affairs; consequently, although another parasite industry in my opinion, until deemed unnecessary, the numbers here are of great consequence.

Administrative and waste (lumped together for some ironic reason) were addressed in the study. One cannot argue much with this area of parasites. A necessary evil if you will. At least it is another area that can't be outsourced.

What the study attempted to do, I presume, was try to explain layoff trends in the hope of solving the issue or at least smoothing it out. It did try to provide information in order to aid in the distribution of funds and services. Should we be concerned about the statistical chicanery inherent in extended mass layoff numbers; or should we maybe be figuring out why it happened and a way to decrease that number? Does the layoff phenomena effect all parts of a country equally? Is there any merit in knowing if this is true? Are the reasons different in certain areas?

Organizations have practiced downsizing for the past three decades with the intent of reducing operating costs and making organizations more competitive. Downsizing is supposed to increase overall levels of efficiency and effectiveness, enhance share price valuations, and generate positive long-term improvements. In other words, to make money. Still, downsizing continues to be one of the most misunderstood, ill-conceived, and misinterpreted contemporary business phenomena. Empirical evidence strongly suggests that downsizing produces considerable negative aftereffects. In addition, these tremendous swings or cycles of growth and contraction by downsizing may have negative consequences. Innovation is seen as a key source of a firm's competitive advantage. The question is "Can downsized firms remain innovative? (Gandolfi & Oster, 2009)

Another general theory leading to downsizing is that corporations need to make changes as the environment evolves. The goal is to cut waste; improve profitability (Gertz & Baptista, 1995); and enhance local, national, or international competitiveness (Cameron K. , 1994). So far so good. The external environment (needs for the product produced or service rendered) determines the optimal population of organizations (Hannan & Freeman, 1977) and economic uncertainty makes institutions choose to be proactive and get ahead of the curve (by downsizing) (DiMaggio & Powell, 1983). There are other reasons thought to cause firms to use downsizing, including; to merely survive by preventing closure, to reduce costs for improved performance, to increase efficiency for improved performance, to redirect strategy and growth for survival, and just to make more money to improve already robust results. People are known followers. The herd mentality. Corporate executives are no exception. Because they've read it in a trade journal (or God forbid, simply a news magazine), they assume some correctness in the statements. Therefore, a technique may take on a life of its own after a while and soon it is taken for gospel. How it began or whether there was any validity to the assumptions are often forgotten over time.

There a number of viewpoints regarding the effects of downsizing that one can chose in order to narrow the scope of any discussion. The attempt is made here to sort out as many as possible in an effort to determine which of the viewpoints, in the opinion of the writer, is most worthy of further research.

Beginning as far back in the causal chain as we can go and still stay within the context of downsizing strictly speaking, the first category might be, why initiate the process in the first place? The answer on the surface would appear to be either; to be competitive and stay in business, or merely to enhance the already existing profits.

Regardless of one's personal opinions, much of the discussion is vague and inclusive. In general the magnitude of the downsizing seems to matter It is hard to compare the same company under different circumstances, or different companies under the same scenario. Many of the studies offer very inconsistent commentaries. Seems that management downsizes because they don't have another solution- in spite of evidence that it doesn't work (De Meuse, Bergmann, Vanderheiden, & Roraff, 2004) The manner in which the organization downsizes has been shown to tentatively mitigate the negative outcomes usually associated with workforce reductions. The findings of the Rondeau and Wagar study suggest that the size of the reductions was less significant than the manner in which the firm dealt with employees during the process. In other words, those firms that considered their employees in the process (e.g., providing long periods of notification, allowing employee input) were able to decrease negative outcomes such as dissatisfaction. (Rondeau & Wagar, 2001)

In Moore's study to learn nurses' reactions to the restructuring process and to assess the impact of restructuring on nurses' well-being suggests that the level of restructuring has a significant effect on the level of nurse stress and burnout. The findings of these quantitative studies suggest that organizations do not always achieve the anticipated outcomes following staff and service reductions. (Moore K. A., 2001). However, the number of empirical studies is small. The ones to suffer may be the patients from the increased nurses' workloads, non-patient responsibilities and a deteriorating work environment. (Aiken, Clarke, & Sloane, 2001). Downsizing affected nurses' satisfaction with career future, hospital identification, supervision, and coworkers. (Armstrong-Strassen, Cameron, & Horsburgh, 1996) In their 2001 follow-up they suggest that nurses transferred to other units were generally less satisfied in their position than the non-transferred nurses, and felt there was a lack of support at the new position (Armstrong-Strassen, Cameron, & Horsburgh, 2001). The size of workforce reductions in Canadian acute and chronic care facilities is less significant than the manner in which workforce restructuring is carried out. Their study also observes that a proactive approach mitigates loss of organizational identity, job dissatisfaction, and efficiency (Rondeau & Wagar, 2001).The study also indicates a strong, negative relationship between employee satisfaction and workforce reduction and suggests that downsizing may be the cause of increased grievances and higher absenteeism. The promises of healthcare facility restructuring do not necessarily translate into improved performance and re-engineering should be part of a long term strategic plan. (Walston, Urden, & Sullivan, 2001)

Downsizing's consequences are commonly divided into financial, organizational, and human effects (Gandolfi F. , 2006). Sadly, the picture of reported financial effects following downsizing is a bleak one (Gandolfi F. , 2008). A multitude of studies has demonstrated that while some firms have reported financial improvements from downsizing, the vast majority of downsized organizations have failed to reap the anticipated improved levels of efficiency, productivity, profitability, and competitiveness (Cascio

W. , 1995). The adoption of downsizing is not only expected to generate financial benefits through a direct increase in shareholder value, but to produce organizational benefits, including lower overheads, less bureaucracy, smoother communications, faster decision-making, and increased levels of employee productivity (Burke & Cooper, 2000). The majority of findings suggests that the adoption of downsizing often falls short of the objectives (Cascio W. F., 2002).

The human costs of downsizing are described as far-reaching (Burke & Greenglass, 2000). The change management literature suggests that three types of people are impacted by downsizing – executioners, victims, and survivors, hence my breakdown in this paper. By definition, an executioner (Burke R. J., 2001) is an individual entrusted with the conduct of downsizing, a victim is a person who is downsized out of a job involuntarily (Allen, Freeman, Russell, Reizenstein, & Rentz, 2001), while a survivor remains with the firm after a downsizing activity (Allen, Freeman, Russell, Reizenstein, & Rentz). Again for emphasis, management, those left behind and those let go. Initially way back in the early 1980s emphasis was on the victims but in the 1990s more focus began to include the survivors. Some studies indicated that victims were doing just fine because they often receive generous outplacement services and financially attractive packages (Allen, Freeman, Russell, Reizenstein, & Rentz), whereas survivors tend to receive very little if any support (Allen, Freeman, Russell, Reizenstein, & Rentz). Let um eat cake, huh, Marie? Do you really think the amount of severance and a little help with a resume makes up for losing one's livelihood?

Positives for Companies

The underlying assumption is that downsizing is designed to increase efficiency, productivity and competitiveness. It is critical that we understand that it doesn't necessarily succeed. It supposedly eliminates unnecessary levels of management, streamlines operations, prunes deadwood, enhances overall effectiveness and makes the corporate more competitive. The question is, does it work and even if it does, is it worthwhile? It is a tool used for change but probably isn't the right tool, except to get rid of dead wood. Even then effort needs to be made to see that they land on their feet somewhere else. Cameron concurs with this line of reasoning (Cameron K. , 1994). Downsizing can be used to improve core competencies (Bruton, Keels, & Shook, 1996). McKinley et al (2000) stated that after three years the downsizers began to financially improve. McKinley "theorizes," but doesn't prove, that it may take more time for financial improvement to improve. McKinley also proposed that downsizing has become an acceptable norm and is therefore legitimate. A Lot of theory here and no proof, and that's even if you are satisfied with a three year result. Thinking long term is certainly a good thing. Bruton et al (1996) indicated that there does seem to be a move away from simple reduction across the board. Whoopee! Now we can be selective as to whose life we can destroy. As stated oftentimes before, advocates say downsizing reduces bureaucracy, lowers overhead, makes communication smoother, and creates greater entrepreneurship and productivity. Critics remain unconvinced and there doesn't seem to be much proof.

The potential problem with that is; things get twisted over time, we have selective memories and, it may be a moot point to those whose lives are destroyed over that time period (5 years or more). Byrne (1994) "contended" the same time theory. One study did find that revenues increased following downsizing. (Chalos & Chen, 2002). The validity of many of these studies is questionable because you might have increased performance anyway with capital expenditures even without downsizing. The study is also refuted by many others mentioned in this paper as to the convoluted reason performance improves, if it does. Some, but not all, scared survivors will step up the pace in fear of being next. That's not a very pleasant way to live and work. Mixed financial performance results are puzzling given the anecdotal reports of productivity gains associated with layoffs in the financial press. Anecdotal reports could mean selective reporting, yellow journalism and unsubstantiated by research. The Chalos study determined that productivity increased in the beginning after downsizing but was then unaffected with later cuts (Chalos & Chen, 2002). And yet many studies say just the opposite. Chalos did find that the process is more positive if done while increasing capital expenditures. He also found that a company can cut costs in ways other than labor, by retooling, refining a process, plant closings (if the labor is kept and moved to another location), that positive results depend greatly on amount of announcing and the announcing timing (Chalos & Chen, 2002). One thing is for sure, if you are going to do it, it can't be done alone (De Meuse, Bergmann, Vanderheiden, & Roraff, 2004). And; it may be OK to shed jobs in weak companies- but protect the worker even still (Boone, Downsizing is bad for business, 2004). A common theme running throughout this research is there are a multitude of opinions, all backed by plausible research. Is it possible that everyone is right?

Numerous writings have purposed that downsizing reduces operating costs, eliminates unnecessary levels of management, streamlines operations, enables organizations to prune deadwood, enhances overall effectiveness and ultimately makes a company more competitive in today's marketplace (McKinley, Sanchez, & Schick, 1995). (Jensen & Svarer, 2003). All of these authors then state that several sources have just the opposite viewpoint, that downsizing reduces profits, slows dividend growth and lowers stock prices among other negative effects. One wonders on initial observation just how both can possibly be true. If reducing costs and streamlining result in reduced profits and therefore stock prices, there is something missing in the analysis. Perhaps, when in doubt, don't!

Downsizing can be and is being used to refine strategic focus, and is a natural response to a dynamic industry (Kilpatrick, 1988). The question is, "Can any other way be found other than destroying the lives of the employees in the process"? It is extremely important to plan before and during downsizing- especially for those being let go. The goal should be to legally discharge those who are not performing and eliminate departments that do not contribute to core competencies; it needs to be selective (Cascio W. , 1995), (Lewin & Johnston, 2000). However, Cascio has researched and written on more than one case in which there appears to be no evidence of financial gain. He suggests growing the firm as an alternative. He also said that the success or failure depends on size and the sickness or wellness of the company. Therefore, according to him, cutting payroll seem logical- "all other things being equal". Of course, we all know all things never are equal. So, responsible restructuring can work; if with the intent to get back to business concept innovation and not done by Wall Street engineering. It's still a question of Cost vs. Asset attitude (Cascio W. F., 2002).

Soliciting input and allowing attrition to occur is another way to smooth out the process (Hudson, 1997). There seems to be no question in some cases that it may be beneficial to the organization to smooth out jolts and crises, improve efficiency and improve core competencies (Bruton, Keels, & Shook, 1996) (Johnson, 1997). In contract, across the board cuts will penalize the most efficient units, especially if done at the suggestion of Wall Street analysts (Leatt, Baker, Halverson, & Aird, 1997).

Studies have shown that getting a jump on an environmental dilemma can be helpful (Gee, 2000). Planned downsizing can also result in improved efficiency because the company may be able to focus on improving core competencies and niche activities (Bruton, Keels, & Shook, 1996). Core competencies are activities in which the company excels and by which it maintains market share and competitive advantage. The actual key to gaining competitive advantage in service industries may be the organization's ability to acquire skilled staff and release those who do not meet performance standards (Charan & Colvin, 2001). One might think, "Gee, really, it took a study to determine that?"

In contrast, reacting in response to a crisis may result in the company making across-the-board cuts. Such cuts, (as Leatt and colleagues suggest), will often penalize the most efficient units of the organization, thus decreasing its competitive advantage. Additionally, cutting in response to suggestions from market analysts or bond insurers may further establish an unhealthy cycle of downsizing, rehiring, and further downsizing that may leave the company in a constant state of flux (Leatt, Baker, Halverson, & Aird, 1997).

Downsizing needs to be selective to avoid harming core competencies and businesses. The process should seek to maintain healthy staff and protect against low morale and productivity losses (Cascio W. , 1995). The goals should be both to legally discharge staff whose performance does not meet standards and to eliminate departments that do not contribute to core business functions. By cutting employees who are low performers, the likelihood of employee morale being hurt decreases. At the same time, cutting non-core services allows an organization to retain its core competencies and to outsource non-core tasks (Lewin & Johnston, 2000). Such cuts are easy to justify and reduce the apprehension of the remaining employees. Leatt et al (1997) agree that across-the-board cuts may not be in the best interest of the company because of the loss of valuable staff. It should be said here, one of many times, that none of this yet addresses the question of what is mankind's function and mandate. To make money or as said in Scrooge, "mankind is our business".

Another component of selective cutting is including employees in the process. Detroit Medical Center provides an example of the benefits of soliciting input from staff to determine which non-core activities and staff to cut (Hudson, 1997). Lehigh Valley Hospital chose to involve its staff in the process from start to completion (Nordhaus-Bike, 1997). Although the network did employ staff reductions, only 29 people out of 3,600 lost their jobs and 55 vacant positions were eliminated. These positive conclusions are generally supported by (Walston, Urden, & Sullivan, 2001), who for six years focused their research on re-engineering in hospitals. However, their research results show that the promises of re-engineering (e.g., improved efficiency, better financial performance, etc.) often did not result in better performance. Consistent with Leatt and colleagues' findings, Walston, Urden, and Sullivan concluded that re-engineering can succeed if sustained over a long period of time as part of an overall strategic plan.

Downsizing works better if there is a focus on the morale of remaining employees through open communication in order to insure customer satisfaction. (Sherer, 1997) Use of outplacement support services is a must (Moore T. , 1994). Helpful also would be to address survivors concerns early on. (Armstrong-Strassen, Cameron, & Horsburgh, 2001), (Kilpatrick, 1988).

To be effective severance should be $100,000 &/or stock options + tuition fees ($20,000), continued health care; and at all levels! Cisco Systems also is taking steps in the right direction. They make the effort to park the best of their employees at a non-profit organization or anywhere for that matter at 1/3rd their pay rather than let them go altogether. This helps both the organization and the employee. Accenture gave their employees 20% pay during a one year sabbatical. Again, not bad, but too little. (Cascio W. F., 2002)

Negatives for Companies

The Workplace has become nasty. "Free markets can exist w/o philistine aggressive individualism found in America. (Kay, 2015). Expected profits are not realized based on ROA. Without substantive evidence of the financial or competitive advantages of downsizing, onlookers may assume that the process is a knee-jerk reaction to either internal or external pressures (Fisher &

White, 2000). Conclusion- the process, if we decide to do it at all, needs to be strategic and focused (Bruton, Keels, & Shook, 1996). This process is riddled with problems including an increase in personnel problems such as absenteeism and lowered morale (Kivimaki, Vahtera, Pentti, & Ferrie, 2000), and greater potential for decreased quality (Murphy & Murphy, 1996). For many businesses downsizing means the loss of employees, positions, departments, or product lines.

One theory espoused is that of Population Ecology, in which environmental pressures dictate size of an organization (Davis, Savage, Stewart, & Thomas, 2003). Population ecology theory examines organizational change from an evolutionary perspective (Hannan & Freeman, 1977). According to this viewpoint, the external environment determines the optimal characteristics of the population of organizations. To survive in their environment, organizations must adapt to the constraints. The adaptation process may force organizations to decrease their size or product and service mix. Population ecology theory posits that rampant downsizing in an industry occurs when the environment imposes an optimal form for organizations--that is, when the population is undergoing metamorphosis. By meeting the demands of the environment through downsizing, an organization increases its chances of survival. Davis also observed that according to Institutional Theories, imitation occurs among corporations when they can't control the environment. Everyone has an idea as to why a company downsizes. From the legitimate reason that they will not stay in business to the far more common reason that top management want that bonus. If you want to be fed a lot of Pablum, here goes: Institutional theory views downsizing as one response to environmental uncertainty. The organization chooses this strategy because it provides a semblance of control. When executives are unable to predict the environment, they are more likely to make adjustments that may be similar or identical to the actions of other organizations. An important nuance of this theory is that imitation can occur among organizations without any credible evidence of a causal link between improved performance and downsizing. Certainly downsizing is associated with environmental change and is a component of the life cycle. The problem is that, unlike the steel and auto industry layoffs of the past that get rehired, these jobs are not reappearing now. (Davis, Savage, Stewart, & Thomas, 2003). It is difficult to tell from Davis' interpretation how it was positive if it did not result in improved performance, unless it meant over a long period and as part of a strategic plan. An important future research question would be, "How long is too long to wait for results"? Clearly, the herd mentality is at work here. It's funny that the auto industry is mentioned. They are one of the worst. Did you ever wonder why a Ford looks like a Volkswagon?

Again, as to cost control, a study of rural hospitals did not find any support for a positive relationship between downsizing and financial performance. (Mick & Wise, 1996). On the other hand, Woodland, Fottler and Kilpatrick (1999) did find that revenues increased following downsizing. (Woodard, Fottler, & Kilpatrick, 1999). It is this kind of conflict in the findings which leads to confusion as to the merits of the process and suggests further research may be necessary to distinguish between the long-term and short-term impact of downsizing among HSOs.

Data collected in 1995, before some nurses were transferred, indicated no significant differences among the nurses on outcome variables such as organizational support, job satisfaction, and organizational identification. However, the data collected in 1997, after some nurses were transferred, suggested that those who were moved to another unit perceived significantly less coworker and organizational support, trust, and overall satisfaction than those who remained on their original unit. (Armstrong-Strassen, Cameron, & Horsburgh, 2001) The same team also studied nurses' satisfaction in three hospitals in Ontario, Canada, in 1991 and 1992. The 1991 study was performed at a time when the hospitals were experiencing a nursing shortage, and the 1992 study measured satisfaction after staff restructuring. The results of these studies showed that overall job satisfaction remained relatively unaffected. However, the nurses did report less satisfaction with certain aspects of their job and work environment, including job security, treatment of laid-off nurses, and supervision. This study emphasizes the necessity for effective communication before and during the downsizing process to mitigate the perceptions that the HSO violated its psychological contract with its employees.

Although hard to prove because you are usually, and perhaps deliberately, not comparing apples to apples, there is little data proving improved financial performance. (De Meuse, Bergmann, Vanderheiden, & Roraff, 2004). Even when more sales are created there is less profit.

America is not alone in the downsizing trend, although the technique is more difficult to implement in Europe because of the union and a generally more caring attitude.

Today's speed of change and non-incremental progress, e.g. faster, better, cheaper, means companies can be left behind in a heartbeat. Large leaps of human imagination make the normal method of operating a company sometimes obsolete. It has become a nonlinear type of progress. Today, business concepts are supposed to be the in thing- which doesn't mean stock buybacks or money sleight of hand. There is a movement indicating down with the financial engineering and up with business concept innovation. The innovation is to create new customers, markets and revenue streams and not downsize. Machines work efficiently but they do not invent. Smart, well trained people invent and are the true long term asset.

One suggested answer to the quandary is to create an environment in which creativity can flourish. This is called responsible restructuring. Companies that downsize see people as costs to be cut while those that restructure see them as assets to be developed. They have a plug in mentality; pull the plug when you don't need them. Evidence suggests that costs are sticky on the downside-meaning they don't go down as fast as the revenue lost. Think in terms of the knowledge base as being a firm's memory and sometimes the memory is like a neural network or Artificial Intelligence grid; if you get rid of one of the links the entire structure may not work. (Cascio W. F., 2002).

The facility may experience loss of institutional expertise and memory (Fisher & White). Schein (1990) also address change as a multi-year effort.

Cameron et al (1993) suggests that retrenchment, cost cutting and productivity improvements are often not successful.

Cascio (1998) said one ominous trend exposed by

the study was that employees got used to downsizing. Even when the survey indicated that the downsizing companies did not do worse, it did not prove they did better. Layoffs alone do not renew or revitalize a company. The independent variable is the % of employment downsized and the dependent variables are Profit margin, ROA, ROE, Asset efficiency and Market to book. The use of these five ratios are subjectively selected from a larger group of at least double that although I agree the ROA and ROE are certainly critical indicators of a company's value. What may be more important is, not which ratios were selected but the comparison of the ratios between those companies who downsized and those who didn't, which is what the authors did. Sequencing trouble results from the data given to this interpretation. It would seem that the data indicated not only did the downsized companies not do better but that they did worse. The author's conclusions left the reader with the impression that there was still doubt as to whether or not downsizing might have produced a positive effect. (De Meuse, Bergmann, Vanderheiden, & Roraff, 2004)

As a pre quall to understanding downsizing more I have inserted a section on the pay scale of those very same CEOs who are firing the average worker. There doesn't seem to be any question that CEOs are paid a lot of money. Just how much is enough?

Positives for Survivors

Cascio (2002) questioned whether or not employees were becoming immune to the layoff experience? I infer this to mean "Can we get away with it over time?" Downsizing works better if a focus on morale of remaining employees through open communication in order to insure patient (it was a hospital study) satisfaction (Sherer, 1997). One might comment that having a stressful job is still better than having none.

Negatives for Survivors

Downsizing causes stress which leads to sickness, absence and heart disease. The results may even be understated as those left behind were generally in better health anyway than those let go, because employees with health problems were more likely to lose their jobs. (Vaherta, 2004). If the employer thinks he can get away with it. There are survivor effects such as lower morale (Armstrong-Stassen M. , Designated redundant but escaping lay-off: A special group of lay-off survivors. , 2002), high stress (Leana & Feldman, 1992), anger, envy and guilt (Noer, Healing the wounds: Overcoming the trauma of layoffs and revitalizing downsized organizations, 1993). Backstabbing, placing the blame and overt failure to cooperate (Moorman, 1991) are all evident in survivors. Stress and uncertainty increase (Tombaugh & White, 1990). Many become dispirited, frustrated and angry at the perceived breach of psychological contract. Works and stress definitely increased for those left behind. (De Meuse, Bergmann, Vanderheiden, & Roraff, 2004)

Work required to be performed by survivors increases greatly. There are ways to mitigate the effects by simply being fair (Brockner J. , Wiesenfeld, Stephan, & Hurley, 1997) and communicate openly (Bridges W. , 1986)

Even University teaching has taken a dramatic turn for the worse. Today is the era of untenured professors with an increased work load forced to attract external funds and publish or perish. (Winefield A. H., 2002). There is no question that this is true, however, to be fair as stated elsewhere, college professors, in other cases, are obscenely overpaid, especially as to pension benefits.

Bridges (1994) warned that only a fool will let their fates be decided by those they work for; the wise will think like entrepreneurs. (Boone, 2004) said the workplace has become a capricious place. Top executives have eliminated millions of employees with the promise that there would be higher productivity and ultimately higher wages for labor. Neither of these has materialized to any great or consistent extent. In most cases, those left behind have had the squeeze put on their wages as well as their workload increased. Assuming any legitimacy to the practice of downsizing, there at least must be better training programs, more sensitivity and a sharing of the pain by higher level management. The anxiety within the organization as to whether or an employee is to be fired kills off any incentive to do a good job, be creative or innovative. The employees spent all their time looking for another job or making sure they kept that one (Boone, 2004), (Brockner J. , Grover, O'Malley, Reed, & M.A., 1993), (Noer, Healing the wounds: Overcoming the trauma of layoffs and revitalizing downsized organizations, 1993), and (Kivimaki, Vahtera, Pentti, & Ferrie, 2000). No doubt downsizing can be hazardous to your health- the stress of more work and the stress of possibly being the next to be downsized would drive a man to drink. Armstrong-Strassen et al (1996) showed that downsizing affected employee satisfaction with career future, company identification, supervision and coworkers. As indicated previously, Wagar (2001) indicates there is a strong negative relationship between employee satisfaction and workforce reduction which causes increased grievances, higher absenteeism and poorer supervisor-union member relations.

There is a nasty dirty laundry list of drawbacks lurking out there, cursing both company and the remaining employees and haunting the halls of the overpaid CEO's. Included on that list would be: less quality work being done, less productivity, less effectiveness, more conflict, low morale, loss of trust, heightened stress, risk of heart disease in all concerned, scapegoating, time spent looking for a new job, loss of team spirit and more individual, every man for himself attitude, a sense of betrayal for both, and feelings of being undervalued and unappreciated for those left behind. For those let go there is loss of self-esteem and sometimes poverty. For the company, they have usually fired the most experienced employees; will experience a "loss of organizational memory", and possibly a loss of customers loyal to the downsized employee. No doubt downsizing causes a disruption to customers and employees (Shah, 2000)

There ought to be a plan! Regardless of the benefits of downsizing or the need for it, strategies are necessary to protect remaining employees. Most everyone agrees that for downsizing to be effective and strategically beneficial, an implementation plan must be in place (Moore T. , 1994). Without some sort of plan, determining who should be discharged and what effects downsizing will have on the HSO is difficult (Kilpatrick, 1988). Arndt and Duchemin (1993) reported on the use of informal support activities as another employee-protection method. These activities were designed as information exchanges that benefit staff and prevent rumors. In addition, management facilitated workshops that were intended to educate staff on the downsizing process.

The downsizing plan should be part of the personnel policy manual. It should provide details about how employees will be chosen for dismissal and should foster a sense of equity (Kilpatrick, 1988). Although opinions differ on the length of time employees should have from announcement to actual termination, the company should provide outplacement support services (Moore 1994). A study by Hershey (1972) found that having advanced knowledge of the pending layoffs does not adversely affect productivity or morale. Providing support for discharged employees will help them move from shock and anger toward acceptance and a focus on their future.

The plan should also include treatment of the survivors. (Armstrong-Strassen, Cameron, & Horsburgh, 1996), (Kilpatrick, 1988). Addressing survivors' concerns and fears early is important, as survivors may feel guilty because they have jobs and they may lose trust and confidence in management. Furthermore, they may attempt sabotage methods ranging from peaceful slowing of production to destruction of property. Reestablishing trust and loyalty and improving morale are vital. Management should have frequent meetings with surviving staff and include them in the rebuilding process.

Positives for the let go

Some scholars suggest that downsizing creates an opportunity for improving their lives. I suggest these scholars live in a tree hut somewhere. Another weak logic postulated is that relief emerges when they realize that the worry is over, especially if they experienced a protracted time of not knowing if they were to be downsized. Bridges (1994) and Noer (1993) both feel that the trend away from the old traditional job security will help individuals achieve autonomy and satisfaction.

Negatives for the let go

The violation of psychological contracts may have a negative effect on the individual's long term attitude toward work in general and their careers. In many, if not most, cases, worker loss exceeds company gains, it's just trendy. (Boone, 2000)

Boone also reported that supposed gains in efficiency did not translate into higher output or employment. Based on the rapid (less than 4 years) re igniting of the real estate bubble and the obscene profits and bonuses obtained by the commercial banks and Wall Street, unless there is a dramatic event akin to a catastrophe, it is unlikely that the huddled masses will gain any measure of fairness in any time frame less than a century or two.

Hickok indicates that cultural change will be the primary effect of downsizing, not finance. Power has shifted from rank and file to the organization (management/shareholders) and relationships have shifted from familial to competitive. Employee/employer relationship has shifted from long term to short term and there is an unsettling distinction between proactive downsizing in advance and reactive to a situation. Even the proactive in advance might have merit if the company is in trouble as opposed to merely anticipating less profit in the future. Hickok suggested that the damage might be mitigated by including workers in discussions and eliminating harsh terminations. (Hickok T. A., 1997)

Downsizing reflects that Institutional shareholders have gotten too greedy. Employees, suppliers, the environment and the community should also be considered. Remember, these shareholders are probably employees somewhere also. If not, and they are only wealthy non workers, then all the more reason to resent and restrict their profits at the expense of the thousands of workers laid off.

In a civilized society we are constantly attempting to improve all manner of our well-being.

Critiques

A brief foray into critiquing some of these research papers is in order if for no other reason than to make me feel good about myself by pointing out their shortcomings. I have selected 3 well written paper for that purpose.

Review - Boone

Boone, Jan. (2004) Downsizing is bad for business; Royal Economic Society Journal

Dr. Boone is a professor at Tilburg U. in the Netherlands. The research question is "Downsizing is Bad for Business" Downsizing has gotten to be trendy, says Boone. Senior executive claim that downsizing was necessary for efficiency- at first that looks to be true and if so then it would all seem to depend on your point of reference or political point of view- are you firing or being fired. But, Dr. Boone's analysis suggests that the worker's loss exceeds the firms gain. Society as a whole would have been better off without as much downsizing. London Business School Professor John Kay suggests that free markets can exist without the philistine, aggressive, individualism that America believes in.

Kay also suggests that financial markets and the fear of them is a major contributing factor and that firms need to somehow get away from Wall Street's death grip. This article mentioned the firing of Durk Jager at Proctor and Gamble after he had cut over 15,000 jobs. I wonder how he was able to do this without anyone being aware of it as he went along. Where were the checks and balances, where was the board, and how much was he given as a Golden Parachute?

The workplace has become a nasty place with unrealized promises of higher productivity, (individuals in America are maintaining their high productivity by simply working more hours).

Boone referenced Joseph Schumpeter's "creative destruction" remark and quickly indicated his disagreement.

His suggestions for improvement are better training, heightened sensitivity to worker anguish and shared sacrifice. He indicated that middle ground is or should be emerging; weak companies should shed jobs and abandon communities. If they do that, they should be penalized- maybe not penalized but not allowed government assistance, self-enrichment or allowed to simply start up again as a new entity(tough to enforce). Strong companies must concede an obligation to care for workers or at least help them through transition. More on this is available in my total overall plan for transition/compensation. Boone cited corporations that seem to work e.g. Starbucks. It would appear that is because of stock options, health insurance, training, and counseling. At Pinnacle Brands employees were able to come up with new product and other cost cutting ideas.

Boone suggests that it is hard to fire people (time spent figuring out who) while coming up with new products and ideas. I interpret this to mean stop firing people! Anxiety kills off any creativity as they spend their time looking for another job. Boone also, like many others, suggests the strange phenomena that efficiency does not translate into higher output, profits or higher employment later.

This is another age old dull platitude- "suffer now for a better tomorrow". Although that may work in suggesting saving money personally for your future, evidence does not suggest that it works in business. This is also a government lie they use when explaining their budgeting decisions. Programs are never eliminated, taxes are rarely lowered, it doesn't "trickle down", and it doesn't get better later.

Boone referenced a Wall Street Journal study which found that in only 9% of cases did downsizing improve quality of products.

As a Literature Reviewer I would have to say that Dr. Boone did handle his paper well. It is relevant, important, convincing and contributes to understanding and development? Not only is all that true but it is germane to my topic and as an added plus, it is likely that I land on the same side of the debate. Dr. Boone is an accomplished writer who rarely has undue limitations on his studies and usually has a sufficient sample size. The methodology used by the author was as follows:

Quantitative (e.g. on the effectiveness of a procedure) or qualitative (e.g. studies)

Primary historical

Statistics- Definition of any population and sample groups

Narratives

Interpretive or critical science research orientation

Evaluate (critique) the appropriateness of method(s)

Objective and evenhanded- Any pertinent date ignored to prove their point?

Credibility- any weaknesses or oversights?

His data was accurately recorded, analyzed and summarized. It also appears to be replicable since it is public information and will not change. As to areas of controversy, there is an entire subset of scholars who believe the process of downsizing is positive. In conclusion, I don't know that I got any new ideas for solutions or resolved any conflicts. By now as I read and gather information it appears to be a re enforcement of my general thesis; that the end did not justify the mean and that with a bit more thought there could have been a better way.

Review - Cascio

Cascio, Wayne F.(2002), Strategies for responsible restructuring. Academy of Management Executive, Aug, Vol.16, Issue3, p80

Dr. Cascio's study was based on the S&P 500 firms from 1982-2000. During this time 80% of the layoffs involved white collar workers. Cascio suggested that; yes, cutting payrolls might be the logical means of reducing expenses and therefore increase earnings (not the same as profits). The key phrase here was "all other things being equal" which of course, they are not. The anticipated benefit of downsizing did not materialize. There was no consistent evidence that downsizing led to improved financial performance as measured by return on assets. This was inconsistent with his earlier study. Only by growing their business do firms do better than stable

companies. One would think this was a given. Those
growing their business did 41% better than downsizers
and 43% better than stable employers by end of year two.
It was indicated that there would be a cost to subsequent
expansion.

The study determined that downsizing was no
longer about large sick companies trying to save
themselves, but companies merely trying to boost
earnings at the expense of laid off employees. It did,
however, observe that small companies will resist layoffs
more due to the invested cost in their employees and the
cost of retraining.

Dr. Cascio makes the following observations: Are
employees becoming immune to the layoff experience?
Temp workers are becoming popular, but at what cost?
America is not alone in the downsizing trend, although it
is more difficult in central Europe.
Today's speed of change and non-incremental progress,
e.g. faster, better, cheaper, mean companies can be left
behind in a heartbeat. Therefore the six sigma quality
enhancement programs are no longer workable. He
speaks to large leaps of human nonlinear-imagination.
This sounds like another hyped idea to me.

Today business concepts are the in thing- which
isn't stock buybacks or money sleight of hand. There is a
movement indicating down with the financial engineering
and up with business concept innovation. The innovation
is to create new customers, markets and revenue streams
and not downsize. Machines work efficiently but they do
not invent, smart well trained people invent. They are the
true long term asset. The suggested answer then is to
create an environment in which creativity can flourish.
This is called responsible restructuring.

Downsizers see people as costs to be cut while restructurers see them as assets to be developed. They have a plug in mentality. Pull plug when you don't need them. Think in terms of the knowledge base as being a firm's memory and sometimes the memory is like a neural network or A.I. - if you get rid of one of the links the entire structure may not work.

Dr. Cascio outlines ten mistakes commonly found in the downsizing process:

Fail to make clear long term goals

Use downsizing as first resort- instead of no new hires, reduce perks, freeze salaries, and promotions

Be non-selective in downsizing- across the board at middle management or below or last in first out

Fail to change the way work is done after downsizing or else just more work piled on others

Fail to get everyone involved

Fail to be open and honest

Fail to treat those who depart with dignity and take care of them

Fail to care for those left behind-

Ignoring other stakeholders

Not evaluating and learning from mistakes

What to do

Before downsizing consider the impact on long term, employees, is it part of a large plan or is it the entire plan –a quick fix, virtues of stability, give employees a chance to find a solution (warn everyone of impending decision without telling who will go so they will all be involved, where in business cycle, product life cycles, communicate, get commitment, train, and trust of all by doing all the right things. See Schwab below.

Dr. Cascio used Charles Schwab as one example where they instituted 50% pay cuts at the top, cut out travel entertainment, catering, and had to take unused vacation. On the other hand numerous people let go received poor severance pay of $7,500. Should be $100,000 &/or stock options + tuition fees ($20,000), continued health care; and at all levels! He mentioned Cisco Systems who came up with an excellent system of parking the best employees at nonprofit organizations at 1/3rd the pay. Nothing was mentioned of making up any or all the difference. Accenture Company gave their employees 20% pay during a one year sabbatical. That may too little. Phillips electronics provided job finding assistance. That assistance needs to be using its contacts to get the employee another job.

In my opinion the employment rate used is unrealistic and totally bogus. It doesn't count underemployed or those who have exhausted their unemployment benefits. They have dropped from the radar. Therefore all references to severance times are also unrealistic and need to be extended. Six months' severance should be 3 years.

The research question was "Is there a long term payoff to downsizing?" Since the study cast serious doubt as to a positive answer to that question, Cascio elected to suggest several alternatives to what he calls restructuring, illustrating mistakes to avoid as well. This work is extremely relevant to the downsizing debate and especially to my particular interests and Cascio appears to be well informed and has written well on the subject. The paper is also important, convincing and, I believe, contributes to understanding and development?

I initially chose this resource only because it fit into the broad definition of my overall topic interest-downsizing and I needed to read all available literature and viewpoints before narrowing down the scope of my research. It was only after reviewing this and other papers that I determined it to be more relevant to my particular detailed interest, which centers on the plight of those having been downsized.

The study had a broad, large size; limited, if at all, to larger companies. Definitions were included to assist the reader.

The methodology used by the author was of a quantitative longitudinal statistical study which was then interpreted by the author to come to conclusions and offer solutions. It was objective and even handed and seemed to be an appropriate method.

The credibility of this paper rests in the time of the study and the breadth of companies involved. The study it replicable since it is public information and will not change. The data was accurately recorded, analyzed and summarized beginning with the logic driving downsizing-future costs are easier to control than future revenues; then discussing the types of downsizing and the consequences-no significant consistent evidence that employment downsizing led to improved financial performance as measured by return on assets, mistakes to avoid

Clearly, there is controversy over the pros and cons of downsizing, usually divided between the corporations and the employees.

Dr. Cascio appears to be a force within the Downsizing community and therefore is always providing new ideas for solutions or resolving conflicts and answering questions.

Review - Hickok

Thomas A. Hickok,(1997), Downsizing and Organizational Culture. Public Administration and

Management Journal.

Hickok indicates that cultural change will be the primary effect of downsizing, not finance.

He addresses those techniques that destabilize and those that reinforce: Power has shifted from rank and file to the organization (mgmt. /shareholders), Relationships have shifted from familial to competitive, Employee/employer relationship has shifted from long term to short term, Downsizing has failed to reduce costs and increase profits. Only a handful were found to have improved the organizational performance, Downsizing fails to consider the future resources needed.

Hickok emphasizes a distinction between proactive in advance and reactive. You should include workers in discussions with no harsh terminations. The "Psychological contract" has been broken (Rousseau, 1995).

Schumpeter (1942) wrote, "downsizing may not be pretty to watch and people will get hurt but that is the way capitalism takes care of the market. There is no job entitlement. Fine, let us concede that and move along in our effort to deal with it. That kind of attitude lends credence to capitalism not being the ultimate system for humanity. Again, are we here to work (a puritan ethic recently born, since the rich did nothing until a few hundred years ago)?

Downsizing creates the appearance of doing something to correct a bad situation. The costs might not bear this out if the cost of hiring outside contractors is more than the savings from employee elimination. Dr. Hickok cited a lack of empirical data on downsizing (Cameron K. , 1994). He stated that with TQM (Total Quality Management) there is an assumption that the first order of business is to thrive and be competitive. It is hard to disagree with this, for; if there is no business there is no job for the employee. This requires further debate as to the fundamental purpose of human beings. I suggest we look to the animal kingdom for examples.

American culture rewards winners, not losers and number one above all others, thereby encouraging employees to hide failures rather than admit and correct them. Where is the happy medium here?

The General Electric study (Tichy & Sherman, 1994) was filled with a nightmare of examples as to the attitudes surrounding downsizing such as the intentional infliction of pain is good. This sounds like "Greed is good". Terms like necessary evil come to mind. It also give the usual credit to Jack Welch for accomplishing great things by merely canning 170,000 people while getting obscenely rich in the process. People do bad things under the guise of a good slogan; in this case it was "the ultimate test of leadership is enhancing the long term value of the organization". If you think about it, just another dull platitude. Profits should be viewed as a means to an end. Handy (2002). Institutional shareholders have gotten too greedy. Employees, suppliers, the environment and the community should also be considered. Remember, these shareholders are probably employees somewhere also. If not, and they are only wealthy non workers, then all the more reason to resent and restrict their profits at the expense on the thousands of workers laid off. In the Xerox study it said one needs to throw a few punches here and there, create dissatisfaction with the status quo. There is an assumption here that the status quo is bad and people will not strive to improve their situation. Hewlett-Packard was successful with a benevolent management attitude toward employees, shareholders and management. (Nohria &

Beer, 2000). Jumping forward to 2013 and many other questions come up regarding HP, although it is likely that their focus and vision of the future direction of their industry is more to blame for their pickle than any management handling of their employees. Hamel and Prahalad (1994) do not question the legitimacy of downsizing but indicate that better to deal with core competencies and restructuring with existing staff than simply cutting. "Make your corporate "Bones" is another humdinger. It usually means cut as much fat as you can and get a bonus. Did you know that CEO pay increased 1000% from 1980 to 1995? What the hell?

Hickok also addressed the Survivor effects- lower morale (Armstrong-Stassen M. , Survivors Reactions to a Workforce Reduction: A Comparison of Blue-collar Workers and their Supervisors, 1993), high stress (Leana & Feldman, Leana, C. R., & Feldman, D. C. (1992). Coping with job loss: How individuals, organizations, and communities respond to layoffs, 1992), anger, envy and guilt (Noer, Healing the wounds: Overcoming the trauma of layoffs and revitalizing downsized organizations, 1993). Backstabbing, placing the blame and overt failure to cooperate (Moorman, 1991) are all evident in survivors.

So how to mitigate effects? Be fair (Brockner J. , Grover, O'Malley, Reed, & M.A., 1993). Communicate openly (Bridges W. , 1986).

What was wrong with the old "Psychological Contract"? (Bridges W. , 1994) and (Noer, Healing the wounds: Overcoming the trauma of layoffs and revitalizing downsized organizations, 1993) both feel that the trend away from the old traditional job security will help individuals achieve autonomy and satisfaction. Easy for them to say, they have a job. That may be true but there has to be a security blanket during an indefinite transition period.

Cultural reinforcing is a term for voluntary reducing by buyouts, job sharing, and attrition. How can it be best accomplished? Advanced notice, shared pain (management suffers also), explicit written criteria as to who stays and who goes, transition assistance-long term, participation in decisions.

Conclusions for Review

Research indicates that for every opinion there is an opposite opinion. Most every economist knows this to be one of the 6 basic economic tenets. Clearly there are conflicting viewpoints on the effects of downsizing; usually depending on how it affects the viewer. Downsizing is a natural response in business that will be difficult to forgo as a tool. It can be used to improve core competencies. It seems worthwhile as a strategic process to control growth. Given increasing competition and continuing pressures to increase profitability, organizations are continually seeking ways to control costs (Greising, 1998). It's only human nature to want to do or be better, and whether good or bad it is unlikely to change. Regardless of whether or not you believe in survival of the fittest, it appears to be Mother Nature's way. Therefore, I will concede the necessity to downsize for just a moment since I'm not up for a battle with Mother Nature and concentrate on baby steps to do it correctly and control it. Momentary concession does not mean agreement. Throughout this paper, however, there will be a running theme that, just like the propaganda espoused by most capitalistic governments, growth would seem to be the better mousetrap. If it's good for the government why not good for a company? You can't have your cake and eat it too. The matter of whether or not the government is correct is a subject for debate another day.

Most opinions are biased depending on which side you are on. Few people are capable of neutral reasoning. So as to downsizing, if you are a corporation you believe downsizing will cut the fat, make you more productive and increase your bottom line. Never mind that it should increase your bonus as well. If you have been left behind, some say you will work harder in fear for your job but more likely than not you are going to be an unhappy camper- looking over your shoulder, looking for another job and generally feeling put upon and looking for ways to get even. If you have been let go, again, there are some who think this is a wonderful opportunity to strike out on a new venture. Usually that thought is harbored by those with a secure job and a lot of money. Most of the time it just destroys your life, causes a divorce, starves your children and causes the dog to get kicked. Future investigation would be helpful to better understand the effects of downsizing.

Observations

Benefits are not trickling down or being distributed to those employees who have lost their jobs.

It is almost impossible to create new products, improve existing ones and come up with new ideas when you are laying off people, thereby stifling the growth potential of the organization.

Contrary to a sales manager's mentality, people do not work at their best under pressure.

Even if shareholders are the most important asset (a very debatable assertion), a more effective order of caring and concern should be: employees first, who take care of the customers, who then buy and create profits, which in turn take care of the shareholders. (Krietner, 2004)

We must be careful that specific cases of a very good company downsizing successfully can be generalized. That might lead us to conclude that downsizing works for everyone when it took a particularly good company to achieve success with it.

There will be long term repercussions because we are penalizing efficient units. Hence, there is a loss of learning, huge opportunity cost and a potential for tremendous labor unrest.

Problems

Lack of monitoring by owners, poor board oversight, and excessive free cash flow allowed managers to expand beyond their efficiency levels, mergers/consolidations and production slowdowns and failure to deal effectively with a global economy and competition. We are giving away our economy in bits and pieces- in manufacturing, engineering, and white collar services. Arguably, however; greed plays a large part as the power gap between top executives and the average worker increases dramatically.

Questions

Is it a good or bad thing to preemptively downsize? This also appears to depend on your point of view.

One burning question. Is downsizing being done to stay alive economically or strictly for extra profit? Why should you destroy lives if you are healthy and profitable just because you want more? As to whether or not there is a long term payoff to downsizing, studies cast serious doubt as to a positive answer to that question. Empirical evidence is still scant and mixed (Chalos & Chen, 2002)but what does exist indicates that long term financial gain doesn't occur. Why does it continue to be viewed as a viable option? Firms downsize for short term gain at the expense of long term productivity. Is the quick fix worth potential long term negative consequences?

Do we wish to live in a world that adheres to a philosophy of "the end justifies the mean"? Do we want to be a nation of temporary workers and do we realize the social cost? Should we ask ourselves, "Is an 80 hour week what we want"? Again, only the top elite will accept that, and that may have some bearing on the pay gap widening.

Would downsized companies have turned themselves around anyway and even quicker if they had not?

If left unchecked, are we becoming a nation of depressed, mean, mad people whose health suffers because of it? We are like rats in a spinning wheel-running faster and faster just to stay in place. Even if you do hire back the people you fired as contract labor, you lose control and loyalty.

Is the elimination of the cost of benefits and ability to dump the contract workers at a moment's notice worth it? The question is; at what price do you hire them back? Care must be taken not to mimic the government that hires contract labor at far more than the cost they saved. Having certain functions outsourced may also have consequences on a national scale in case of a war. We will no longer have the plants and factories to provide the equipment that served us so well in past unfortunate crises.

Alternatives

Why not challenge workers to come up with ways to solve the problem and invent new products, increase revenues by growing the business and cut costs in other areas such as supplies, materials and redesigned work flow of machinery? Create adequate severance packages and outplacement services. Don't hire so quickly in good times.

In observing the effects of downsizing on those employees let go, data has been gathered and analyzed concerning the unemployment rate, since it is a direct result of the downsizing process. Further research needs to be performed regarding the validity of this statistical data and whether it is accurate and takes into consideration all of the important aspects. It would appear that it does not, since there is no inclusion of underemployment statistics. It also may be lacking in validity because it does not fully account for those who have exhausted their unemployment benefits and have dropped from the radar. The benefits obtained from unemployment insurance are quite possibly for far too short a period.

If you must downsize, there is a right way to implement the technique, beginning with planning for it long before the event is to occur. Planning must continue during and after the process with a clear vision of long term horizon thinking. The process must: be part of an overall strategic plan, it must reinforce company goals and values, communicate to employees at all time, specifically eliminate those who are under performing and not contributing to core competencies, eliminate from vacancies and attrition (assuming no hardship on those remaining.), deal with honesty and dignity at all times, have compassion, seek input from employees, provide outplacement services, provide education for those leaving and those staying, attempt to refocus product line w/o downsizing or plant closings, and most of all, keep executive pay in line. A 10 million dollar executive equals 300 employees laid off or 300 times the average salaried workers pay.

Because of the mixed evidence regarding the long-term benefits of downsizing, further studies are needed to assess if and when downsizing is beneficial. Both quantitative and qualitative studies indicate that there is much room for study and improvement. Future studies should investigate (and suggest) the types of downsizing practices that improve organizational survival and prosperity.

CHAPTER 3 METHODOLOGY

Research Question

Does the negative emotional effect of downsizing on workers in the United States (or the industrialized nations of Western Europe) who; are already fired, think they may be fired, or who will not be eliminated but are working twice as hard and feeling the stress, far outweigh any short term positive effect or profit for the organization?

Why do we need to know the answer? Because workers are suffering and it is morally right to deal with it. How is it timely? Because America is in trouble, and has been since the 1980's. Will it be representative? The Meta-Analysis should give as good a representation as any methodology. Are these Ethical or political issues? Certainly. Even though the one side (Management) usually doesn't consider ethical issues when justifying the process from a profit standpoint, an advanced civilized society, needs to be concerned about all its citizens, or it will not survive. As to politics, everything is politics. Or it begs the question, "Where have you been the last 5,000 years?"

Hypothesis

A Theory is a generally accepted explanation of events. A theory comes from repeated observation and testing and incorporates facts, laws, predictions, and tested hypotheses that are widely accepted. It is stronger than an Hypotheses. It has already undergone testing.

A Hypothesis is a specific, testable prediction

about what you expect to happen in your study. A proposed explanation of a phenomenon still to be tested. For example, a study designed to look at the relationship between study habits and test anxiety might have a hypothesis that states, "Students with better study habits will suffer less test anxiety." Unless your study is exploratory in nature, your hypothesis should always explain what you expect to happen during the course of your experiment. A speculative guess yet to be tested. A tentative explanation or idea about how things work. It guides you into further work to get a better answer. A provisional idea whose merit requires evaluation.

Hypothesis 1
Corporate executive officers have no incentive to keep workers when eliminating jobs is the easiest way to increase (short term) profits.

Hypothesis 2 Management is guided by financial market demands for short term (quarterly) profits at the expense of the employee and long term health of the company.

Hypothesis 3 Entire plants being moved to lesser developed countries, thus eliminating numerous jobs and an economic base in the first country, have negative short term effects on the workers and long term negative effects on the country and quite possibly the corporations themselves.

Hypothesis 4 The benefits of downsizing are going to a limited group (Corporations and their Corporate officers), and not being equally distributed among other members of the work force. This explains why the economic numbers of the United States look good while the average person is struggling.

As a guideline for addressing any hypothesis I have made an effort to determine: Is the hypothesis stated clearly and is it testable? Yes. Can it be accomplished?

Yes, although still somewhat subjective. Is the scope correct? Probably still too broad. This writer has a macro persuasion with a view toward the big picture. Further studies can be more precise as to industry, department, country, or field. Will analysis accept or reject the hypothesis? Can data be collected? Yes. Downsizing is a subject much in discussion and practice. The explicit methods of data collection will be a Meta-Analysis, so as to obtain as much diverse information as possible. In other words, a large sample size.

Is the population receptive to investigation? That depends on which of the player categories you ask; the corporation, those let go or those left behind. It is unlikely that Corporate will be receptive. Why kill the golden goose?

Will I be able to measure job satisfaction, motivation etc. These are measured by stress levels, profits, and productivity.

How can we increase the performance of employees? Give them job security. Since there are three billion Indians and Chinese willing to work for less than the average American worker, that seems to be a nonstarter. More money. Not likely for the same reason. A share in the profits? Maybe.

It appears that without serious work on human nature, narrow mindedness will continue to cloud everyone's judgment depending on their personal objectives and point of view. This seriously impairs the ability to improve strategic vision as to the effects of downsizing.

From a culture and ideology standpoint it appears that the United States is moving in the wrong direction, becoming more like a banana republic than an advanced caring society. Our work ethic is shot, we are lazy, we feel entitled and we have far too many people either not working or working on a meaningless job that is none productive. Think of all the Real estate Agents, Car Dealers, Insurance Salesmen, Lawyers and the hordes of Government workers who are overpaid and doing little or nothing.

The impact on society? Eventual doom. The end of society as we know it. A far less affluent society with a much lower standard of living.

The Research Design

Many writers just seem to be in love with numbers crunching. A serious question, after reading these writers, would have to be "who cares and where is this leading us and who is it helping?" It is just information for information's sake.

Deductive Reasoning

Deductive reasoning draws from general laws to a specific conclusion (guaranteed), from knowledge to new knowledge. Aristotelian logic from the Meta-Analysis of others. The conclusion must be true if all of the premises, propositions and assertions are true. This is not to be confused with a logically valid argument using false premises

Inductive reasoning stems from evaluating specific, actual experiences/ observations to making a new general principle. It is based on empirical evidence and is pragmatic. It's based upon facts, experiment or evidence, not on science or proven theory.

Quantitative

According to Mark Easterby Smith et al (1991)

there are 5 design choices, each broken down between the two philosophical camps- the positivist and the phenomenologists.

Positivism- measures the external world objectively. It bases things on facts. It values freedom and, although claiming to be independent, still influenced by outside power forces. It looks at basic laws and is measurement concerned (quantitative). It questions what, is it, how much, and does it, not why or how. It tests an existing theory/hypothesis, often by Field Study and asks what. It's hard to address innovation, customer satisfaction and unknown variables. It is more concerned with the process.

Qualitative

Phenomenology (also known as social constructionist), is Qualitative. It generates a theory/hypothesis-uses Cases mostly, and asks How/why. It can't generalize as well and interpretation can be subjective. It is more concerned with the outcome. The world and reality are not objective and exterior but socially constructed and given meaning by people, ergo, inferring things through sensation, reflection or intuition. Also, judgments, perceptions and emotions. Phenomenology intends to be scientific, but isn't looking at things through clinical psychology or neurology. Instead, it reflects on experience. Phenomenologists are not so much fact gatherers but address how and why people react to situations/ circumstances. Human action comes from how different peoples' senses allow them to react to things, not from something external. Human beliefs, behaviors, perceptions and values are considered. Phenomenology states, therefore, that science etc. is driven by human interest and is part of what one observes. It concentrates on concepts rather than numbers. (Checkland, 1999). The Efficient Market Theory in the stock market isn't as valid as people would have you believe because the emotions of people enter into market movements. (Walker, 1985). Qualitative are more subject to interpretation mistakes, unlike quantitative researchers. Case studies in which participants are observed can be misleading because when participants find out what you're doing, they can change their reactions.

Design Choices

1. **Independent** (Positivists/objectivist) - people are objects under external influence) versus get involved as Phenomenologists

2. **Sample size**-Large versus small-cross sectional (Positivist) versus longitudinal-(Phenomenologist), which takes a long time and requires more skill by the researcher.

3. **Testing** the various theories. For example, existing (Quantitative) versus generating new (Qualitative) theories (through hypotheses). Generating is Grounded theory (looking at the same event in different situations) Phenomenologists. Substantive theory (Developmental theories) versus formal theory. The quality of a theory should be analytical enough to enable some generalizations to take place and yet possible for people to relate to their own experiences. (Glaser & Strauss, 1967). Melvin Dalton (1959), a phenomenology advocate said scientific method was inappropriate for his work- meaning hypothesis, observation, testing, confirm or not confirm- because when you quantify and reduce variables to their smallest component they lose the real meaning of the situation. He is not opposed to

using a certain amount of quantitative data which he got secondarily. It was clear that Dalton did not start his research with any preconceived hypothesis or theories to test, it grew out of his confusion and irritation. He contented himself with framing simple questions about things he didn't understand. Discuss pros and cons of the Scientific Method -Object being to discover truth and extend knowledge. Major scientific discoveries are not produced by logical and rational application of the scientific method but by independent and creative thinking outside the boundaries of existing ideas. Thorpe (1991). Confusion, irritation, things I don't understand, secondary quantitative information, questioning the scientific Method because of its possible loss of meaning as it is refined. I guess that pretty much sums up my research as well.

Testing starts with a theory or hypothesis. It's Positivist, has more clarity and can be followed better. It might be more trivial. It is also a little more what than why.

Geert Hofstede (1980) in his positivist research on the effect of national cultures on social and work behavior asked the following:

> Individualism- does society emphasize this, or the good of the group?
> Masculinity-how much roles of men and women are differentiated
> Power distance- inequality between lowest and highest paid
> Uncertainty avoidance- concern for law and order

4. **Experiment** (Phenomenologist) versus Fieldwork (Positivist).

Experiment- Assigns a control group and experimental group. The problem is to be fully matched. Measure attitudes before and after the course. Again, quality of survey is important.

Fieldwork- Get involved with the group. Watch out for buzz words and "in phrases".

5. **Verification** versus Falsification (Check for what doesn't work)

We should also be reminded of the types of Methodology as defined below:

Meta-analysis- statistical pooling of many studies

Field studies- practical and relevant -Population- Existing CEO's who want to find a competitive solution before a new outside hatchet man comes in, fires half the people and looks like a hero. Employees in fear of losing their job.

Lab studies-precise, in controlled situation. May not transfer to organization

Sample surveys- from questionnaires-depends on quality of sample and the question technique.

Historical, Descriptive, Analytical, and Experimental Case studies- narrow but accurate. It cannot be generalized usually.

Why Researchers Do This

Instrumental-To apply it to an existing problem

Conceptual- more general just for enlightenment

Symbolic-to justify a position already held, e.g. the tobacco industry,

Goal setting. As part of a perceived plan for profits

Forms

Exploratory- raises questions, understand what's going

on, Delphi technique, what do you think (ask experts).
Descriptive- what, how, where questions, measuring
effects or trends, if you are not sure of the scale.
Longitudinal- follow a group, panel survey
Causal- does x cause y, over time.

Just as within the corporation itself, does attitude
and policy trickle down from the hierarchy? If so, is there
a correlation between corporate actions and National
policy? Much has been said about the "Trickle-Down
Theory" espoused during the Reagan years. That didn't
work over the last 30 years, did it? According to most
every study known to man, the rich have gotten
significantly richer, both in term of raw amounts and in
terms of the overall percentage they control.

Social engineering model- results are fed into
specific decisions and then supply the answers needed to
enable decision makers to take the right course.
Quantitative. This is usually past oriented.

Enlightenment model- think of many different
viewpoints. Qualitative.

A Critical incident technique is used for
collecting observations of human behavior downsizing in
an office environment, in order to make predictions about
the person or group doing the action (Thorpe & Smith,
1991). It is critical when you are fairly certain of the
purpose or reasons for that act. (Flanagan, 1954). This is
Objectivist, therefore positivists.

I initially expect to pursue the following design/
methodology: In order to learn as much as I can about the
subject I have worked with both major methodologies as
well as a number of the sub sets. The questions will be
qualitative-How and why, not what. Yet by acting as an
Independent and not getting involved I will lean toward
being a positivist. My sample size will be both large and

long due first to the Meta-Analysis methodology of significant scholarly works- which is quantitative and second to the fact that I have been able to observe this phenomenon over almost twenty years. I will be generating, not testing the Hypothesis, therefore, qualitative. Generalization- would like to be able to generalize, but know I can't get from qualitative except at a conceptual level, which is what I will do. Case studies makes this hard also, only if I were to do one myself. Within a meta-analysis is OK though. My Meta-Analysis is also accepted as "research evidence, correlation studies using archival data" (McGrath, 1982, pg 79).

Scope

Again, the problem of downsizing is not country or industry specific. Concentration is on those industries in the United States, England, and Western Europe that are losing significant amounts of employees.

The time period to be considered is from the early 1980's through 2016, with the findings to address the consequences of the present and the immediate next 10 year period.

The broader issue to ultimately be addressed, of which downsizing is a major part, is whether or not the loss of jobs in these industrialized nations, specifically those of a manufacturing base, can effectively be replaced at all with anything meaningful; or will the net job drain eventually spell economic doom and collapse for those nations permanently, or at least for a generation or more. My work will be but a beginning, a baby step, from which to build toward the broader problems.

CHAPTER 4 ANALYSIS

Identify the problem

Is it worth studying? Since so much pain has occurred and so much hype has surrounded the process as to it being a legitimate (and acceptable) method of management, this is certainly a subject worth studying. Not as much a question of legitimacy as to acceptability.

What I expect to get from it. It would be nice to obtain a solution whereby everyone wins at this game. Not very likely so I expect I might hope to gain and be able to commit more knowledge to paper concerning the subject; in the hopes of coming up with suggestions for compromises.

Causes

Lack of monitoring by owners, poor board oversight, and excessive free cash flow allowed managers to expand beyond their efficiency levels, consolidations, mergers and production slowdowns, and failure to deal effectively with a global economy and competition. We are giving away our economy in bits and pieces- in manufacturing, engineering, and white collar services. Arguably, however; greed plays a large part as the power gap between top executives and the average worker increases dramatically.

Unintended Consequences

When dealing with Downsizing I am reminded of the above mentioned law. This is really a pretty good example. The idea of unintended consequences dates back at least to Adam Smith and the Scottish Enlightenment and popularized by Robert Merton, a sociologist. (Smith, 1776), (Merton, 1936). Similar to Murphy's Law, it is sort of a warning against the huberistic belief that humans can fully control the world around them. As to downsizing, the five suggested causes react as follows: Ignorance (It is impossible to anticipate everything, thereby leading to incomplete analysis-which may mean downsizing might not be the right thing to do), Error (Incorrect analysis of the problem, or maybe following habits that worked in the past but may not apply now)(this is not in conflict with the idea that "those who fail to study their history are doomed to repeat it"- which means downsizing may not be the right thing to do), Immediate interest, which may override long-term interests (CEO's steering their flock toward quarterly goals at the expense of long term profits by getting rid of qualified workers-), Basic values (meaning one's innate greed and self-preservation) may require or prohibit certain actions even if the long-term result might be unfavorable, and Self -defeating prophecy (think of the guy selling apples. If he takes fewer apples to work because things were slow yesterday, since he has fewer apples to sell, he will surely sell fewer. If you fire good people to save money, you will be unable to expand and make money when things get better because you decimated your intellectual stock).

Men such as Nobel have been read and studied because of the "unintended consequences" illustrated by dynamite, just like downsizing.

A few things have stood out from this analysis. The downsizing trend has not produced the financial rewards expected. Corporate executive officers have no incentive to keep workers when eliminating jobs is the easiest way to increase (short term) profits. Management is guided by financial market demands for short term (quarterly) profits at the expense of the employee and long term health of the company.

Confirmation bias

This is the tendency of people to favor information that confirms their beliefs or hypothesis. People display this bias when they gather or remember information selectively, or when they interpret it in a biased way. The effect is stronger for emotionally charged issues and for deeply entrenched beliefs. They also tend to interpret ambiguous evidence as supporting their existing position. Beliefs persist after the evidence for them is shown to be false. Does Confirmation bias exist in research? Absolutely. It is hard to be impartial.

When a practice destroys lives as downsizing does, only an insensitive robot would not want to study this phenomena in the hope of mitigating the effects, as a bare minimum and possible substituting for it in some fashion.

Everyone has their own agenda, their own opinion, their own cause and their own way of looking at things. If you are a manager you want your bonus, and the only way most know to get it is to lay off workers to cut costs. Do some people end up being forced to get a better job, or start a successful business? Sure. Does that happiness dividend hold for most people? It doesn't appear likely. For one more Mercedes, management just ruins lives.

Should corporations, i.e. CEOs, have a heart? Is that what we want and where we should be heading? Or, is survival of the fittest still the norm, never to change and not supposed to.

Outsourcing

The Walmart Story

What would any discussion be without the company we all love to hate, everybody's best bud, Walmart- the Wicked Witch of the West? This company epitomizes all that is bad about downsizing, morally and socially, mostly due to outsourcing. We really need a ground swell of social change to uproot the beliefs this company holds. We need to ask ourselves what kind of country we want to be. Walmart's version is one in which you drive down wages, cheat on taxes and go the cheap on health care (27% less than the industry average) and other benefits including retirement security (Trickery leaves about 500,000 Walmart workers ineligible for any retirement benefits-Rebutting the charge of no retirement security, the spokesman said Wal-Mart offers a combined profit sharing/401(k) plan and contributes up to 4 percent of an employee's wages, whether the employee contributes his own money or not. The secret to the discrepancy in information here is that, in order to qualify for these goodies, workers are not eligible to participate in the plan until after completing 13 months of service and 1,000 hours. This company lives on part timers and turnover), ship jobs overseas and buy overseas (so they participate in Sweatshop labor), all in the name of the almighty dollar. There big box mentality destroys small businesses in communities and downtown areas- take a look at the shells of thousands of these downtown areas across the United States (Fishman, 2006). Not that they are the only ones, just the poster boy for the practices. This needs no references, it just what it is, and it's in every forum across the nation.

The United Food and Commercial Workers Union lists Walmart average wage at $9.68 versus Costco's at $16.72 per hour. Of course, to Walmart, the glass is half full, saying that their wage is higher than the minimum wage and that somehow they are the Messiah come to save the working man. They think they are doing the world a favor by removing people from the public assistance roles. Granted, that is a psychological step up for many, but the upward move must be to a level that is greater than the public assistance after taxes and child care (Greenhouse, 2015). I don't think these people have a clear understanding of what the minimum wage is really meant for. Walmart. Another Walmart spokesman, in response to the destruction of other businesses charge, tried to justify their existence by saying that other businesses want to be near them (and are therefore cropping up). Again, missing the point here. If you are in a sinking ship you will try for a life boat. What they mean is that the few businesses they haven't destroyed want to be near them. Sure, we are our own worst enemy, we shop there. No one is willing to be the first to jump ship and stand up to be counted. This is a good time to designate the mantra screamed over and over again throughout this paper. Certeris Parabis (all other things being equal), if the average person knew that by paying 10% more for everything, unemployment would go away, his/her neighbors would have security and communities would be able to afford services again, would they do it? You betchem, Red Ryder.

Another spokesperson for Walmart said they purchased more than $150 billion in goods from suppliers in the United States. What they failed to mention was that they purchased over double that from overseas.

As for "sprawl," a spokesman said, "Look at a Wal-Mart super center. You can do your shopping, get an oil change for your car, get prescriptions filled, and get a haircut. It is the truly the convenience of a one-stop shopping experience" (Soderquist, 2005).True, there is some merit to that. If only the benefit of whatever time saved translated to a better lifestyle here in the United States.

The company is widely known for requiring workers to do off the clock work, and social service organizations can attest that Walmart workers need to rely on the "kindness of other"- friends, the community or the government. At least the government and community are there for them. The company aggressively opposes unions (Greenhouse, 2015).

Basically the company is a two time loser; they buy from overseas producers of products that could be made here, creating jobs, and by their very big box nature, they put Mom and Pop stores out of business. Few rational thinkers believe an equivalent number of people are then hired by Walmart.

China

Horrible and corrupt as we seem, are we letting the world pick our pocket? China, India, Vietnam, Saudi Arabia- you name them, are making deals with U.S. companies that will provide tons of jobs overseas-- work Americans could be doing. What is the U.S. doing to fight back? Appears to be nothing. The troubling part is that developing countries don't just have cheap wages. They're also offering government-backed incentives of cheap land, lower taxes and low-cost capital to win jobs in cases where they don't have a compelling market advantage. So, minus the cheap wages, why can't we do those things? Currently, we don't seem to know what our competitive strengths are (if any) and we also don't seem to have a long term plan to correct the situation. (Fallows, 2012)

It's not just profit, but huge profit that is an obsession of most of today's large and small corporations. As an example, General Electric decided that it could get a better return on its capital by putting it to work in one of its other businesses. In the fourth quarter of 2006, they were looking at around an 8% profit. This compared with a 19% operating profit for both the company's infrastructure and health-care divisions (Fallows, 2012). So, here's where I'm stumped, mystified and irritated. What's wrong with 8%? I know people with savings who would kill for 8%! Their point was that it makes solid free-market sense then for General Electric to put its plastics business on the block so it can take the estimated $10 billion to $12 billion that would be generated by the sale and reinvest it in a business showing 19% operating profit rather than one generating just 8% profit. True enough. Then sell it to an American company- or sell it to me! Saudi Basic Industries, the largest public company in the Middle East, with 2006 revenues of more than $23 billion, has been buying chemical businesses even as U.S. companies shed these assets. They are reported to have hired Citigroup to put in a bid for General Electric's plastics business (Fallows, 2012). They do this, so they say, in order to provide large numbers of jobs for the country's population. I ask you, don't we need the jobs also? Our Unemployment rate, regardless of what it is, is misleading because the jobs are now lesser paying jobs and less fulfilling. How many have actually lost their jobs to outsourcing? If relatively few, then care for them won't be very costly. If a significant amount then I rest my case and it is serious.

Intel's announcement around 2006, that it would build a chip plant in China also makes perfect free-market sense from Intel's perspective (Jubak, 2007). It's a $2.5 billion plant! Although it does put the company closer to a fast-growing market, which makes good business sense, the key was profit. Those tax breaks, cheap land and access to cheap credit mentioned above mean it will cost about $1 billion less to build the plant in China than in the United States. Again, all things we could offer here in the United States.

Where is the US government with its national interest's philosophy when you need them? Who's representing the long-term U.S. national interest in the creation of more decent-paying jobs?

This isn't a problem unique to the United States. All the so-called developed world faces the same challenges: How to create jobs at home when cheap wages are pulling them overseas. But charity begins at home so let's deal with our problems here at home.

I concede that it is easier for developing countries such as Saudi Arabia and China to come up with a strategy for catching up with the developed world than it is for a developed country such as the United States or France to devise a plan for staying on top.

There is little dispute that most products are made in China today. Necessary items such as shirts, pants, and shoes as well as the toys of today e.g. IPad, IPhone (Fallows, 2012). A reasonable and positive question would be "what would it take to get American companies to come back to the United States to do their manufacturing? Another question might be "Can a country continue to be a leader long term by just servicing and outsourcing what little they do produce? (Weil, 2005). Two very different questions. Think Apple, Google, Facebook. Think Wall Street and Amazon. Consulting, Finance, Software. No manufacturing.

The Shenzhen manufacturing zone in Southern China has over 450,000 workers. (Fallows, 2012). That's only one of several zones. If the total is only one million just think of the one million jobs lost in the United States. That may be a simplification but clearly a number and situation worthy of consideration. From the early 1980s on, manufacturing in America was known as "Rust Belt" industries, especially in the North Eastern cities. Think of all the vacant downtown sections in Akron, Cleveland, Detroit, Rochester, Corning, Manchester etc. One in five jobs were manufacturing related. Thirty years later that number was one in ten. Those "Rust Belt" jobs are looking pretty good now. Manufacturing has been leaving America since the end of WWII. Seriously, is the profit gained by a few worth the heartache spread among many?

The good news is that now the trend appears to be slowing reversing. Part of this is due to Chinese wages increasing. Part is due to labor prices becoming more attractive in the United States. (Fallows, 2012).

Part is due to technological improvements, communication improvements and productivity improvements here in the United States. Some manufacturers have determined that the cost saving doesn't make up for the time delay, inefficiency, poor quality, and inconvenience of not being able to design and refine the products close to the manufacturing (Maniscalco, 2004)

In China, wages are rising quickly. Environmental concerns are beginning to take hold in China. The currency is increasing in value against the dollar. Also, China's "investment model" is showing strain. China has created jobs by building factories, highways, railroads, dams and airports where there are no cities, and cities where there are no people. At that level, as hard as it is to believe, it would seem that there is such a thing as too much savings and investment and infrastructure (Brown A. S., 2005). The solution would appear to be coordinating peoples' savings with needed work/projects. The United States did this during the New Deal in the 1930's so there should be some anecdotal evidence as to the success or failure of such an endeavor. Even then it appeared to take a war to get us out of the doldrums. Or did it? Consensus would have us believe the Chinese need to create more domestic consumption while the United States needs to become more competitive in exports. I suppose it's possible for both to be true but one should ask, "How can both be possible- which is the right way?" Perhaps a little bit of Aristotelian "Golden Mean" or everything in moderation.

There is actually more good news for the United States. China has other issues which, even if they solve them, can only help our cause over time. Displacement of farm working adults, migration into the cities, 14-year-old "apprentices" and political pressure to reform environmentally and socially, are all issues that need the full attention of the government. It is worth remembering though that the government has met this challenge many times before over the last 30 years (Schuman, Woo, & Overland, 2008). (Fallows, 2012) is a firm believer that you can learn a lot by visiting a countries factories. He alluded to learning a lot about the England of Charles Dickens and Friedrich Engels by seeing its factories, and the America of Theodore Dreiser and Upton Sinclair by seeing ours a little later. An inspection of the factory conditions does reveal a few problems. Crowded rooms, fast paced assembly lines and the presence of hazardous materials. Lastly, the 60% turnover rate is a problem to deal with. Why would workers put themselves through the poor conditions at some of the larger companies with bad reputations? Because at least they will get paid a reasonable wage and not be underpaid or even cheated and not paid at all. It is important to note that just like in the United States, different factories and different areas will show different degrees of improvement.

But again, the Chinese are addressing these issues with cafeterias, exercise rooms, training rooms, shuttle buses, coffee shops, convenience stores, and campus type environments and cleaner/more comfortable work areas. Not all, but many. Still to be consider and implemented would be the "have a life" concern. The Chinese worker doesn't mind working a few extra hours but they would like some help with their social life. Maybe some mixers, some singles nights and other organized activities. Cleaver people if they decide to accede to these wishes (Engardio,

Roberts, & Bremner, 2004)

Outsourcing/Downsizing has been good for American companies overall but bad for America's low-skilled manufacturers. Draw your own conclusions as to who gets rich. The only problem with this logic, which would seem to lean toward American soft type jobs, is that there are very few of these jobs, mostly at the top while the bulk of workers in either country are in production. Even if they are lower paying, at least they are working.

There have been a number of efforts to re kick start the small manufacturing section. Good press goes to those taking place in The Bay Area. Any effort is great; however, San Francisco seems to represent all of America's imbalances, intensified. Tech and venture-capital billionaires on the Peninsula, hipsters in the East Bay and the city, rich naturalists in Marin, and ordinary families priced out of anything not a distant commute away. This is the perceived view of a hollowed-out and unequal modern United States (Fallows, 2012). It reminds me of Ayn Rand's *Atlas Shrugged*. (Discussed at greater length later). It certainly seems that in the not too distant future, the large (rich) cities will operate on one level while the outer areas – the rest of the country will be a wilderness or wasteland. Similar to "Logan's Run" with the same sheltered inner city and wilderness beyond. Whether or not the wilderness is good or bad isn't the question. Clearly we are, or fast becoming, a divided nation of rich and poor. Let's cross out fingers that the rebirth comes before anarchy. Into the standard American urban mix—high-end tech and finance, low-end service or tourist work, the professional class from universities and hospital complexes, we need to stir a renaissance of small-scale manufacturing. And not in

San Francisco.

The strategy needed is one that combines quick response, local skills, and a global marketplace to foster manufacturing in U.S. Cities. Being careful to protect intellectual property. The result needs to be a greater probability than Apples of creating jobs in the United States. You need a "quick iteration" way of deciding which ideas will work best in manufacturing. "You iterate and adapt quickly based on consumer demand. You learn to 'fail fast (Fallows, 2012). With this in mind, the politically controversial decision to keep General Motors operating saved hundreds of thousands of manufacturing jobs from being needlessly lost looks like a pretty smart move.

Is there any truth to the rumor that China uses prison workers and peasants as cheap labor? (Hebron, 2006). After determining whether it's true of not, can we check to see if we do it too? Or, perhaps, should we be doing it too? I have little doubt that China will do whatever is expedient to get ahead- and I'm equally sure that they probably got the idea from us.

A Progressive View

"Don't worry; they'll get better jobs in the service sector." That's what the free-trade supporters always say (Anderson, 2004). Easy for them to say, they have a job. "What do you suppose goes through their minds as jobs shift to Mexico or China? That line doesn't work very well anymore, since service jobs, including high-skill computer programming and financial analysis, are now going overseas also." (Anderson) Someday we will have to get it right when deciding whether and how much to assist our corporations with globalization. "US government's corporate-friendly approach to globalization requires a fundamental reorientation of policy that will aid workers at home and abroad." (Anderson) Remember, only a small portion of our economy exports.

What to do, what to do? How about elimination of taxpayer subsidies, among other things. Ban foreign outsourcing of state and federal government contract work, give tax credits to those that do not outsource- and double credits if a job is created. Any program that encourages overseas investment could also be targeted. Take a page from European firms who pay severance or negotiate with unions over plans to move jobs overseas.

Place the incentive where it belongs- with those who will keep the work and products in America. You can't imagine that corporations will "do the right thing" and stay at home. "Greed is good". These corporations, with rare exceptions, do not have a nationalistic bent. They have a self-serving agenda. That means it's up to someone else to make them.

The Chinese government a few years ago estimated that reforms required by the World Trade Organization would destroy the livelihoods of 20 million farmers (Anderson, 2004). Cute, coming from a nation that is encouraging farmers to move into urban areas-to fill all the empty buildings and to work in the many factories. Now that would appear to destroy the livelihoods of farmers, don't you think? Supposedly to upgrade their standard of living. Shades of the Industrial Revolution in the United States and England 150 years ago. Mexico said they lost 1 .3 million agricultural jobs under the North American Free Trade Agreement, according to the Carnegie Endowment for International Peace. (Scott & Ratner, 2010) Yet the United States whines that so have we. So, if they lost jobs and we lost jobs, WHERE ARE ALL THE JOBS? That would make it a race to see who could lie the most between the United States and Mexico, or make you wonder why we did that deal.

I keep hearing about the tremendous gap between the United States and so many of these other countries. Yet, when I go on vacation things are at least as expensive as they are here. I've always wondered how people in China and India, not to mention the Western European countries, are able to exist when prices are ridiculous yet wages are not. What am I missing?

The Dubya Bush Administration did anything but produce a full employment economy. On the contrary, it cobbled together one of the most inefficient sets of economic policies imaginable-tax cuts mostly for the rich over ten years and rapid increases in military spending (Anderson, 2004). It just doesn't get any crummier than that. They also never addressed seriously the large numbers of dislocated workers, and poor wages. All of which is supposed to be a positive outcome of free trade.

The government should, as a bare minimum, provide a protective blanket for those workers who have been downsized. This can be accomplished through unemployment benefits, free retraining to increase their current skills or for a new skill, health-care etc. It is important to note in fairness that some of these workers lost their jobs because they were grossly overpaid and had obscene pension plans that hastened the downfall of many companies. Again, the Bush Administration tried everything in its power to not expand unemployment benefits. (Anderson) This man was clearly out of touch with normal human beings.

Arrogance and stupidity are dangerous bedfellows. His administration also did not adequately funded its education program and made no serious effort to expand public health care coverage.

Bush, and people like him, say "if you don't have a job, it's your fault because you don't want one or don't try hard enough. This kind of rhetoric coming from a man who was given everything on a silver platter and still screwed up everything he ever touched. There should be a requirement that every politician should work summers in a canning factory. The fact is that most politicians, and people in general, operate by their own little set of rules- and simply change them when it suits them or the rules become inconvenient. I am truly amazed that no one put a bullet in this spoiled ex hippie's stupid brain.

How about wage insurance that would make up any difference if a worker had to take a pay cut upon finding another job? This for a limited time (a few years?) and with the understanding that seeking further education would be a requirement.

Don't you get tired of hearing that your reward will be in heaven while others seem to have their cake and eat it?

The major reason is the same as it's been for decades: Machines are doing more of the work and people less. Which is fine if, as promised, that would mean more free time for workers while earning the same amount of money. There may have been a time when we felt the expansion of the service sector would outweigh the losses in the manufacturing sector. If so, those thoughts are now long gone.

So what's is the problem? We don't know for sure. But it's possible that this is the best we can expect from now on. Since its bubble burst in 1989, Japan has lived through more than two decades of economic stagflation.

Why is it that we cannot learn from others? Isn't that exactly what is going on here in the United States? Which brings up the question of who caused this dilemma again? Easy money, one of the culprits, was brought about by the Federal government. With all that easy money the firms had a great excuse to expand and naturally hire more people. It was the Government's fault for the loose money and the corporations fault for hiring too many people. The easiest way for both Wall Street and the corporation to increase profits is to squeeze workers and make then work harder. Any Grimms' Fairy tale would take a back seat to the horror story of survivors who must now do the work of all those let go. To listen to the rich and powerful, you would think all this is evidence of a productivity miracle. More like a Scrooge environment, working harder and longer for less pay-- with no coal! I picture the mouse running on the treadmill.

Our treatment of the unemployed is nothing short of a crime. Cruelty to match any fairy tale. As a percentage, our expenditures on retraining and job creation is relatively small compared to other developed nations.

BP built an addition to a Frederick, Maryland solar plant and then tore it down because they got a better deal overseas? Must be nice to have all that money, or are they using yours? If the cost of materials is high compared to labor, the outsourcing/downsizing strategy makes even less sense. How did Europe manage while they sent their manufacturing to the US up until 1970- or did they? Actually, with all their socialism, how have they managed to stay afloat for the last 100 years? Clinton, a Democrat, helped to push through NAFTA, which has seemed to not be a good thing for either side. Why not? It seemed like a good idea at the time.

There are ways to perhaps address downsizing in a more humane way. Even the wrong approach would be a step in the right direction. Key objectives of outsourcing (downsizing's little brother), such as reducing costs and gaining flexibility, can also be met by floating workers, using part time workers, independent contractors and setting up joint-ventures." (Khanna & New, 2008). Floating workers refers to cross training employees so that they can be utilized somewhere else. (Khanna & New). That seems like a reasonably good idea. Employing part time workers is a great technique that is cost efficient for dealing with the seasonal spikes that can occur within the business. That does not make it an acceptable long term solution, although better than outsourcing. Part time jobs also act as a screening for finding future permanent employees. Also a good idea. The downside is that the employers don't have to pay benefits to part timers. Hiring independent contractors taps into a level of expertise in a given field that the organization may not otherwise have. (Khanna & New). Finally the approach of setting up a joint venture with another organization can help to achieve business goals while building up a long term symbiotic relationship between the two organizations which can lead to future success (Khanna & New). Good idea, but rarely implemented well. If there is a poor partnership, workers overseas are less likely to care about the product. Didn't anyone ever tell these people partnerships are generally doomed? That doesn't even begin to address the piracy issue in which one member of the partnership steals the technology of the other, and then dumps the partner. Was it made clear that the partnerships should be between two companies here in the United States? Any effort to keeping the work on our own soil is better than giving business to a foreign job market.

No doubt that from management's standpoint there is merit to moving job overseas. Too bad most of them don't have a good game plan.

It bears repeating many times that the analysis of the cost to stay in US and manufacture versus sending the work and job overseas is a difficult choice. Not for the CEO's mind you, but from a more realistic viewpoint of a third party. There is no question that with a minimum wage of around a dollar, the Chinese (and many others) can certainly produce cheaply. Depending on the industry, that figure can drop as low as 33 cents in India. In some cases even the raw materials are cheaper. Against those numbers would be the cost of shipping. The time delay and lack of ability to see and touch and therefore turn on a dime has to be factored in to the equation. If not, then why all the fuss over Just in Time inventor (JIT) that the Japanese used so successfully to compete against us in a previous turf war. Suffice it to say, there is debate (as well there should be) as to the feasibility of the practice of outsourcing. None of this so far has taken into consideration, the human toll in jobs lost in the United States.

Companies, granted, are run by smarter than average people. They are becoming global entities with a market not solely based in America because it is in their best interest. Diana Farrell, a Director for McKinsey, argues that there is inherent risk in sending our companies overseas, including abuses, and loss of jobs in the U.S- and that some countries will lose out. What a cavalier attitude! However, she argues that this is all in the short term and that our job is to find ways to work out the kinks in the practice. In principle this idea can help everybody on Earth so long as countries can find their competitive edge. I'm glad she said "in principle". How about "in fact"? A country can certainly decide to turn inward but its citizens may face skyrocketing costs, and suddenly cheaper products made elsewhere will look much more appetizing. This entire world is interconnected and there is not much we can do about that anymore (Heffes, 2004).

Jobs lost here and created elsewhere doesn't wash. (Heffes, 2004). It's kind of hard to be fair and reasonable when you're out of work and hungry.

Companies that are not managed well will fail. That doesn't mean that those at the top don't make a killing while destroying the company. The middle class is exploding in many developing countries (Heffes, 2004). Great for that country- not so great for the country that is losing the jobs. Unfortunately, outsourcing is probably here to stay. There are just too many positives to be ignored. And greed is a powerful motivator.

Dewhurst points out that normally big corporations justify offshoring by explaining that it improves quarterly revenue as costs decrease. (Dewhurst, 2008) That issue would seem to be a short term fix as well as a foregone conclusion. After a company has chosen to offshore it is almost impossible to improve upon that initial cost reduction, but management doesn't seem to have any regard for long term prospects.

It would seem that importing cheap goods should be better, but the cost of items only drops by 10%, which doesn't really help or isn't noticed by consumer; yet the farming out of the job to do the work costs the U.S. one career. What good are cheap goods if no one has a job to pay for the goods?

Paul Craig Roberts told the Bookings Institution in January 2004 that "The US would be a third world economy within 20 years- the economic outcome of the US labor force being denied first world employment and forced into low productivity occupations. By 2024 the US will be a "Has Been" country. We will have no economic base. We will not be self-sufficient" (Roberts, 2005). Heaven forbid if another conventional World War occurs. In case we have forgotten, depth of industrial base is likely what won it for us before.

Maybe you wouldn't have to downsize if the CEO didn't make so much. All I ever hear from corporate crybabies is, poor us, we can't compete. Therefore, we have to downsize. That means firing many $35,000 average workers so the CEO can make $10,000,000. If that doesn't make your blood boil, shame on you. Legendary venture capitalist Tom Perkins compared "the progressive war on the American one percent" to Nazi Germany (Kovach, 2014). Nicole Miller CEO Bud Konheim said on CNBC that "Americans making $35,000 a year should stop complaining because they're much better off than people in India and China. We've got a country that the poverty level is wealth in 99 percent of the rest of the world, he said" (Frank, 2014). First of all, you can't take that $35,000 you are making here and simply go to one of these so called other places. Someone really ought to put a bullet in this SOB's head! The French Revolution is looking pretty good. That kind of attitude is likely why people like Hitler can come to power.

"These people are wrong on moral grounds and wrong on policy grounds," says Steven Rattner, who currently oversees former NYC Mayor Michael Bloomberg's investments as chairman of Willett Advisors LLC. "On a practical level, if the people in the 1% don't recognize the 99% are hurting, they're going to end up with far more severe consequences then if they were simply willing to do something now. Those consequences could include civil unrest and tougher legislation, such as much higher tax rates for the wealthiest," he says. (Task, 2014)

"On a moral level, the whining of the 1% is particularly appalling", Rattner continues, "noting overall median incomes have fallen about 7% in the past 12 years on an inflation-adjusted basis and by 25% since 1979 for the average American without a high school diploma." "This is not what America is about, he says" (Task, 2014)

What kind of logic dictates that when you are bleeding money you hire a new CEO and pay him/her millions first thing. After reducing the CEO pay by 90% you might even want to consider promoting CEO's from within!

The benefits of downsizing are going to a limited group (corporations and their corporate officers), and not being equally distributed among other members of the work force. A horrible side effect of our outrageous practices is that the disease spreads to these other countries and there is nowhere to go and hide. The perils of globalization almost always seem to outweigh any benefits.

The benefits of Technology have not made life easier for workers as was promised, merely reduced the number of jobs available without a plan for other work or more affordable leisure.

The point is, who cares if the average worker makes a difference or not? Concede (only for a moment) the argument that the CEO is all that matters. First, let's all quit and see how well he does without workers. No? OK, then go at it from a more macro humanitarian level. Yes, human nature is lousy but are we not trying to improve it all the time? Isn't that what civilization is all about?

Boone (2000) said that since top management's time is limited, the time spent in the downsizing effort detracts from time spent inventing new products and improving existing ones.

It appears that downsizing has become an acceptable management practice despite evidence that it doesn't work financially. Most authors do not advocate downsizing as a universally good practice. Organizations should not exist solely for profits- it should be a means to an end- happiness, leisure, security; (Handy, 2002).

Most corporations and especially those in the banking industry and Wall Street could use a good shower. Or maybe I need one after reading about their antics. How about a good laugh? Let's call it self-governing. Are you nuts? People in positions of power and responsibility need to be held accountable for their actions and especially for their part in the 2006-2011 recession. These people are parasites feeding at the trough for their own benefit. Instead of hiding behind the corporate entity, there needs to be some individual responsibility. A good place to start would be the boards of directors.

Minimum Wage

One of the reasons given by management for downsizing is that there isn't enough work. I guess they forgot that the reason there isn't enough is because they have farmed out the work overseas. They did that because they could get it done cheaper overseas. So, how come the average worker is overpaid so much and still can't make a living here in the United States? The simple answer is that costs other than labor need to come down here in the United States. Something needs to be done about lower income workers scrapping by.

What does minimum wage have to do with downsizing? The argument goes that raise wages and people will be laid off or not hired. In the fast food workers minimum wage battle, the industry argued that the pay hike would lead to job loss and higher unemployment (Downsizing).

A recent study found that higher pay is associated with sharp reductions in turnover, which means lower costs for employers. Hence, no downsizing.

"The minimum wage can actually *increase* employment, owing to additional money in the pockets of workers, which they will spend in the economy, which in turn causes greater demand for goods and services, and more employment for workers" (Widmaier, 2013). Less downsizing.

The Australians pay a higher minimum wage ($16) have low unemployment and a Big Mac costs less. (Noor, 2013). That ought to tell you that it can be done; we just don't want to at the decision making level. End of story.

From a governmental macro level, better to have people working than to have to pay them welfare benefits and unemployment. That would seem to put the government on the side of the worker and against downsizing. Reduce the benefits or raise the wages.

Widmaier (2013) said minimum wage laws operate to reduce labor demand for low-skilled workers, along with the employment opportunities for low-skilled people. Whoever gave him that idea? Minimum wage exists to prevent lower income people from starving. Heaven forbid if the Unions, even with all their faults, get eliminated. Management will run roughshod and we will be back in 1850.

Dr. Diana Pearce produced a study indicating that lower income folks do not have enough money and that even programs developed for them are not adequate. She also found what a minimum subsistence might look like, with and without subsidies. Pearce said that self-sufficiency was around $10.45/hr. for each of two people working or $3677/month or $44,123. A single adult must earn 18.35/hr. to earn $3230/month for that same minimum subsistence. (Solman, 2013)

Age Discrimination

Another group suffering from an inequitable society which includes downsizing as one of its methodologies is the older worker. Traditional theories of human capital include assumptions that it declines with age.

There is a dilemma in financing the pension and lifestyle expectations of the increasing number of people moving into the middle and older age ranges. I don't doubt that people expect a better lifestyle than they earned, but as to financing the pensions, didn't I put that money into Social security all those years?

Ironically, these older workers who were formally considered to be declining in value, are actually valuable to their companies, who are having trouble obtaining certain skills.

Yes, older workers are paid more. That's the seniority system of employment. So, structure an acceptable incentive program that satisfies both the employer and employee for an exit strategy. This may possibly be true in technological environments (Bartel & Sicherman, 1993), where older workers are assumed to be less adaptable. The research identified overall positive inducements for supporting investments in older workers, contrary to historic thinking and conventional human capital theories (Bartel & Sicherman). Incidentally, many other studies have determined that older workers, due to a better work attitude, have better absenteeism records than younger workers. Older workers are also inclined in general to work more consistently while on the job. Just ask any young worker and they will tell you that you'd be lucky to get 3.5 hours a day from them. So why do older workers get downsized more?

Education and experience are obviously important elements of human capital. Middle aged and older workers can have trouble finding new jobs at their previous wages because their old wages many times reflected firm-specific human capital. However this logic seems to be assuming that their firm-specific capital is either not transferable or is of lower value to competitors. The cost of learning new skills and proximity to retirement may reduce the perceived expected return from investing in learning new skills. This is felt to threaten the economic return for an employer when hiring older workers.

If knowledge is part of human capital and information is power then the long-term motives for sharing and transfer must be part of the organizations game plan otherwise competition between individuals will cause information and knowledge not to be shared and will hurt the firm. The role of older workers and mentors becomes clear both as custodians of knowledge and transfer agents. They also have a role as motivators and in providing evidence that sharing knowledge improves rather than damages individual careers. If that is, in fact, true.

Never let it be said that there are not 66 year olds walking around out there who never matured beyond the age of 18.

The question of human capital and the elderly is germane because in the example of cyber businesses, they operate globally and have fewer employees. Who is doing the work? Somebody is going to be downsized.

There may be another glitch for the older worker however. Today's world is changing as to the permanency of any position. It isn't the old AT&T for a 40 year career. Due to many reasons, the loyalty is gone- first from the employer and as a result, from the employee. Many older workers may find it harder to want to adapt to this more transient type of work place. The younger workers expect to work for many firms, to have their performance and payment assessed on short term results. They want expertise, not position. That's going to be tough on some older workers. "No one likes change" applies more to the elderly. Age also means a safer pair of hands and better social skills. If the older worker maintained contemporary technical skills they would be unstoppable- assuming given a chance.

In today's world, work that was once thought to be for young unskilled and desperate workers are being taken by older workers who have largely forgone the value of their accumulated experiences. Think about it. They have foregone the value of their accumulated experiences. How sad. It makes for a curmudgeonly group of people and a poor commentary on our society.

A new underclass of marginalized older workers of both genders is emerging within developed economies. They say that this is happening at the very time when the experiences and appreciated human capital of such people are needed to reinforce the shrinking skilled labor pool. Why are the two not getting together, and when will it begin to happen?

Developed economies may not be able to keep growing and to finance pensions unless retirement is both deferred and made partial. This means older workers have to be re-engaged, re-trained and retooled to keep them working at high levels of economic utility. In turn this means their particular skills and related values must be understood and sustained. Evidence from many sources shows that common perceptions of declining skills and downward changes of physical capacity with age are incorrect in both absolute terms and impact upon work performance. There are no intrinsic biological limitations to full time work at standard full capacity until at least the age of 65 years. This needs to be urgently incorporated into academic theories and recognized in human resource management. The fact that longevity is no longer the norm in jobs, the low pay/high pay system assuming even true, may need attention.

There is a lot to criticize in both these economic approaches to human capital. In most technical and professional occupations the job holders will only accept training that is specific to their own view of their long-term worth. In that sense it is probably going to be transferable learning and unfortunately, moves with the employee, usually to competitors. By the way, good corporations have always known that the better the employee, the greater the risk that he/she will move on eventually. That's just a cost of doing business.

In some industries such as accounting and engineering specific human capital can evolve into general human capital. In these industries one gets designations when certain specific technical experiences and levels are achieved. Once you get the designation it can be transferred.

How about this? Older workers should be paid more because they spend the money in a more socially responsible manner, e.g. for their children's education, for savings, for housing. Young people spend money on drinking and partying. Yeah, yeah, I know that's generalizing but that is what's being done to older people.

There a number of viewpoints regarding the effects of downsizing that one can chose in order to narrow the scope of any discussion. The attempt is made here to sort out as many as possible in an effort to determine which of the viewpoints, in the opinion of the writer, is most worthy of further research.

Beginning as far back in the causal chain as we can go and still stay within the context of downsizing strictly speaking, the first category might be, why initiate the process in the first place? The answer on the surface would appear to be either; to be competitive and stay in business, or merely to enhance the already existing profits.

Positives for Companies

Certainly, no work would be complete without reference to Schumpeter and his infamous comments that "downsizing may not be pretty to watch and people will get hurt for sure, but this is the way the market takes care of itself in capitalism." Schumpeter stated that there is no entitlement to a job. That's easy for him to say. Maybe there should be. He coined the phrase "Capitalism is creative destruction." (Schumpeter J. A., 1950)

This, of course, is viewed by many as a positive result of downsizing if one is the recipient of bottom line savings because of the practice. It is still difficult to equate the practice in any way to Schumpeter since his is an advocate for the growth and expanding of companies, not downsizing. (Schumpeter J. A., 1950)

Certainly technology upgrades or changes in market situations have made some workers redundant.

Sheraton Hotels downsized successfully when they went from a 300 room hotel needing 40 managers and 200 employees to that same facility now needing only 14 managers and 140 employees (Harari, 1993). Many companies are finding themselves overstaffed because increasing technology has led them to require less time and fewer workers to get the job done. Promeon, which is a division of Medtronics, used to require 112 workers to produce 80,000 pacemaker components. However, increased technology in producing these pacemakers has now led the company to only require 23 workers to produce 105,000 units in the exact same time. Furthermore, the manufacturing cycle time has gone from 60 days to 1 day with these 23 workers (Harari). In Promeon's case, if they didn't resort to layoffs, they would have ultimately been beat out by more innovative competitors (Harari). No one condemns companies for struggling to stay in business. After all, each company is competing with others companies, and those who do not make money eventually go out of business and all the jobs are lost. The desire is to get these companies to care for the employees let go in a better manner and spread the pain around to upper management more. Whether, and which, technology is good or bad remains to be seen.

In the unfortunate event that a company would determine layoffs to be the only appropriate solution, the biggest mistake a company can make is their lack of honesty. If a company has any plans for layoffs in the future they should let the employees know. They should tell them exactly why layoffs are a possibility, who will be affected, and when. If the layoffs are not going to create any other improvement than cost cuts, such as organizational growth and success, then there is not a significant motivation to be laying employees off. Companies need to keep their workers educated throughout the whole laying-off process so that they know exactly what to expect. Managers should be willing to answer any questions and show statistical data to support their reasons that layoffs are necessary. If managers are honest with their employees, then there is no reason why the workers within the organization should feel mistrust or anger towards the company (Harari).

Another mistake made by companies in the process of laying-off employees is their lack of sensitivity, counseling, and placement assistance. People who are dealing with a layoff need help both emotionally and professionally and it can really help a company to be sensitive to these issues. If an organization takes on an "out of sight, out of mind" attitude, they will ultimately get a bad reputation and therefore face problems when it comes to recruiting top employees. Most company's face large challenges in finding top talent employees, mostly because people with top talent have unlimited choices, and if a company acquires a bad reputation, it isn't likely that these top workers will be interested in working there. Stroh's Brewery helped find employment for 98% of their employees who were dismissed from layoffs. Other helping tactics can also be done, such as Herman Miller who offers an entire years pay for any employee who faces a layoff (Harari, 1993).

The third mistake that is often made during layoffs is the lack of attention to the survivors. Many companies make a huge error in believing that once they are done with layoffs that business will just go on as usual. If there are a large amount of layoffs then it is obvious that there will be a lot more responsibility added to the survivor's work load. If a company wants the survivors to perform their best, then it is very important for them to be aware of why they are still there. Whether it was luck, due to their performance, or just didn't involve them, it is important for them to know (Harari, 1993). If a company expects the survivor's to be satisfied with their job then it's necessary for them to feel like there is a reason they are taking on more responsibilities. Management needs to make them feel like they are highly valued in the company for their work. Money usually conveys that sentiment.

When Charles Schwab took a 50% pay cut in order to set the example, it was a good first step but the severance of $7,500 given to some employees still left a lot to be desired. Phillips electronics provides not just out placement services but job finding assistance. Companies need to use their contacts to get the employee another job. (Harari, 1993)

In Oren Harari's article in *the Management Review,* he states that, "Too many people on the payroll are draining costs, inhibiting speed and curtailing innovation—among others as well as themselves". Employees want better pay, pensions, and health insurance that add to other factors and eventually cost the company its profits. The company loses momentum along with the business edge to compete. This threatens the company's existence.

Just like humans, corporations naturally overreact to good times by hiring fast, in bulk and too much. Then they go about weeding out those not fitting in It appears to be a foregone conclusion that there will be a sign curve cycle of ups and downs that can only bring misery to employees (Love & Nohria, 2005). It begs the question of whether it doesn't bring unnecessary misery and unnecessary work to the corporation as well. Wouldn't it be more prudent for all concerned to take a closer look, hire the right amount in the first place, take care of them once on board and not have to go through the pain of laying them off later? This phenomenon appeals to target management and white collar staff, not manufacturing blue collar workers as proponents of the practice would have you believe (Love & Nohria). These authors also indicate that firms have rehired some laid off employees after finding out they possessed specific, critical or tactic skills or knowledge needed. It shows them willing to reconsider decisions but the fact is they made the wrong decision in the first place and it cost them time, manpower and money. It has been suggested that owners figure out the characteristics that top performers possess and consider these when looking at prospective

employees. Somehow I thought we had been doing these
for the last several decades.

HR Strategies

No one is saying that the pain of downsizing-
related lay-offs could be avoided entirely, but it sure
could be minimized somewhat. Somewhere, someone in
an organization could and should be following the trends
of the marketplace, and from observation, anticipate to a
certain extent the next downturn. A little preparation
would go a long way. Over the years the destructive
practice of downsizing has been the standard response to
financially difficult times. In spite of the fact that little
evidence exists that the process actually works, at least to
the extent anticipated, they still do it. The consequences
are costly and devastating to individuals and entire
communities.

Assuming absolutely necessary, one should at
least make the practice that of last resort. Defer, minimize
or even avoid should be the goal. Do studies. Think of
alternatives. Maybe a short term temporary cost cut might
work and prevent future problems. This would be in the
case of a temporary setback such a drop in sales. Get on it
early.

Concentrate on efficiency- which you should be
doing anyway in business (but aren't). Be flexible,
implement a hiring freeze (hiring new people while
laying off others is not only expensive but sends a poor
message to employees (Maxon, 2008). Use a hiring
freeze to eliminate redundant positions. Use Incentives
such as early retirement and reasonable buyouts
(Bumbaugh, 1998). It seems that it would be easier not to
hire than to fire. Require employees to take their
vacations, and also require some unpaid vacations

(Govreau, 2008). Reduce the workweek hours. Some pay is better than none at all (George, 2004) (De Bono, 2008). As to how the work still gets done – there is supposed to be less of it.

Reduce or eliminate altogether any overtime. Reduce salaries. This is a nasty call and might backfire. You risk creating poor morale, lack of loyalty, and having top people leave. Even a temporary plant shutdowns would be better than firing people (Gandolfi F. , 2008a).

As a gesture of good will, and with the hope that you may obtain other good ideas, don't overlook soliciting cost reduction ideas from employees (Vernon, 2003). Not only do the workers feel included but it's hard for them to complain when it was their idea. These employees are a good source for ideas because they are on the front line and know better than anyone else what could be done to improve things.

One excellent idea some firms have found works well in appeasing workers is that of issuing stock options. Perhaps a promise (and delivery) of a bonus when things turn around might work (Morss, 2008). Voluntary sabbaticals sometimes work either with a reduced pay or even none at all. Sabbaticals are a two edged sword though. Some workers return energized and chomping at the bit, while others lose their edge, having been out of the loop. Then there are those who don't come back at all, having found better situations. Ironically, firms offer sabbaticals during goof times yet not so much during economic downturns (Vernon, 2003). The whole point here is to be able to reduce costs without losing high performing employees during a downturn.

Employees could be farmed out to another firm for a set period, like a contract worker almost, with each firm picking up a portion of the salary and benefits

(Morss, 2008). A good firm will also think of transferring the employee within the company itself. Internal job fairs are a great way to make employees aware and available (Vlasic, 2008).

Then there is an offering of a severance package or early retirement. This is not a bad idea as it recognizes employees for their service and creates goodwill with both those going and those left behind. The flip side is that it can be costly up front and those left behind may develop an entitlement mentality (George, 2004).

The only time Downsizing is unavoidable is if there is a prolonged business downturn (Vernon, 2003). Many studies suggest that mass layoffs should still be avoided (Gandolfi F. , 2006). As mentioned above regarding honesty, it is critical to instill loyalty and commitment in both the remaining and the laid off workers (Vernon, 2003), mostly because, remaining positive about the long term prospects of the economy and the firm, one wants to be able to re hire those let go and retain those left behind (who maintained a good attitude). One way to make these workers happy is with a re hiring bonus, which is great; however, oftentimes the rehire takes the form of hiring external consultants, and not those left go. There are many pros and cons to this form of employment. In some cases, the consulting contract pays even better, but there is the issue of a lack of benefits (Gandolfi F. , 2006). In some cases, good salaried workers do not have the proper mentality in order to be consultants. Or they don't know how to go about seeking that kind of work. In the case of the bonus, one must be careful to be sincere in the offer.

In any case, the firm needs to maintain communication with the laid off worker. Monitor everything to catch mistakes as soon as possible. Today, with the internet (Facebook!), 24-7 hotlines, and e-mails, it takes very little time and therefore, there is no excuse for not maintaining contact and good relationships (Lublin J. , 2007). Is it just me or is it offensive to receive critical messages by email or Facebook? All of this in addition to the outplacement assistance mentioned above.

The impression shouldn't be given here that this will be an easy task. Life in the corporation is complex. Dealing with responsibilities for making money, human beings, human nature, and just the ordinary every day organizational challenges does require effort

General Motors has been downsizing since the 1980's. That's long enough to have made an impact. It didn't. Let's see, didn't they go bankrupt? That would indicate that they should have considered something else, like: suspend dividends, cut CEO pay, get government help, share components across brand lines, better quality cars and reduced models. GM builds gas guzzlers while Toyota build hybrids. GM still does not produce the quality cars that Toyota does. Part of the problem may also be huge pension costs and ridiculous promotions and discounts.

In GM's case, like so many others, the justification given by biased management for their actions was that the costs of downsizing would not outweigh the saving of cutting 25,000 jobs (Harari, 1993). What a joke! Now you will have a smaller company with fewer people earning less money still responsible for the same bloated pension costs from a previous era. If you are making fewer cars with fewer people what makes you think you will make more money than before? Seems like expansion would be a better idea. Isn't that what the government tells us is necessary to survive?

If you look around and see that because of technology updates one worker can do the work of two (without killing himself!) then the key is to find another task for the other person. Either a different task or more of the same.

Notwithstanding the pilferage of pension funds, most of the time companies still keep pension plans while downsizing. Not in question is the fact that the pensions are in many cases far too large (Kerr, 1975).

Challenge workers to come up with ways to solve the problem and invent new products, increase revenues by growing the business and cut costs in other areas such as supplies, materials and redesigned work flow of machinery.   American companies are busily outsourcing workers when they should be in sourcing CEOs from other countries. U.S. CEOs are way too expensive (Sklar, 2004).

Don't lay off on a flat percentage or those with seniority. Different departments require different number of employees and seniority brings with it intellectual capital.

Again, how tough is it to provide feedback, rewards and recognition to survivors Treat them fairly and with respect.

Use multiple strategies and techniques. Not all downsizing strategies worked as planned, and you may have to change and experiment.

Ayn Rand

Downsizing is just another capitalistic management technique that we have been lead to believe is perfectly OK, because "Greed is Good", and the pursuit of money, especially in the United States, is an American pastime. It's another example of, "say it often enough and people begin to believe it." A number of things over the years have caused this attitude. One in particular is the philosophy of Ayn Rand. It's hard to believe that she wrote *Atlas Shrugged* in 1947. I guess that just goes to show you greed has been around a long time. In *Atlas Shrugged*, and in her opinion obviously, she recounts how industrious, self-reliant, and capable people become the villain in society. Turning logic on its head, she says, these people are seen as the height of what ails the economy because they work to enrich themselves while neither asking anyone for help nor offering to allow others to freeload on their success (Rand, 1947). How dare they! Individualism means we will do whatever is necessary to get ahead, including downsizing. She leaves little room for sympathy for others. Let the chips fall where they may and those who can't keep up can, and should, fall by the wayside. In Rand's philosophy there is no room for compassion and empathy. Sounds pretty much like the attitude most of those at the top have today. Nothing is important except the almighty dollar.

Like so many of us- probably most of us- she is subjective and dismissive of things she feels no need for, or disagrees with. (Rand, 1947)That sounds like exactly what must be going through the minds of those who downsize. Who cares who I hurt as long as I make money? The philosophy is over simplified. Black or white. Right or wrong. With me or against me. It doesn't seem to allow for catastrophe or bad luck.

Can you imagine the United States without the collective effort that provided the Social Security blanket? What about making sure everyone is healthy and has a good education? No matter how nice things are in some valley in Colorado for John Galt, physical security is still an issue as long as human nature demands violence to take something from others. Keep downsizing and you won't be safe from the angry, hungry mobs no matter where that magic valley is. Besides, if we provide some sort of security blanket for citizens because we care, wouldn't it be the same to take care of workers in other ways, like provide jobs for them?

Rand thinks private enterprise will take care of roads, schools, hospitals etc. (Rand, 1947). History says otherwise. Private enterprise, until the greed factor is addressed and corrected, will go where there is a profit to be made, which means increasing technology and using the cheapest labor possible- usually not you. Ergo, your job just went overseas. It's possible this globalization thing isn't the panacea it was made out to be.

Negatives for Companies

Firing people has gotten to be trendy- it is how you make your corporate "bones" (Hickok T. , 1995). Sloan (1996). An important future research question would be, "How long is too long to wait for results"?

There is clearly a lack of conclusive evidence supporting the long term benefits of downsizing (Bailey, Bartelsman, & Haltiwanger, 1994), (Cascio W. , 1995); (Lewin & Johnston, 2000), (Armstrong-Stassen M. , 1998), (Madrick, 1995). Armstrong et al (2001) discussed nurses who were transferred and experienced negative job feelings and results. Wagar (2001) observed that a reduction in workforce resulted in decreased performance. The study suggested that: more grievances were filed, a poorer supervisor union employee relationship developed, there was more absenteeism, and lower overall employee satisfaction was evident. Because of guilt and lost trust in management, survivors may sabotage the organization with decreased productivity

Downsizing has failed to reduce costs and increase profits (Cameron, Freeman, & Mishra, 1991). Collins and Noble (1992) indicated that cost savings could be achieved by methods other than layoffs. Rosenstein (2000) reported that significant savings could be achieved through material and supply cost reduction. Hamel and Prahalad (1994) stated that downsizing for the sake of cost reduction alone is intellectually shortsighted and neglectful of what resources will be needed to increase revenue streams of the future. Hamel and Prahalad do not question the legitimacy of downsizing but indicate that it would be better to deal with core competencies and restructuring with existing staff than simply cutting. Downsizing fails to consider the future resources needed (Hickok T. , 1995). Little has been written on this, but increased workload and a deteriorating work environment may have adverse effects on customers. Walston, Urden and Sullivan (2001) discovered that downsizing does not translate into improved performance and that it should only be used as part of a long term strategic plan. Cascio (1998) found no financial improvement from downsizing. In fairness, he found no detriment either. Dr. Cascio's study was based on the S&P 500 firms from 1982-2000. During this time 80% of the layoffs involved white collar workers. Cascio suggested that; yes, cutting payrolls might be the logical means of reducing expenses and therefore increase earnings (not the same as profits). The key phrase here was "all other things being equal" which of course, they are not. The anticipated benefit of downsizing did not materialize. There was no consistent evidence that downsizing led to improved financial performance as measured by return on assets. This was inconsistent with his earlier study. Only by growing their business do firms do better than stable companies, not by downsizing. Those growing their business did 41% better than downsizers and 43% better than stable employers by the end of year two (Cascio W.). The study hits on a huge issue; that not only does downsizing not solve the problem, but expansion is the way to go. It is important to note that for downsizing to win the argument it must do better than the stable organizational environment, not just break even. Otherwise, why do it and destroy lives? The study determined that downsizing was no longer about large sick companies trying to save themselves, but companies merely trying to boost earnings at the expense of laid off employees. It did, however, observe that small companies will resist layoffs more due to the invested cost in their employees and the cost of retraining. (Cascio W.)

America is not alone in the downsizing trend, although the technique is more difficult to implement in Europe because of their attitude of concern for the worker backed up by a strong union presence.

Today's speed of change means companies can be left behind in a heartbeat. The goal of a good company should be to create new customers, markets and revenue streams and not downsize. Machines work efficiently but they do not invent. Until the rise of the machines becomes a reality, smart, well trained people invent and are the true long term asset.

Downsizers see people as costs to be cut while restructurers see them as assets to be developed. Evidence suggests that costs don't go down as fast as the revenue lost. It is possible that if you lay off the knowledge base (employee), you have removed an important link and the entire structure may not work. (Cascio W. F., 2002) He hit on most of the mistakes in the downsizing process: failure to make clear long term goals, use of downsizing as first resort- instead of no new hires, reduce perks, freeze salaries, and promotions, being non-selective in downsizing- across the board at middle management or below, failure to change the way work is done after downsizing or else just piling more work on others, failure to get everyone involved, failure to be open and honest, failure to treat those who depart with dignity and take care of them, failure to care of those left behind, ignoring other stakeholders, and not evaluating and learning from mistakes (Cascio W. F.). Before downsizing, consider the impact on long term employees. Is it part of a large plan or is it the entire plan –a quick fix? Don't underestimate the virtues of stability and give employees a chance to find a solution (warn every one of the impending decision without telling who will go so they will all be involved. This last one is questionable and refuted by other studies. Communicate, train, and get commitment and trust (Bridges W. , 1994). Only the foolish will let their fates be decided by those they work for. Cameron et al (1993) and Auerbach et al (2000) have all presented ways to prevent staff reductions.

In 1991 Wyatt Company surveyed 1005 companies and found that less than 1/3rd experienced expected profit increases. 46% found that reducing employees did not reduce expenses as much as expected. It may have reduced it some, however. This is not a complete argument unless we can show the other detrimental effects that were incurred. Only 21% achieved satisfactory return on investment increases.

Downsizing is frequently shortsighted, a knee jerk
reaction. (Bruton, Keels, & Shook, 1996). Bruton also
indicated that strong opinions mixed with scant data
provide a dangerous brew for strategic decision making.
Especially when that data is used to justify an already
held opinion. As in most things, successful downsizing
may depend more on the specifics of a particular
company. The study addressed efficiency vs.
effectiveness (fewer employees or narrowing scope of
core competencies). Doing an existing job with less was
not as successful as altering the range of what you do-
diversifying or selling off non-productive units. This
seems to be a reversal of the trend to buy all you can
prevalent in the 60's and 70's. Some successful
downsizers do pursue efficiency gains. They do it in
conjunction with refocusing on core competencies
(maybe keeping people on in a different role) and not
extracting wage concessions from remaining workers.
Cuts might have to be deep if in an ailing firm. The
bottom line seems to be to match the size to the specific
case or needs of the company. Should you cut R&D?
Common sense would tell us that research is the life
blood of your firm. Then again, no one ever said common
sense ruled the day. Bruton joined the hardliners in
saying the ultimate goal is the improvement of financial
performance. Should that be, and not mankind's welfare?
Besides, De Meuse et al (1997) found that financial
performance decreased with layoffs from 1987-1991. We
live in a "Culture of narcissism". (Lasch, 1979)
Corporations have only one objective- profit. David
Packard at HP advocates keeping shareholders,
management and employees in balance, whatever that
means. Fisher and White (2000) find that only 41% of
downsized companies reported increased productivity

and only 37% realized long term shareholder value. Is this a poor showing at only 41% and therefore a testimonial against downsizing, or could it be said that if almost one half of the companies realized improvement it's worth the attempt? They also found that downsizing affected learning capacity.

Chalos (2002) made the effort to explain the paradox between ongoing downsizing and inconclusive empirical evidence to support the practice. His study was inconclusive, showing success in some and failure in others. Market studies by (Lee & Alexander, 1999), found negative price reactions to employee downsizing announcements. Chalos (2002)said a corporation has a right to profit. Not really. Just like life, liberty and the pursuit of happiness, they only have the right to try for profits. Which brings us back again to the burning question, are we heading in the right social direction and is money really how we ultimately wish to judge ourselves? Even if one wishes to hang their hats on the positive quantitative numbers, assuming there are any, any college course in finance will question the validity of these numbers. Even though net income looks good, it isn't necessarily the same as positive cash flow. Chan (1995) found that plant closing did not significantly improve performance. Yet, Chan found cost cutting earned significantly positive returns. Go figure. In addition to the negative market reaction to plant closings, closing plants and cost cutting did not improve performance. Refocusing did better than cost cutting Chalos (2002). Clearly strategies are needed to improve performance, such as revenue refocusing, cost cutting and plant closings, product line down scoping instead of downsizing, and get rid of unprofitable or unrelated lines. Hopefully there is a place for the employees on the remaining lines. Cost cutting can be retooling or refining a process in a product line as well as layoffs. Buying cheaper, outsourcing, trimming R&D, trimming selling and administrative expense are all alternatives to downsizing. Not that they are all perfect or to be sought either.

DeMeuse et al (2004) in their 12 year study of 100 firms from 1987-1998 asked "do firms that downsize experience better financial performance, and if so, how much and what time period is required to see results?" It would seem to be open to interpretation. Their introduction states that it has been "proposed" that downsizing reduces operating costs, eliminates unnecessary levels of management, streamlines operations,, prunes deadwood, enhances overall effectiveness and makes the corp. more competitive. First of all, the above efforts appear to be overlapping. You don't get credit for all of them. I find that eliminating unnecessary levels of management is much the same as streamlining operations and pruning deadwood, which then reduces operating costs, which enhances overall effectiveness and makes the corporation more competitive. The key word here is purposed. There is no proof. Very little data supports the reliability of this strategy. DeMeuse admitted that relatively few empirical (actual experience or experimental) studies existed at the time of this paper. His hypothesis that financials of those that downsized would be significantly different did prove to be the case. Those that practiced double digit downsizing performed much poorer. Even though more sales were generated in some cases it did not translate into profit. The study found that corporations that downsized three or more times did poorer than those that didn't. DeMeuse et al (1997) said when management perceives labor as a cost they will downsize again. Even when the survey indicated that the downsizing com. Looks like layoffs alone do not renew or revitalize a company.

Investment Return

Corporate executives and shareholders seem to take it as an article of faith that reductions in force and the savings they generate are a necessary evil when earnings numbers are declining. Others start with a given from empirical evidence that downsizing is wrong because of the damage inflicted on individuals, communities, and society.

Most people with any financial background only think of one thing when confronted with these words. How much money did I make? They never ask, are the workers important? Are workers thought of as a cost or as an asset? Will taking care of them better increase the overall corporate harmony, and the bottom line?

Granted, you have to make money to continue to exist as an entity. How much is enough? Is the bottom line the only mandate for a company? Who really owns a company and who is a stakeholder to be concerned about?

Is the practice of downsizing going away any time soon? If so, what are the ways to accomplish your goals without it? If not, then what options are there to make the process less painful?

Good health, good wages, job security, retirement pension plan, and pleasant working conditions are all critical, but you must still make money. The pendulum can't swing too far either way.

Community college programs and other retraining facilities and efforts are costly and often only correct for unskilled and perhaps some semi- skilled workers. Companies that downsize therefore, can help themselves best by providing a better service through a higher Quality Outplacement. That not only helps them financially but creates a better image in the community

Unfortunately, many companies, in thinking about costs, downsize their outplacement at the same time as their people, in order to reduce costs. And sadly, if it's an inferior outplacement plan you're looking for, they are abundant. If done poorly it could take forever.

High-quality outplacement programs would include proactive mental health and counseling support for discharged workers, plus tailored coaching in job finding skills. Services often merely have facilities available for clients to conduct their own job searches. By going with high-quality outplacement services, companies cut the costs of a downsizing action by reducing overlooked losses in absenteeism, unemployment insurance, health care insurance premiums, turnover, and litigation.

Proponents of downsizing would have you believe that organizational change is unavoidable. That Restructuring and Downsizing have become a necessity. This in spite of the fact that the hidden costs of organizational change of both discharged and remaining employees consistently outstrip the savings gained from reductions in personnel. Studies show that absenteeism and turnover among remaining employees always increase after downsizing, translating into lost productivity and lower profitability.

Like a catastrophe in your life, of which this is one, talking about it helps, and the correct way of talking about it helps a lot more. These are skills not possessed by many of the outplacement groups. Studies show that addressing psychological needs helps former employees find jobs faster. Clay (1998) cited research by psychologist and University of Texas professor James W. Pennebaker, PhD to that effect. It permeates to those left behind as well, for, in seeing that their former coworkers are being taken care of, trust that they will be treated fairly as well. And for management- no lawsuits and a good reputation for the company. It may mitigate the bad taste in everyone's mouth but it isn't going to bring back your job or any feeling of well-being that was present before the carnage. Let's not hope for too much and get ridiculous. The problem with American management is, American management. Management has been spoon fed so much clap trap for so long from MBA classes and the capitalistic financial world, they wouldn't know a fair deal if it slapped them in the face. From their financial perspective, it will seem counter intuitive that investing in the welfare of ex-employees will help profits, especially because the reason for downsizing is to improve productivity by cutting costs. Financial executives may ask, "Why should I spend more money on discharged employees and dip into the savings from letting them go?" Not so much a long term thinker here. The answer is, there are hidden costs as mentioned which could negate the entire process. In addition to those costs, we have the morale issues and the sabotage that often accompanies it. That can only mean more sick days, lower productivity, and higher turnover. Not to mention a propensity to destroy things. Then there's hiring temporary substitutes, the costs of both replacing employees that leave and training their new substitutes. Also, discharged employees continue to cost money after being laid off in the form of health insurance until they land on their feet, or the requisite time has elapsed. And let's not forget Uncle Sam's cut. Unemployment insurance tax rates will increase. How about litigation? Not everyone is a Mr. Milktoast who will take this lying down. Cost will be incurred even if the case is dismissed or settled out of court. If the company goes to trial and loses, whoop de do! Financial injustice is finally given its comeuppance.

As a third party, it's easier for outplacement firms to stay the course for others. Besides they are getting paid for it, after all. Like anything else, the slightest spark can ignite a storm of outrage. Making contact and working with the employee before that fateful day would be great. How about some interview practice? Workers are not going to want to do this. Most people hate the process. Like heroes, only a fool would really want to put themselves through it. If this outplacement firm is any good, they should know who the players are, and which ones are the closers. There are tricks to doing interviews. Remember to picture them naked.

Those left behind also need counseling and help. Decreased morale translates into survivors being disgruntled enough to go elsewhere for a new job. (Makawatsakul & Kleiner, 2003). Although it's not easy to quantify things like lack of loyalty and low morale, you can bet it affects the bottom line. The absence rate from sickness as well as the risk of serious health problems will more than double after a major downsizing (Kivimaki, Vahtera, Pentti, & Ferrie, 2000). "In a survey of 909 firms that had been through downsizing, 70 percent of retained employees were afraid of losing their jobs. Asked if they still trusted their organization after downsizing, 31 percent said they did not." (Houston, 1992). Not only do the survivors feel pain for their friends let go, but they feel guilt from being spared. According to Tangri (2003), "Stress costs American businesses more than $300 billion annually in lost productivity, absenteeism, accidents, employee turnover, and medical, legal and insurance fees, and workers' compensation awards. That doesn't even count the effect on stock prices and profitability." Jude Rich of Sibson Consulting, Princeton, NJ, in a 2002 article for *Financial Executive Online,* "cited the example of a large hotel chain experiencing annual employee turnover of 60 percent, which cost the company $350 million annually from hiring and training replacements, lower productivity during ramp-up time for new employees, and reduced occupancy rates due to poor guest satisfaction levels." The Third Annual Industry Week Census of Manufacturers survey from over 1,750 manufacturing plants determined that, "Productivity at plants with turnover of less than 3 percent was 66 percent higher than it was at plants with turnover of more than 20 percent." (Tangri, 2003).

A 1998 *USA Today* article cited Edgewater Holdings, a Chicago insurance company offering wrongful termination coverage, as estimating that "more than 50,000 wrongful termination cases were filed in 1997." Besides the direct costs of jury awards and attorney fees, lawsuits cost a firm in productivity dollars as management spends time preparing a defense. One study by Detrouzous et al (1992) of The Rand Corporation, stated that these "indirect effects of wrongful termination doctrines are 100 times more costly than the direct legal costs of jury awards, settlements, and attorney fees." It is possible that good quality outplacement may assist in the legal end because people getting new jobs quicker will have less time to fester and think about law suits, especially if the law suit was filed mostly due to the financial hardship caused the ex-employee by the loss of the job. That may not apply if the suit was filed over a loss of dignity. It's humiliating to lose a job. Right up there with a divorce, loss of a loved one, or being robbed.

According to a Kaiser Family Foundation report, Challenger (2005), cutting reemployment time also saves companies the cost of continued health insurance coverage for discharged employees. And we all know how expensive health insurance is. Just like the unemployment insurance, it pays to get the people back to work as soon as possible.

If you are in an economy where downsizing is prevalent, what makes you think there are a bunch of good jobs out there? The dull platitude spewed from corporate is that the unemployed do not match the jobs available and that's why we hire foreign workers. Assuming one does not believe that one group of people is innately better than another, why not train the laid off worker instead?

The cost of turnover is monstrous. Some employees start the job hunt while still at work (with the employer's permission). There is the cost of the exit interview plus all the administrative costs, hiring a temporary substitute, cost to recruitment such as advertising, and interviewing, and finally, training and orientation costs (instruction manuals, coaching, and decreased productivity at first.

We live in America, by far the most litigious country on the planet. So, regardless of who's at fault, chances are high that you as an employer will get sued. Outplacement can help, as can calming employees on the day they are let go and giving them hope. That is a lot of risk to take for a bonus. But I guess it's because you get the bonus individually and the cost of litigation is borne by the corporation.

Though any help should be better than none, better (high quality) is the way to go.

Providers of high-quality outplacement services go the extra mile and try to understand each company's culture, objectives, and needs, as well as each client's beliefs, goals, and aspirations. That's asking a lot of human beings so I hope you get one of the good ones. Ultimately however, the company chooses which outplacement provider to use so shame on you if you decide to be cheap. Remember, research shows that investment in the right quality of outplacement services helps returns on profits, human capital, and community relations.

The Future

Mr. Hamel and Mr. Prahalad urge senior managers to look toward the future and ponder their ability to shape their companies in the years and decades to come. (Hamel & Prahalad, 1994)

How do you do that? It's a great turn of phrase more easily said than answered

Change is inevitable. How are you going to handle it? In a crisis mode or in a calm rational method? The latter usually means don't wait until the last minute or after things have good south and success is over. Managers must recognize not only what their core competencies are but that somehow they should look forward to the chance to compete. That appears to

be an academic supposition espoused by someone
living in Neverland and never having to be responsible
for a bottom line. Look around your company- at your
track record, your initiatives. Look at your employees
and see if they understand what the 10 year plan is for
your company. Ask yourself if your senior managers
are doing the same thing as others or are they being
farsighted. Are they re-engineering or are they ordering
paperclips and toilet paper Are they rule makers or
followers and are they efficient and innovative? Are
they playing catch up all the time or getting out in front
of new strategies? And who sets the agenda- your
competitors or your own foresight? Are you sharing and
brainstorming the future with colleagues or going it
alone. Some of the questions Prahalad suggests should
be addressed are: What new core competencies will we
need to build? What new product concepts should we
pioneer? What alliances will we need to form? What
new development programs should we undertake? Over
the last few decades upper management has not been
able to keep up with the acceleration of change. There
is no question that the computer age has brought with it
that acceleration. This study hints that these large
companies were run by managers and maintenance
engineers and not leaders and architects. You can't be a
bystander (Hamel & Prahalad, 1994). If a company is
not keeping up with change then the bad organizational
traits such as downsizing kick in, along with strategies
such as employee empowerment, which sounds good
but oftentimes means more work and responsibility for
the same or less reward. Then the overpaid CEO
becomes a hero by simply firing everyone.

     According to Prahalad, "despite excuses about
global competition and the impact of productivity-

enhancing technology, most layoffs at large U.S. companies have been the fault of senior managers who fell asleep at the wheel and missed the turnoff for the future." (Hamel & Prahalad, 1994)

Why is it economists have become convinced that without growth we will die as a company or a country?

Shareholders, not realizing that "the enemy is them", are coming up with the new trite phrases such as: "Make this company lean and mean;" "Make the assets sweat;" "Get back to basics." It all sounds so simple. They apparently spend their time being cute rather than holding management accountable. Prahalad states that "Although perhaps inescapable and in many cases commendable, restructuring has destroyed lives, homes, and communities in the name of efficiency and productivity. While it is very difficult to argue with such objectives, pursuing them single-mindedly does the cause of competitiveness as much harm as good." (Hamel & Prahalad, 1994) He gets 3 brownie points for recognizing the idea but has 2 taken away for the "commendable" remark. Executives must consider this restructuring because otherwise he/she will be replaced by someone who will. Shareholders keep clamoring for more profit. Prahalad goes on to discuss "Denominator Management" whereby management always fiddles with the denominator of the Return on Investment formula in an attempt to improve their numbers. The numerator is income while the denominator consists of assets, like plant, capital, equipment, or, as is usually the case, people. It would appear that they address the denominator because it is easier. To earn more income they would actually have to do their job and do it well. I suspect many of them aren't that good.

The theme running through much corporate policy seems to be capitalism at any cost. There is no question that is has been successful – at least at accomplishing a profitable bottom line. We would all do well to take a lesson from the past and remember how long one can get away with folly before failing, and how long a dark period might follow.

Prahalad cites success in Britain during the Thatcher years as proof that downsizing sometimes works. (Hamel & Prahalad, 1994).Perhaps if you wander around England today (2016) you would find there are a lot of people not working (on the dole). The country is a shell of its former self and these policies may have contributed greatly to that. Prahalad's comment was that the only remaining worker in Britain was the most productive in the world.

The problem with the ROI fiscal method is that it doesn't address any social issues. Some of these issues in the study arose in the late 1980's and the effects are still seem in 2013. Areas of Manchester, Liverpool and even Newcastle (Coal to Newcastle), to mention just a few, are blighted.

Prahalad goes on to quote studies that indicate how share price increases are temporary. (Hamel & Prahalad, 1994). That should be a wake up but more importantly, maybe we should stop using share price as a measure of company value.

Re-structuring is merely reducing staff while re-engineering is that plus coming up with some better ideas for the company. That's just dandy for the company but not so good for those let go. Even that has holes though as the re-engineering of many American companies is just playing catching up and not coming up with anything new. An example of this is the auto industry. For several decades now the United States Car Industry has been trying to learn how to be quality oriented and cost conscious. The problem is that countries like the Japanese have already moved on from that. In their minds quality is now the price of entry to the table, no longer an end objective. Plus, again, the social cost has been enormous as thousands of jobs have been lost and market share for these American companies has been reduced significantly. We are just getting our butts handed to us. That new Ford Fusion is a great looking car. Too bad it copied most of its styling from Volkswagen and Toyota.

You can't just get smaller, you have to get better and then you can't just get better, you have to change with the times. Change means you need to think "Who will be your customers in the future, how will you reach them, what skills you will need and what competitive advantages can you bring to the table?" One way you do this is to get everyone involved in the discussion. Maybe small think tank

High Anxiety

There are certain changes in society which affect the work environment and bring about techniques such as downsizing. In the developed countries at least, we have changed from a manufacturing base, in existence since the middle of the 1800's. Before that we had an agricultural base where, although physically more difficult, it was probably a better quality of life with closer family ties.
The unions have diminished in power, leaving an information gap and apparently less involvement in decision making. When decisions are unilateral without

recourse, only trouble and vulnerability can be the outcome (Greenhalgh & Rosenblatt, 1984). Sometimes these feelings have more of a detrimental effect on people than the actual termination. (Dekker & Schaufelt, 1995).

Today, employees are faced with tremendous job insecurity. Is that one reason substance abuse is so prevalent? Loss of self-esteem is a sure fire formula for suicide. Feelings such as shame, depression, desperation and guilt are not uncommon. Counselors should help explore grief and loss issues, ways to handle stress, job searching support, and assist workers in handling self-esteem. They should be attuned to the symptoms of anxiety, anger, depression, adjustment issues, and grief as well and make sure to discuss all information from the beginning. (Holm & Hovland, 1999)

Counselors can act as mediators in interventions with family matters also. Canaff (2004) stated that many clients become mired in the anger stage, which makes the job-hunting process almost impossible. Hard as it is to believe, the sit com story is true of a person getting so stuck in the denial stage that they get up and pretend to go to work each day, without informing their spouses or friends that they have been downsized. The spouse must be involved and supportive. Heaven forbid the worker has been downsized more than once and even a new job still leaves them "waiting for the other shoe to drop" (Holm & Hovland, 1999).

Westman et al. (2001) found that wives experienced more effects from their husbands' downsizing during this period than did their husbands. The wives stressed feelings continued after the husband found another job even as it lessened for husbands once they found new jobs. They concluded that wives may act as "shock absorbers taking on the men's stress and protecting them". This addresses the structural differences between men and women as to how they handle stress

Regardless, increased health and emotional difficulties were experienced by somebody as a result of high stress levels due to downsizing (Wilson, Larson, & Stone, 1993). The ability to provide mutual support during these trying times mitigate and help weather many negative effects. There is an age factor present here as younger couples are more affected. It appears that maturity really does come with age, although it might have something to do with having put something aside for a rainy day. Parent--child roles follow similar patterns as children are asked to give up friends in a relocation, do without bobbles they were accustomed to before the downsizing, extra-curricular activities and perhaps witness the tension existing between Mom and Dad. (Small & Riley, 1990).

The trick seems to be to provide social support, which is "information that leads a person to believe that he or she is cared for, esteemed, valued and belongs to a network of communication and mutual obligation" (Lim, 1996).

Rumor mills and "water cooler" talk is usually inaccurate and anxiety provoking for the employee. Stay away from the water cooler.

A word to the wise. The shift toward self-management/self-employment may be here to stay, and will be hard on the counselors and the workers (Schein, 1990). The alternative is to become a second rate citizen.

Powerful and wealthy individuals underestimate the importance of food in your stomach and a warm bed.

It would be naive to believe that any practice that makes the perpetrator money will stop- at least without strong coercion from an independent source. There is no incentive for executives to do anything but look to the bottom line financially. That's how they are rewarded. Self-policing is a joke. So, human nature being what it is- rather self-serving at best- we are in trouble for the long haul. The human nature part will probably take another 5000 years to work out so it looks like the immediate solution is up to the outside independent source. Just because it's an uphill battle doesn't mean we have to stick out head in the sand.

It isn't helping that every hack writer is now advocating that school is a waste of time since there are no jobs. Plus it's expensive. I can't say I disagree with the latter, as it follows the pattern of most capitalistic and democratic societies. Stick it to um and gouge as much as possible.

The introduction of technology which can do the work much quicker has not translated into profits; or if it has, those profits have gone into corporate and executive coffers.

Companies have a habit of hiring too fast and too many in good times. Naturally there will be too many people and some will not be appropriate. Downsizing gives the company a chance to weed out those employees that do not live up to expectations (Love & Nohria, 2005). In other words, their mistakes. What a poor excuse for a management strategy. No wonder we are losing the economic battle for world leadership. That still is no excuse. Might it not be better to hire correctly in the first place? Not only that but these companies sometimes rehire employees they laid off later if it is determined that they have needed skills. Why didn't they figure that out before they let the employee go instead of jerking their heartstrings and potentially destroying their lives? It is said that this demonstrates that business sometimes makes the wrong decision and is willing to reconsider. Bully for them. They get a C- for the effort. It has also been suggested that owners should figure out characteristics that top performers possess and consider these characteristics when looking at prospective employees. I would have thought this conversation would have taken place sometime around 1873.

In a capitalistic society, it is said, where some companies grow and expand, it is only natural that others will have to cut back in order to keep their company in business at all. Creative destruction again. Thank you Mr. Schumpeter. Why don't more people ask if this is really the best system?

Incidentally, that isn't what is happening in these companies. Jobs are constantly being redefined and new levels of production are being forced on employees, requiring more work to be done in less time while the idea of job security is obsolete. After several hundred years of improvement we are now going backward in improving the workplace.

"We have found through studies that a 10% reduction in workforce results in only a 1.5% reduction in cost. We also found that currently (2016) corporations have very bad reputations with the public which devastates social networks. We found that customers who worked with a certain employee may not deal with the firm again and Wayne Baker's paper states that 2/3rd of downsized companies fail to realize productivity gains" (Love & Nohria, 2005).

Some companies have no reason to downsize, they just run with the CEO pack- the thought of being left behind boggles the mind of some CEO's. Remember, these guys/gals are supposed to be the cream of the crop. I feel like there is a locust attack coming to this crop. To make matters worse, much of the time size isn't the problem- imagination or innovation or quality is.

An often used excuse heard is "this will open up a whole new lease on life for you." What a load of clap trap. You got fired! If it's so good, you do it! Or, here another one- "It opens a window of opportunity". It is a rare occurrence when people profit from being laid off. There is a direct correlation between downsizing and decline in income due to a lower paying job.

Even if shareholders are the most important asset (a debatable assertion), a more effective order of caring and concern might be: employees first, who take care of the customers, who then buy and create profits, which in turn take care of the shareholders. (Krietner, 2004).

There will be long term repercussions because we are penalizing efficient units. Hence, there is a loss of learning, huge opportunity cost and a potential for tremendous labor unrest.

Productive/Creative

What does Lean and Mean really indicate? Supposedly one can adapt better and be more flexible. In reality the specter of job insecurity lurks. So how does that sword of Damocles (job insecurity) hanging over one's head affect the creativity and productivity of the workers? Productivity increased slightly in one study with higher levels of job insecurity, whereas creative problem solving decreased (Probst, Stewart, Gruys, & Tierney, 2007). "In 2001-2002 43% of all corporations restructured, resulting in a 10-15% permanent reduction in employees" Probst (2007).

"These corporate reductions are often undertaken with the aim of producing a 'lean and mean' organization – one that is flexible, 'able to turn on a dime', and quick to adapt to changing environmental needs" (Landsbergis, Cahill, & Schnall, 1999). The thought was that being smaller, more flexible, and agile as opposed to the large, hierarchical, rigid organizations was the only way to be competitive in today's global market place (Lewin & Johnston, 2000). Often, actual organizational downsizing is preceded by the threat of lay-offs via formal announcements or the spreading of rumors of such plans. Actual downsizing and the threat of lay-offs have been repeatedly found to result in subsequent employee perceptions of job insecurity (e.g. (Ashford, Lee, & Bobko, 1989), (Probst T. M., 2003), (Roskies & Louis-Guerin, 1990).

The foundation of creativity and creative problem solving is often argued to be divergent thinking, or the ability to 'think outside the box' to produce novel solutions (Vincent, Decker, & Mumford, 2002). Employee creativity is vital for entrepreneurial activities and long-term economic growth (Amabile, 1997), (Simonton, 1999), (Wise, 1992). While many organizations cite increased flexibility and enhanced innovation as benefits of restructuring and downsizing, many researchers argue the exact opposite may occur. Pech (2001) reasons that while organizations may claim to encourage innovation and creative behavior, organizational cost cutting and downsizing serve to counter such behavior. Similarly, researchers have argued that innovation is likely to suffer as a result of downsizing due to an increase in risk-averse thinking and behavioral rigidity (Cameron, Sutton, & Whetton, 1988).

Amabile and Conti (1999) found that the work environment for creativity significantly declined during downsizing. What is a reasonable percentage by which to determine significant? It is only natural that attention to creativity will be diminished and diverted if one is focused on job insecurity; especially if the creative process is complex (Sanders & Baron, 1975). Generally, most studies support the theory that downsizing has negative effects on creativity (Cameron, Sutton, & Whetton, 1988). Negotiators who were faced with a competitive upcoming negotiation were less able to solve similar creative problem-solving tasks and exhibited less flexible cognitive thinking than negotiators who were led to expect a cooperative negotiation. (Carnevale & Probst, 1998), (Staw, L. E. Sandelands, & Dutton, 1981). This may indicate further that stress of any kind is not good for creativity. Shanteau and Dino (1993) found a negative relationship between environmental stress (e.g. disrupted sleep patterns, noise, and overheating) and the ability to solve novel creative tasks. However, these same participants were able to complete rote decision-making tasks. It's like trying to concentrate heavily while having a migraine.

If any of this is the least bit true, it is important that corporations be made aware because they are thinking just the opposite, in many cases hoping to obtain increased flexibility and enhanced innovation.

Productivity can be determined in a variety of ways; stock prices (one of the favorites), other financial indicators, and individual performance. Madrick (1995), Rubach (1995), Morris et al (1999) also found no consistent evidence that downsizing led to improved financial performance. Job insecurity has negative effects on worker health and attitudes (Kuhnert, Sims, & Lacey, 1989), (Roskies & Louis-Guerin, 1990), (Sverke, Hellgren, & Naswall, 2002).

Inappropriate comparisons may contribute to the confusion also (Jex, 1998). Do you get credit for work effort or being good at your job? Both seem to be important (although the latter is more often used as a benchmark for promotion), but mixing them in the same cauldron is a no no. However, Probst (2002) found that participants were more productive (as measured by their output) when threatened with lay-offs, but those increased outputs were lower in quality and had more safety violations. Most of us will no doubt relate to maniacal managers threatening dismissal in order to force us to work harder. Any study based on only proficiency without taking into consideration quality or safety would not be valid

According to a study by Farr and Ford (1990), Employees will gravitate toward routine tasks and, by elimination then, avoid creative tasks which are harder to get credit for. They are more likely to be rewarded by the organization (Probst & Brubaker, 2001).

Counter productivity may include verbal harassment, assault, and the spreading of rumors, as well as harmful acts directed against the company or its systems, such as sabotaging equipment, stealing, and wasting resources (Hollinger, 1986), (Neuman & Baron, 1997), (O'Leary-Kelly, Griffin, & Glew, 1996), (Robinson & Bennett, 1995). Stressful working conditions may contribute to employees engaging in counterproductive work behaviors such as absenteeism and tardiness (Chisholm, Kasl, & Eskanazi, 1983), (Gupta & Beehr, 1979), interpersonal aggression, hostility, sabotage, and complaints (Chen & Spector,

1992).

It also makes sense that fear of termination and loss of income might prevent employees from being counterproductive. This would be more true the more egregious the offense such as anything against the rules of the company, theft (Hollinger & Clark, 1983) and sexual harassment (Dekker & Barling, 1998).

The Biggest Losers

"What happens when companies shed not just fat, but brain cells?" "Extreme downsizing is what management Professor Wayne Cascio says companies engage in when they cut their workforce by more than 20 percent." In the recent recession (2006-2009), almost half the larger companies downsized aggressively. (Galagan, 2010)

Cascio, in his 300 firm study at the University of Denver, looked at the financials three years after the cuts and found that nothing had worked! The costs, ROI, and profits had not improved. Those are not acceptable numbers for any lay off scheme. (Cascio W. , 1993)

The question is then, why do they continue to do it? Ignorance of the facts, lack of foresight, copycat? Maybe. Simple answer: because they get rewarded unjustly for it. Galagan (2010) illustrated his point with the example of Mark Hurd at HP. All of Hurd's financial numbers were just fine. Unfortunately Hurd followed the typical game plan and simply got rid of 26,000 people to achieve the results. The real result was a loss of intellectual brain power. Take a look at HP today. They're a company that's floundering. They can't compete because they have no bright minds to come up

with innovative ideas. Not only was the innovation not
there but morale was horrible (so people slacking off)
and the budget for Research and Development was
reduced. Sum it up- short term gain-maybe, long term
performance consequences – severe. Cascio indicated
that he found these lay off gurus and their companies
lag the industry for up to nine years. All the usual
suspects – burn out, stress, turnover, cost to rehire, lost
trust, lawsuits, sabotage, and violence. " In knowledge-
driven organizations, such as consulting firms and
technology companies the negative effects are even
worse. These colleagues depend on social networks
where ideas are generated and that is disrupted by the
departures. Good companies like Google, Apple and
Southwest Airlines all protected their employees and
found other ways to cut costs (Cascio W. , 1993). It's
just easier to fire people and measure the immediate
results than the long-term negative effects of too little
brainpower or too much disillusionment.

There is perhaps one exception to this. A
company in an industry that is permanently shrinking.
Some better solutions? Attrition, redeployment,
growing, changing competencies.

Innovation

For innovation to occur you have to be ready for
it. That means attempting to align employee and
corporate values. The values can be acquired through
education, observation, and experiences, and taught or
influenced by parents, friends, work associates,
religious institutions, community, or culture.

Many people feel that innovation occurs better
in a diverse group (Amabile & Conti, 1999). It's

amazing that we advocate the very acrimonious disagreeable personalities. Perhaps that kind of thinking is at the heart of why we are an unfair and dysfunctional society. Successful, innovative companies seek to harness the power of divergent viewpoints despite the creative friction between employees that routinely occurs (Amabile & Conti). Here is at least an acknowledgment that friction does occur. The question is, "can you harness that power with friction existing? Also, is the price worth it? If not from a profit standpoint then from a stress related humane environment.

It would go without saying that innovation must be done correctly. Keeping the size manageable and cost down would seem to be a good idea. It wouldn't hurt to have some checkpoints along the way also. It's unsettling to get all the way to the end and find ugly surprises.

In some cases it seems the innovation is geared only to making money. That attitude is likely more prevalent at the corporate office than in the laboratory

Can a corporation innovate and downsize at the same time? It's tough. Downsizing has an immediate and severe effect on the innovation activities of companies and ultimately renders them dysfunctional. (Gandolfi & Oster, 2009)

Efficiency has a hard time existing in the same environment as arrogance and disruptiveness (Amabile & Conti, 1999). Self-interest trumps a lot of good ideas also. Sprinkle in a little fear and the game is afoot.

Another stumbling block to innovation is that new hires are often chosen in the (old) company image (Kanter, 1977), (Sutton & Callahan, 1987). Incoming executives (brought in to fire everyone else) seldom know any other way to increase profit numbers than to toe the line, fire people and increase the bottom line.

Bommer et al (1999) observed four organizational consequences upon the conduct of downsizing; *reduced* levels of risk-taking, a *decreased* willingness to make suggestions, a *drop* in motivation, and *increased* levels of fear among employees through its effects on organizational knowledge. It was observed that downsizing may seriously *damage* the learning capacity of organizations. Rightner et al (2006) studied the impact of downsizing on various components of innovation management and found that downsizing had an overall *negative* effect on innovation.

Layoffs

Committed and motivated employees serve customers better; customers happy with your company's products or services are likely to express their satisfaction, making your employees feel better about their work. Then they buy! It's a virtuous rather than a vicious circle. A positive one. But you can bet that it's a circle that can be broken when you start slashing employees. When there are fewer employees to share the load *and* those employees are anxious and demotivated after seeing their colleagues laid off, service quality can suffer, prompting customers to go where they are treated better.

The downsizing crowd insists that in a recession you must eliminate jobs to get smaller because there is less work. Others feel that's the very problem with business. The second group feels that employees are assets, not costs and there should be other ways to cut "costs" e.g. growth, innovation, retooling the process etc. Setting aside the second theory, if one insists on getting rid of people then without undermining either the quality of your service or the morale of your workforce. This group still thinks they can do it. Good luck with that. For a moment assume that it is possible. If so, treating both the employees and the customers respectfully would be the first step. There is a distinction between being loyal by hanging on to unproductive workers (the wrong way) and protecting the interests of good productive works (and therefore customers) "Protecting the unproductive is just being paternal, and doing that is a recipe for disaster. Loyalty means putting the welfare of customers and employees ahead of short-term interests." (Reichheld, 2006) Reichheld says you should be doing it in good times as well as in bad. It's just a lot more difficult doing it to good workers in tough times. Whether it is inherently disloyal to let good workers go is up for debate. It does make sense however, to exhaust all other avenues first and make sure that communication has occurred frequently and quickly. James L. Heskett, professor emeritus at Harvard Business School. In his book *The Service Profit Chain* (Free Press, 1997), speaks to the positive virtuous circle that results when companies have both satisfied customers and motivated employees. "Those who take the easy, immediate approach of downsizing without sizing up opportunities to do something more imaginative are going to have problems," he says. He also said "The smartest companies today, even when they're in trouble, are moving employees around, having them share jobs, having them work reduced hours so the company can preserve jobs.. That creates trust between employees and management, and that's going to affect how these employees deal with customers." Although the jobs may change and the hours may be fewer or the pay may be cut, at least you still have a job. Remember, all this takes place only after all other avenues have been explored as to ways to cut costs. (Heskett, 1997)

"Everyone has layoffs," notes Patricia Seybold, CEO of the Patricia Seybold Group in Boston and author of *Outside Innovation: How Your Customers Will Co-Design Your Company's Future.* The better companies just focus on keeping customers happy. As a result, she says, she's seeing more companies make the quality of the customer experience a significant factor in determining performance-based pay (Seybold, 2006). This attitude is wonderful and makes complete sense, but it would be presumptuous to believe that it is widespread yet. Heskett (1997) said that for those who must go, the best procedure is to "lay off people as if they were future customers. "When you let someone go, try to put together a safety net, do the best you can to provide relocation support. Treat these people as potential future customers and potential future employees—as if they will one day be in a position to send business to your company." He also said that it would be nice to scrounge up some extra money for those left behind.

Rather than firing employees why not fire non-productive customers? By that is meant "demanding customers" Even though consensus is that demanding customers push us to be better, they aren't all profitable. Fred Wiersema, a consultant and author of The New Market Leaders: *Who's Winning and How, in the Battle for Customers* (Simon & Schuster, 2002) says you have to size up your customers and decide who to keep. If you have customers who don't offer substantial revenue, and they're not strategically important and if they're more

trouble than they're worth, then get rid of them. Just
like employees though, these customers must be let go in a
decent fashion, not just dumped. (Wiersema, 2002). Reicheld
(2006) indicates that "most leaders can't tell you what it
means to be loyal—that failure has led to mediocre service
and high prices that alienate customers and employees
alike."

The playing field isn't all one sided however, and it
may be wise to remember that in good times employees can
leave and get a raise, or threaten to leave and get a raise. It's
hard to get any loyalty during these times. Perhaps the
employees may think longer and harder about a move if
the company treats them with a little more loyalty and
kindness during the bad times.

A Special Envoy

These are the people who are in charge of the
firing or laying off. Talk about pitting us against each
other. Even though we know most of these people are
only doing it because they were told to and will lose
their jobs if they don't, those let go will find it hard to
forgive them. If the one's doing the letting go have any
sense of fairness and emotional empathy at all it will
make their lives miserable also, although not as much.
There has to be repercussions in society when this
happens. There are particular skills and experience
needed for managers to break bad news well. Would
you take the job if offered? Maybe it's not an offer but a
requirement. Since the job appears to be a necessary
evil, then it becomes important to do the job as well as
we can. Downsizing should involve sensitivity,
discretion, and the ability to mediate. Ashman (2012)
states "it is imperative that: the message is
communicated accurately, with sensitivity, with

fairness and in a humane manner. People leaving
should be able to do so with dignity, and those workers
left behind are transferred into roles for which they are
suited.

In public organizations, notwithstanding any
incompetence they might be known for, their approach
was always to downsize through a combination of
hiring freezes, voluntary severance (redundancy and
retirement) and redeployment. Without exception,
compulsory redundancy was considered to be the last
option. In the private sector, no such pattern exists.
Taking the public sector approach takes longer and the
longer the process, the greater the demands are on
the envoys. That may be stressful for envoys but could
be constructive for the organization. The question
would be, "do you pull the band aid off instantly" or do
you give everyone time to adjust and get used to the
idea?

The envoy process was generally described as
traumatic, nerve wracking, dreadful, very upsetting,
hideous, and ultimately, stressful. Generally, the worst
job one could ever have. Except not having any job.

These envoys, in order to cope as well as
possible, need to separate themselves from the havoc
they are creating. (Ashman, 2012).That may relieve
some stress on them but, an employee immune to the
feelings of others would not seem to be desired.

Is it wiser to have envoys come from HR or
from the production line? HR would be more aloof to
the situation but maybe bad news is received better
from someone close to you. Good for the employee let
go, bad for the envoy. The fact that the envoy might be
next in line to be let go would increase his or her
genuine concern. HR managers need to learn not to lord

it" over other employees.

Should people be given ongoing training for this envoy task? Training is always a good idea. How else would you know what to do? The envoy needs to know the legalities, how to feel for people, how to prepare the let go employee for a future career, how to help with getting financial assistance, and how to get the let go employee involved

Dangerous Ploys

Critics of the downsizing process think it is a ploy and a dangerous one at that. There are quite a few reasons given for downsizing and they all sound good on the surface. They include: decreasing the number of management layers, in order to improve communication and speed up the decision-making process, eliminate duplication of responsibility, get rid of bureaucratic slowdown by subcontracting traditional staff responsibilities to external support organizations- all of which is supposed to enhance productivity and cut costs. Sometimes; however, things don't always work out as planned. It's true that laying people off will cut costs. That however, is often offset by the cost of laying them off- unemployment, benefits, new hire training, retooling, intellectual property loss etc. Additionally, productivity does not necessarily follow. The attitudes and atmosphere in the plant or office can be so poisoned that work can actually suffer. According to a Society for Human Resource Management study of companies that downsized, less than half the respondents showed improved productivity as a result (Henkotf, 1990).

The danger is that the trend will not change. The

reasons are simple. Corporations are not learning from the past, leaders always believe that they can do what others cannot, and because downsizing is the most appealing alternative managers can think of when trying to improve the bottom line and make their quarterly bonuses. It's no skin off their nose

In general older employees are targeted. The rationalization sometimes offered to justify this, though little data exists to support it, is that because of their age these employees have less energy and, therefore, are less productive. Plus they make more money and can be replaced more cheaply. The huge downside is the loss of valuable experience.

Business students at Shippensburg University and Gettysburg College were queried from 2004 through 2009 by the author. The population consisted of three to four classes per semester with approximately 30 students in each class for a total sample of approximately 1000 students. The following reactions were observed and recorded: The students determined that after a downsizing program employees begin hoarding information to increase their value. Intra departmental and interdepartmental contacts begin to dissolve. Units tend to draw protectively inward and to focus on solving their own problems, ignoring the possible negative affects their solutions might have on other units. After a downsizing, employees frequently have difficulty finding required information because the responsibility for it has been shifted. Those given control over additional files can't gain access to them.

The students also agreed that employees have less trust in the information they receive following downsizing. Messages from top level management is automatically suspect. Information gained from other areas of the organization is also viewed as questionable. Reports and numbers have probably been altered to make those writing and tabulating them look impressive. Everyone now mistrusts everyone else. All communication is considered a smoke screen and memos are especially suspect. The buck is passed whenever possible. Rumors are everywhere. Everything is thought to have a hidden meaning. There is an immediate overload of work for everybody. One reason for this overwork is the confusion caused by people suddenly having to take on additional responsibilities without proper preparation. This confusion causes inefficiencies throughout the organization because employees too often have to learn through trial and error. Concerning decision making and problem solving, the students said that, following a downsizing, emphasis shifts to the elimination of risk. Decisions are not as likely to be based on employees' best judgment. They are designed to please bosses. The quality of employees' work usually deteriorates because they frequently lack the necessary experience or training and because a sincere effort now seems pointless because of their impression that the company believes everyone is expendable.

To make matters worse, while the workload and number of work hours required goes up, pay often stays the same or goes down. Top level management's rationalization is that the employees allowed to keep their jobs won't mind. The students and I felt that the added burden increases already strong feelings of resentment toward bosses.

Job security, a major reward in business and an accepted norm for decades, is gone. Employees no longer feel in control of their lives. Any promises by upper level management of better days to come is viewed skeptically. People able to look for a job with another company frequently begin doing so, which adds to the drain on expertise.

Because of strained relations between management and employees and the resultant uneasiness felt by managers, discipline either becomes more severe or totally disappears. Some managers use the insinuation that "You could be next" to drive employees. A reminder of a school yard bully atmosphere. Others tolerate performance shortcomings that shouldn't be tolerated in their efforts to regain employee trust. A "jungle attitude" predominates. Both managers and employees do what they must to survive.

Finally, while responsibilities increase, there is less training. At a survey of personnel managers at companies that recently downsized, Ninety four percent of the respondents said that they were given less than two months to plan and implement their downsizing-related activities. (Roth, 1993). Therefore, there is no time for anything like training. There is an increased work load. Training departments are often reduced during a downsizing. The employee's perspective on training and job-related development also changes. The chief purpose of training frequently evolves into gaining the skills necessary to find a job elsewhere. In terms of career development, employees begin opting for "safe" jobs, rather than ones in which they can realize their potential or take the lead in somewhat risky but challenging and rewarding projects.

Is there an alternative and can these reactions be avoided or softened with better preparation? Most of the literature agrees that the Passage of time is the key ingredient for improved morale and productivity for a post downsizing morale and productivity slump. In most cases it would take years. Some merely hope for an eventual change in upper level management. Employees hope that new leaders will have different agendas and that job security for workers will be one of their top priorities. Talk about naive! The agenda of a CEO is to look good and make money for themselves.

Roth (1993) did give equal time to the downsizers. Their reasons for downsizing were: Decrease the number of management layers in order to improve communication and speed up the decision-making process, Eliminate duplication of responsibility Get rid of bureaucratic slowdown by subcontracting traditional staff responsibilities to external support organizations. Gee, no mention of bonuses. What great guys. Just the type to bring home to Mamma.

Sometimes the bottom line initially improves after a downsizing, but because of the ongoing problems this improvement tends to taper off. At the same time, attempts to increase productivity are hampered by a lack of employee commitment, so that top level management is forced back into the cost-cutting mode. The most convenient vehicle at its disposal is a second go at downsizing. However, there are now fewer resources to juggle. Also, an awareness may develop that the company might either be in serious trouble or be about to change its structure permanently.

So, knowing the pitfalls of downsizing, why do top level executives keep doing it? A majority of CEOs are quantitatively oriented (Henkotf, 1990). These people are more comfortable with quantitative solutions to corporate problems than with qualitative ones so downsizing is their solution for everything for short-term improvement to the bottom line. Also, few of our current CEOs have received the training necessary to successfully generate employee-driven productivity improvement efforts. They have not received this training on the job because a majority of them have been locked into their areas of expertise most of the way up the career ladder. They may have attended corporate sponsored seminars and workshops on the subject and developed some of the understanding and skills required, but not nearly enough to be effective. Those with MBAs have not received the requisite training in their classes because, emphasis in most MBA programs remains on the quantitative aspects of management; on the improvement of specialized skills such as marketing, production, human resources, accounting and technology. Maybe we should rethink our approach to executive training and spend more time on developing the ability to increase the productivity of employees as cost cutters, innovators, and quality enhancers. Remember however, that we still need more of that same technical expertise in order to be competitive.

Some U.S. corporate leaders are beginning to realize, that cost-cutting can also be achieved by involving employees more fully in improvement of the products, and anything which leads to increased productivity.

Good CEOs understand that, if structured properly, this approach starts producing positive, bottom-line results almost immediately and that these results, rather than tapering off, snowball.

Downsizing has proven to be a short term, short-sighted approach to improving the bottom line. There does not seem to be a way to handle downsizing without adversely affecting employee morale and creating a level of confusion in key management systems. Short-term savings will eventually be offset by long term problems. Some corporations and individuals in other parts of the world already understand this and as a consequence, are rapidly increasing their economic lead on us. Either too many of our corporate leaders do not get this, or they lack the skills necessary to define and implement better alternatives. Which is strange because we pay them like royalty, supposedly because they are so rare and valuable.

Legal

What about the legal aspect of the downsizing phenomenon? Hot dog! More work for the lawyers. There are legal ramifications of most any act, and when people truly suffer from a loss of income and job security, there is no reason to think it will not be at least as bad. Potential jurors have indicated that an employer forced to defend a discrimination claim is at a disadvantage before ever entering the courtroom. In the survey conducted by the Minority Corporate Counsel Association and DecisionQuest in 2002, it was revealed that more than 75 percent of white males, who are usually regarded as most supportive of corporations, report distrusting corporations due to events such as the Enron scandal. 85 percent of the survey respondents indicated a belief that large corporations hide information about their products until they are caught by the government or in a lawsuit, and 75 percent of respondents indicated a belief that managers and senior executives are more likely to perjure themselves than lower-level employees. (Galina Davidoff & Neufer,

2002). The *National Law Journal* (2001) indicated that close to half of the survey respondents disagreed with the statement that most big companies treat all employees fairly and only 29.8 percent of agreed with the statement. Overall, 42.3 percent of respondents agreed that older workers and minorities are the first to lose their jobs in a layoff. (Schwartz, 2005). I suppose the conclusion obtained from all this is that "where there's smoke, there's fire", meaning that if true, it is likely that the world is an unfair place. It is probably worth a cautionary comment that legal does not mean justice. On the flip side, however, there is hope for compensation for a great deal of that unfairness. So both sides are guilty and the legal system is corrupt. No news there.

One has to wonder, with all the government watchdogs, just how a corporation can get away with downsizing/firing, legally and still stay away from discrimination regarding race, religion, marital status, gender, age, or disability

Who is right or wrong in this case is up for grabs. One never realizes how many protective laws there are in the name of goodness and mercy; and yet, with a bevy of lawyers, the corporate world still manages to do it. Who did we leave out above? Oh yeah, a white, Angle Saxon, male, protestant, over 40. How would you like to be one of those?

In order to avoid violating any of these groups rights, a corporation must not treat an employee not in a protected class any differently than one in the protected class. The loophole probably comes in that it must be proven intentional and timely. There are any number of wiggle clauses. If the person doing the laying off is in the same protected group the corporation might have a problem also. The burden of proof is almost always on the employee. (LeBlanc v. Great American Insurance Company, 1993). Then the plaintiff has to prove that the employer's reason for the layoff decision is phony and the real reason is unlawful discrimination. (Reeves v. Sanderson Plumbing Products, 2000). Good luck with that.

All an employer has to do is say the protected class employee is less qualified, because it is hard for the laid off employee to prove otherwise and the courts know that and will side with the employer (Turner v. North American Rubber, 1992). Courts have determined that seniority and high pay are not the same as age discrimination. (Allen v. Diebold & Thomure v. Phillips Furniture Co., 1994); (Bialas v. Greyhound Lines, 1995); (Bay v. Times Mirror Magazines, 1991).

You can prove discrimination even without evidence if the claim is that a policy on its face adversely affects a protected class of individuals. Reverse discrimination reared its ugly head again when The Supreme Court once judged that Duke Power could be held liable under Title VII for race discrimination based solely on statistical evidence. Duke Power required that entry-level job applicants have a high school diploma and achieve a satisfactory test score on an exam administered during the application process, but these requirements resulted in a statistically significant screening-out of black applicants. Again, the system has flaws- as long as you're black. Somehow it doesn't work as well for the older worker. Using statistics usually involves lawyers trying to 'spin' their own analysis to convince a judge or jury that discrimination likely did or did not occur (Hazelwood School District v. United States) Once again, government meddling has given the upper hand to a minority group in spite of the fact that they did not qualify. Well and good for the minorities but not so much for the remaining employees. (Schwartz, 2005).

An employer still has a chance to prove no wrongdoing by showing that the action taken was job-related for the position in question (whatever that means) and a business necessity. (42 U.S.C. § 2000e-2(k) (1) (A) (I)). Anything that has to do with business judgment, such as teamwork or positive attitude, is hard for the courts to refute- a big stumbling block if you are thinking of suing as an employee. Financial numbers can also be manipulated and then interpreted many different ways leading to whatever conclusion one desires. Got to love the legal system. Bottom line, it's tough to cover all your bases; but it should be, shouldn't it, if you're getting ready to destroy someone's life?

One of the best things to do to cover yourself in an RIF is to pay severance in exchange for a written agreement not to sue, which, if you have ever been let go, you remember the piece of paper shoved under your nose. At which time any little morsel you can get seems better than nothing. That's exactly what the employer is counting on. (Schwartz, 2005). This is why lawyers go to law school.

What world do you live in where people like losing their livelihood? Legalities play a role in the Downsizing process. It's not going to end up being fair and can end up rewarding the wrong group.

If you lay someone off and shortly thereafter, rehire someone else for the position you can probably expect trouble. Equally troubling would be if you eliminated the position under the premise that a product line were going to be eliminated, and that never happened. Again, you have a problem.

A voluntary exit incentive programs might be the way to go. This might protect your trade secrets and proprietary information better. Don't forget to include the unions in talks. They may be willing to help in some way.

Does the law require fairness? No. Will the judge instruct the jury that it must decide the case based on fairness? No. But fairness and witness credibility will be the difference between winning and losing a trial. Therefore, extraordinary attention should be given to the "tone" of the entire reduction procedure and how it is conducted. "Humane" is the watchword for a corporation seeking a positive outcome.

Reallocation

The reallocation of labor and capital will have consequences. There is a strong possibility that both resources will diminish during and after any transition. This happens because the capital may not be deployed as well in its new surroundings and the labor may not be as qualified in the new setting. Now, I'm not insinuating that this is worse than being fired by any means. This is more a cautionary tale for the corporation than the individual. The scenario is best analogized by the "Peter Principle" in which an employee is constantly promoted because he/she is doing a good job. The minute they stop doing a promotable job they are stuck in that position- doing a less than desirable job. In this case then, whenever you or your money move into a new environment, in which you aren't as good, the results are not as good.

As a result there could and probably would be

either lower productivity or higher unemployment, or both. There is some question as to whether the slowness of the workers to re-establish themselves in a new environment caused the elongation of the recession or the recession caused the elongation of the hiring process for displaced workers. Outside the academic world or the corporate boardroom the answer to the displaced worker is "who cares?" Productivity did rise after the downsizing bloodbath. Again, an academic question of little consequence is "were the laborers reallocated because of productivity gains or were there productivity gains because of the reallocation? Good Lord, get a life! There was one firm fact established by the study however; the destruction of significant amounts of specific human, physical, and organizational capital. Displaced workers who were re-employed outside their original industries experienced a huge drop in earnings. Huge means on the magnitude of 15% if they stayed in the same industry to 20% if they switched industries. (Burroughs, Bing, & James, 1998), That hurts the individual displaced, their families both emotionally and financially, the company due to loss of intellectual capital, and the governmental system because there is likely a larger strain on the welfare system to make up the slack. Of course displaced workers in non-downsized industries also experienced a decline in earnings, just not as severe. Capital also suffers similar consequences when moved and employed outside its element.

In speaking of capital, if it's human capital much of it is specific to a certain industry and the cost to reallocate could be large. (Ruhm & Sum, 1988), (Topel, 1991), (Neal, 1995). As to the organizational and intangible capital, why corporations do not realize that if they downsize they will not have people with specific knowledge ready for the next upswing in the economy, and the brand recognition, and relationships built with suppliers and clients will have been lost (Bahk & Gort, 1993), (Corrado, Hulten, & Sichel, 2005)

There have been many times when the cost of reorganization was too high (Koenders, Kathryn; Rogerson, Richard, 2005). Only the greediest CEO's consider downsizing in good times. As always, the thought of worker's welfare is never a factor for consideration, it's always "bottom line."

Of course, sometimes workers are protected when they shouldn't be protected and policies subsidize inefficient firms.

The Displaced Worker Surveys (DWS) by the U.S. Bureau of Labor Statistics are a good tool to determine if more workers were displaced in downsized industries and also whether they were unemployed longer than for workers displaced from other industries. These studies indicate that the rate was 4 times as great as in other industries.

In principal, reallocation is not without benefits. In an economy with changing preferences and technologies, reallocation may be necessary in order to allocate scarce resources to their more productive uses. Just so the corporations remember there can be significant costs when capital is specific to a firm or industry.

Even if redeployment of personal is successful, it takes a considerable amount of time for these resources to be re-employed elsewhere.

As always, it would take very little tweaking of the data to skew information and results in another direction

Positives for Survivors

Cascio (2002) questioned whether or not employees were becoming immune to the layoff experience? One could infer this to mean "Can we get away with it over time?" Downsizing works better if there is a focus on the morale of remaining employees through open communication (Sherer, 1997). Having a stressful job is still better than having none.
A small percentage of survivors might feel good about themselves. Since they made it through they may become more productive and committed. This feeling is enhanced when the survivors feel they have a say in the restructuring (Amundson, Borgen, Jordan, & Erlebach, 2004).

Survivors

In either changing times or bad economic times top executive always scramble to fix the situation. To a certain extent that's what they are paid to do. Nevertheless, the solution always seems to be the same-chop the work force. No matter how many times good sources indicate that innovation or growth or a different type of re-structuring may be a better solution, employees are always the first to suffer.

Corporate downsizing has become a cure all for business owners, but a catastrophe for workers and the overall economy (Cameron, Freeman, & Mishra, 1993), (Cameron K. , 1994) Most companies do little to prepare their employees for a reduction or help survivors deal with the situation after the downsizing (Armstrong-Stassen M. , 1993).

Studies have found increased stress (Armstrong-Stassen M. , 1993); (Mishra & Spreitzer, 1998), decreased motivation; reduced performance with extra workload (Brockner, Grover, & Blonder, 1988), (Davy, Kinicki, & Scheck, 1991), (Meyer, Allen, & Topolnytsky, 1998), distrust/withdrawal of management/leader; and anger, sadness, guilt, loss of self-esteem, insecurity, and fear. Armstrong-Stassen (1998) found that the managers reported a significant decrease in their job performance and organizational commitment which certainly had a bearing on the effectiveness and quality of services provided by the organization. This all leads to an intent to leave the organization (Mone M. A., 1994), (Evans, 1995), (Noer, 1993)

Is the relationship between employers and the workers changing? (Kets de Vries & Balazs, 1997) say yes, as do Rousseau & Wade-Benzoni, (1995). Back in the day one went to work for Ma Bell right out of high school or college and stayed there for their entire working career. The worker was well cared for and respected, and in return, gave his/her all to the company. Long gone. (Borgen, 1997), (Borgen, Amundson, & Tench, 1996). There now exists a tremendous amount of grieving and bereavement (Kubler-Ross, 1969) and emotional upheaval of the survivors (Bridges W. , 1986).

Survivors have mixed and conflicting reactions. By far, the reaction is negative. Downsizing is perceived to be unfair, usually is poorly prepared for, and communicated poorly. Additionally there is the fear of the possible loss of one's job, lack of organizational support programs, poor or self-serving leadership, and the impact work changes had on their lives at home. Survivors wished to understand and be involved in shaping the restructuring process. These survivors clearly saw themselves as having a stake in the success of their organization's transition. They indicated that they were reassured when they could understand and could have a voice in the process. Many felt that they could be of help in the process. The feeling also was that the company didn't realize how much extra work that the survivors did. Survivors were also not happy with counter- productive measures, and wasting of resources. Finally, there was a feeling that one high executive laid off would save more money (and be more fair) than a number of lower level employees. (Amundson, Borgen, Jordan, & Erlebach, 2004). Those who were transferred away from their colleagues experienced isolation and loneliness as well as guilt (Brockner J. , Grover, Reed, & DeWitt, 1992). There were some positive indicators that coworkers supported each other through the uncertainty and found ways to stay in touch with each other after downsizing. Many times, in the name of corporate trade secrets or security, laid off workers are rushed out the door like criminals. They are made to feel dirty, like they did something wrong. Very demeaning.

There are managers who would try to do the right thing and will initially try to look out for employees but, ultimately, self-interest kicks in. Access to supervisors during the process is extremely important. The access would be even better if proactive by the boss, even if only social. And when the boss comes, he better be smiling with a note of sincerity. Inadequate, contradictory, or vague communication increased confusion, anxiety, mistrust, and speculation.

One employee in a recent study questioned whether management would give any consideration to being close to retirement, or other significant benchmarks. Really? Put your head back in the sand, my friend. Executives don't care how old you are, how long you've been here, or how near you were to a key milestone; you could be gone in a minute. It's not in the mandate or the modern culture. How do hard work, commitment, and loyalty fit into the picture? They don't. Extra time put in? Not likely. Those attitudes on either side do not bode well for a society. I suspect there will be fewer friendly folks walking down the street with head held high looking you in the eyes and saying "Hi".

As to morale in general, survivors sense feelings of anger, cynicism, resentment, fear, and anxiety in themselves and among their coworkers. The suggestion that a positive attitude will alleviate these feelings would make a good subplot in a Marvel comic book but is unlikely to carry much credibility to either those let go or those left behind in a downsized corporation.

Another age old dilemma that has been exacerbated by the downsizing trend is how to cope with the stress of the job after leaving work in the evening. There has never been a good answer for this. "The Soccer Dad" image has always been difficult to pull off and a myth in all likelihood. Most of us (not all because there are people who just love their work more than anything else), would like to spend more good quality time with our families. The reality of it is that it

is almost impossible. We chose which camp to land in.
Even the discrimination of women plays into this
scenario. The truth of the matter is that it is asking a lot
to care for children and be on top of your game at work.
Perhaps no one means to discriminate but when you
look around for guidance and the person isn't there, that
person falls a rung or two down the ladder. Now that
downsizing has entered the picture, everyone and
anyone who is faced with the difficult decisions is
suffering. We are torn between needing a sounding
board to hear about the lousy day we had so we can
relieve some of the stress, and wanting to shield our
loved ones from the misery we have faced all day long.
We want the emotional support from spouses, families,
and friends; distractions from work by children; and
activities that provided relaxation and relief from stress,
yet are unable to accept them when they are offered.
Speculation has it that if you are able to separate work
from your home life plus do a good job of being a good
provider, then you are probably lacking in an energy
level and dedication necessary to get ahead. The happy
go lucky charmer normally isn't up to the work place
rigor. Nor does he/she want to be. Survivors find
themselves in this unenviable position in spades. A
simple conversation explaining the problems you are
going through might help. Letting your family know
you may be acting a little down and depressed and that
it isn't their fault will solve a vast majority of the
tension and problems at home.

  If we were better human beings we would do
what the books tell us to do and acknowledge our work
troubles but limit the time spent worrying about them.
Easy to say, tough to do. It goes without saying that if
you are able to psych yourself well, you can either

convince yourself that you can cope with the job lose or
that you are so good that it will not happen to you.
Ditto-easy to say. If you can assess your skills, contacts,
age, and the current job market and come away feeling
that you will have no problem finding another job then
everyone will come up roses. Downsizing, like so many
other negatives in our society disproportionately affects
the little guy who needs help the most. Especially in the
United States today where money seems to be more
important.

A general feeling that one has the support of the
company is a critical aspect for those left behind. Some
helpful policies would be flexible hours (unpaid leave
of absence, or even paid for that matter) good training
programs, good assistance programs (these for those let
go as well), and just a general acknowledgment of the
stress that you as an employee are going through. Being
sensitive and proactive is paramount. Get out ahead of
it.

Customer service is bound to be effected. New
working relationships take time to develop, and hard
when new people are learning new systems at the same
time. Then there is the frustration of training new
people, some of which either lack skills or even the
ability to adapt at all. In some cases, organizations
appeared to make no effort to help remaining
employees meet and work with new colleagues, leaving
employees to struggle alone in an unfamiliar, unfriendly
environment. The atmosphere can be very depressing. It
creates tension, mistrust and anger everywhere.

Ways to assist this transition period along might
include formal team-building sessions in the workplace
and maybe a social after hour's effort to build personal
relationships. Sometimes the physical move, if it means

condensing groups together rather than spread out over different areas ends up helping the overall effort. Of course, the reverse is also true so be careful not to take a cohesive group and separate them.

Conflicted feelings arise in most of us as we try to determine what to do with the expertise and knowledge that you've gained over the years. Do you give it away to the employer in order to keep in their good graces or hold out and make them pay somehow. The corporation on the other hand would do well to garner this expert knowledge from you at all costs, especially if their intent is to can you anyway.

People better learn to get along or they become their own worst enemy. We all know it's a terrible situation, but the guy/gal next to you is not the enemy.

Negatives for Survivors

Few remaining employees in a downsized company easily adapt to the change, and some never do. They feel anger, fear or distrust toward the company. Starting with this premise I can't help wondering again who this helps? Of course I know the answer. It helps money make more money.

Distrust and heartache sometimes begin before the actual downsizing because of the company letting the employees know about the upcoming cuts they are going to be making. This is done because a percentage of the studies and management books indicated that they should- because people need warning. Not always a good idea. Two sides to every coin. Employees may become paranoid, and their top priority is their own career rather than the bottom line of their employer. And rightly so.

Only at Disneyland does someone else look out for your interests more than you do. This can cause the employee to be unfocused and prevent them from performing their jobs efficiently. Based on human nature, many workers would also be perfectly willing to stab their associates in the back in hopes of keeping their job. Usually when a downsizing is complete, morale in the company is at an all-time low because in almost every merger, acquisition or downsize, employees are faced with uncertainty about their jobs before and after the restructure. Further internal problems result from employees who survive with the company, but cannot adapt to their new settings and expectations, and eventually quit their job.

This is commonly referred to as the survivor syndrome. Many people who survive as a result of downsizing often live with the fear that they too will be terminated in the future. They are often shell shocked and distrustful. They are mentally scared survivors of a restructuring of a company that they have never seen before. In this climate of economic insecurity, their jobs are constantly being redefined. They are forced to meet new levels of production criteria, requiring them to do more work in less time, plus the idea of job security is obsolete. The employees are uncertain about what will be happening in the future in regards to their job and their financial health. A simple means of communication can be very important for the company. One of the major reasons for employee problems after a downsizing is the mistrust in the management and lack of knowledge regarding their job status. If the employees are informed of what is transpiring within their company, they might not be fearful of losing their job, or so quick to stab a fellow employee in the back. This will also allow the employee to work towards the common goals of the company and not just work to make themselves look good. Workers have been conned into settling for lower wages and little or no benefits in exchange for supposed higher job security.

Another negative effect that organizations have seen after downsizing is low morale. This then equates to lower productivity and profits for the organization. After downsizing, the remaining employees work with anxiety and lose the trust that they once had in their employer. This results in less initiative to get work done, with the feeling of why bother trying to do the job when they could be the next to be laid off. Downsizing can also create competition and rivalries between employees. One will do anything to get an edge over another to maintain their job. They devote less effort to working and concentrate on doing things that will protect themselves. This increases workloads for the other employees and the company loses the family atmosphere and creates a workplace of tension and uneasiness. The goals of the organization are put on hold to try to keep the organization running smoothly and efficiently. The company also loses employees experience, talent, and relationships with customers. These things may not always be replaced easily. It may take a lot of time to rebuild experience and talent within the corporation, if it is even possible at all. The employees who are left will have to learn to do these tasks as well as perform their everyday jobs from before. This can lead to a large loss in productivity within the company.

There are many managers in the business world today that believe cutting jobs is a fast and easy way to control costs and boost their financial status. They don't take into consideration how it effects not only the people they are laying off, but the people who survived the layoffs in the company. While it is obvious that losing one's job is going to be devastating to that person, it can also create a huge wave of emotion to the remaining employees. It can make people feel paranoid about their own job security or could even cause them to become angry and feel disloyal to their organization because they feel the layoffs were unfairly done due to bad decision-making by managers (Harari, 1993).

Corporate downsizing is supposed to make a company lean and mean, and spur rapid financial growth. While the letting go of a lot of overhead may make a company's short-term financial statements look better, it does not always lead to success in the future. The short-term rise in the stock of the corporation may be erased in the future. Some problems associated with downsizing could lead to the demise of a company down the road. In many of these cases the overall performance of the company diminished after the downsizing and the company was actually less profitable than it was before

Negatives include: less quality work being done, less productivity, less effectiveness, more conflict, low morale, loss of trust, heightened stress, risk of heart disease in all concerned, scapegoating, time spent looking for a new job, loss of team spirit and more individual, every man for himself attitude, a sense of betrayal, and feelings of being undervalued and unappreciated for those left behind.

A survivor of downsizing may react with low risk taking, withdrawal, absenteeism, aggression, and low commitment to the job. (Boone, 2000) After an initial coping period the survivor goes through a recovery period in which he/she may feel grief for those who lost their jobs, grief for the loss of job security, grief for the loss of the trusted relationship with supervisors and managers, and grief for loss of one's own self-esteem and belief in oneself (Bumbaugh, 1998).

Designated Redundant

In the world of downsizing, if any of us had to speculate what would make us unhappy, it would be tough to imagine anything worse than losing your job. However, there is little doubt that there are consequences for those left behind. In particular, there is even a subset of those left behind whose heads were on the chopping block and they escaped. No doubt all groups are affected.

There has been a great deal of research, beginning with the Depression up through the 1990s, on redundant employees who have lost their jobs (e.g. (Cobb & Kasl, 1977), (DeFrank & Ivancevich, 1986); (Fryer & Payne, 1986), (Hanisch, 1999), (Hartley & Fryer, 1987), (Leana & Feldman, 1994), (Swinburne, 1981)

Marjorie Armstrong-Stassen (2002) determined that during the downsizing period those declared redundant experienced significant decline in organizational trust and commitment compared with those who were not designated redundant. After the downsizing was completed, however, that group reported a significant increase in their job satisfaction, trust in the organization and organizational commitment. Not discussed was why that might be. How about, the weight of the world had been lifted from their shoulders? Job performance went down and stayed down. Even though perceived organizational morale increased in both in the post-downsizing period, it never recovered to pre- downsizing levels.

In summary, the results of this study indicate that in the first year after downsizing some of the dissatisfaction begins to go away. But that refers only to job security and is likely because some of those who were designated redundant and were not let go now feel more secure. The researchers then generalized that organizational downsizing does not have a long-term effect on survivors. There is no logical evolution from the results to the conclusion because the positive result of job security is only one part of the overall analysis and also has other logical reasons for occurring which don't address this conclusion. Organizational morale and trust were not taken into account and in fact, were significantly below acceptable and previous levels, which alone would render this study conclusions inaccurate. This is substantiated by other studies by this author, (Armstrong-Stasson, 1997) Having found similarly low levels of organizational morale and trust following organizational restructuring and downsizing. Morale and trust are immediately, and seriously, undermined by organizational downsizing. (American Management Association , 1996)

Kozlowski, Chao, Smith, and Hedlund (1993) suggested that survivors' reactions to organizational downsizing are probably influenced by the extent to which the downsizing directly affects them. Gee, ya think?

There is a large body of work indicating negative consequences with the downsizing process. Research has found organizational downsizing to be associated with: a significant decline in job satisfaction (Armstrong-Strassen, Cameron, & Horsburgh, 1996), reduced job performance (Armstrong-Stassen M. ,

1998), increased job insecurity (Cameron, Freeman, & Mishra, 1993), a deterioration in organizational morale (Cameron, Freeman, & Mishra, 1993), (Cooper, 1999), decreased trust in the organization (Kets de Vries & Balazs, 1997), and reduced commitment to the organization (Kets de Vries & Balazs, 1997), (Luthans & M., 1999). Downsizing violates the psychological contract of job security. Employees who are declared redundant would perceive that their organization has reneged on its obligation to them (Robinson & Bennett, 1995). Actions such as fair treatment, open and honest communication, and supportive behaviors will not only promote trust but will also improve organizational morale. (Mone & V., 1996), (Mone M. A., 1994)

The legacy

The consequences of downsizing will be felt for a long time.

Survivors who still hold their jobs after cutbacks should feel lucky. But they don't. They feel threatened, abandoned, burdened with more work, and subject to greater job stress. Even if the bad feelings do subside with the passage of time, the hair on the back of your neck is always on guard for the other shoe to fall. It would seem to be a lousy way to live and work. Anxiety all the time about when you will love your job affects your health, your personal life, and your attitude. Hopelessness is common.

The American Management Association (AMA) concluded that once you downsize, you have a taste for blood. Do it once, you will do it again. (Greenberg E. , 1989)

Downsizing is almost always conceived and administered at the top. Employees are considered part of the problem - not part of the solution. Consequently, there is little employee involvement in the process. In most cases, any downsizing plans are a well-guarded secret, and the rumor mill is left to do its damage. (Hays, 1994)

Managers emphasize team-building, learning, and innovation, talking terms like self-managing teams, re-engineering, empowerment, cooperation and innovation. All baloney. The reality is very different. Think about more work, fewer people to do it, the fear of losing their job, and a management team totally out of touch. (Cameron, Freeman, & Mishra, 1991)

Managers just do not admit there is a problem. Denial is a wonderful shield. Part of that is because then they do not have to deal with it. Bye, Bye to good morale and trust. (Ironson, 1992) The aggressive behavior found in CEOs has now worked its way down to the lower levels of business.

Of the people who have experienced downsizing in the past and expect more in the next year, 92 percent reported symptoms in one or more of these categories (Shore, 1996)

The good to come from all this is a lot of employees now spend more time with their families. The effect on families can be a burden also. Not having a job or money can be a real downer when it comes to marital tension. The employee is stressed all the time and either becomes irritable and takes it out on family members or spends less time with them.

The goal of downsizing is to improve productivity by eliminating some jobs and combining others. Or is it to increase bonuses? Even from the perspective of the company, downsizing has not been an overwhelming success. (Rose, 1994)

All of these risks lead to many problems. One being the potential exodus of the best performers. Why should these people put up with the company crap? First chance, they will jump ship. At the same time, management will cut the high cost positions filled by experienced people. That's a two edged sword that erodes a corporations' brightest and best base.

One thought is that the weak are singled out as candidates for downsizing. Cruel as that may be, it does happen. Survival of the fittest in a flock of sheep or cattle. Except we are not sheep or cattle. Because of that stigma many employees are concerned about being labeled as complainers or weak employees. Like the general public, after a while of getting dumped on you become resigned to your fate and give up. What's the use or why bother?

Why can't management see that a happy balance must be obtained between addressing cost cutting and taking care of employees?

Try to get employees involved. In spite of knowing this is the thing to do, most manager are afraid that the employee will rebel if they find out about upcoming layoff. That may be partially true but the other way (not telling them) is doomed regardless. At least there is a chance the told employee will understand. Those left behind may also feel a bit better about the situation. Bear in mind that the situation sucks regardless.

Dealing with employees truthfully and upfront will reducing anxieties. Management should also be proactive in gently guiding employees into counseling.

When downsizing (again, if you must) you need to change the work programs around so as to at least appear to be rightsizing. (Vollmann & Brazas, 1993)

This is little more than a psychological ploy, but it may work. Perceived unfairness can destroy an otherwise good plan. (Brockner J. , Grover, Reed, & DeWitt, 1992) Just be aware that being open means being prepared for confrontation and criticism. (Diamond, 1996)

No doubt low morale, decreased productivity, and loss of talent would seem to be troublesome in trying to be an innovative organization.

Survivor reactions

Many studies indicate that downsizing had a significant impact on work attitudes. Gee, did you think life would just go on as usual having twice the work with half the people to do it and also seeing many of your friends and colleagues canned? Plus when you ask the managers what they think, do you really believe you will get any decent answer? I'm not entirely comfortable with the validity of any study using the enemy as a sounding board.

As time went on white collar workers were beginning to be effected as well as the blue collar workers, which upset a lot of assumptions. More than one million white-collar workers were laid off between 1979 and around 1992 (Kozlowski S. , Chao, Smith, & Hedlund, 1993). There is some irony in the fact that those survivors are expected to make the company whole again and better, with fewer personnel (Kozlowski S. , Chao, Smith, & Hedlund). It would be great if it were determined that the downsizing pain were short lived and eventually things got back to normal. (Mishra & Spreitzer, 1998).Then maybe there might be some justification for the process. Research to date says just the opposite. Things get worse. (Bergh,

1993). Most current studies deal with job insecurity (Brockner J. , Grover, Reed, & DeWitt, 1992), and trust in the organization (Brockner J. , Wiesenfeld, Stephan, & Hurley, 1997)

Survivors are likely to find that their job has been significantly modified or even eliminated (Tombaugh & White, 1990). It would not be unusual to then find survivors in denial and withdrawal.

The experience of survivors is a stressful life-event as bad as a divorce or loss of a loved one (Newman & Krzystofiak, 1993). Some individuals may experience a downsizing as an opportunity to grow and develop in their job, liking a challenge and the new freedom that may become available with fewer layers of management (Stewart, 1989). My guess is that is a very small group of people. In general the survivors experience guilt, fear and lack of commitment (Noer, 1993), (Noer, 1998). (Noer, 1990). lack of job satisfaction, and less job involvement (Kozlowski S. , Chao, Smith, & Hedlund, 1993).

Some hypothesized that bad feelings would subside over time (Nicholson & West, 1988).The results of this study that over time attitudes improve could be viewed as corporate trickery. This may be similar to governments slowly introducing negative policies so that the recipient doesn't notice. Pretty soon you're living in a Fascist state with no rights. This is a classic example of the fable of the frog being placed in boiling water upon which time he would immediately jump out, yet upon being placed into a pan and having the heat turned up gradually, he   doesn't notice and eventually dies. So, as people become more comfortable with their new roles and teammates, they would also become less disenchanted with top management. The human being is known to be forgetful over time regardless of the situation so I'm not sure how much credibility to give to the study results.

Mishra and Spreitzer (1998) found that trust in management and work redesign play a powerful role in determining survivor responses. If survivors do not trust that the top management is competent and honest with employees through the downsizing, they are likely to respond in a destructive way. Additionally, if work is not redesigned in a manner that will minimize overload, survivors are more likely to respond negatively (Lodahl & Kejner, 1965), (Frone, Russell, & Cooper, 1965) found that high involvement individuals had a tendency to be susceptible to the use of alcohol and let their health deteriorate. In the contrary scenario, the less involved an individual is in her or his work, the less likely it is that changes in work conditions will influence changes in organizational commitment. In other words, they didn't care about the organization before, why should anything change?

"I am willing to put in a great deal of effort beyond that normally expected in order to help this organization succeed." Wouldn't it be nice to have about a dozen of those?

It would be just plain naïve to believe that downsizing had no effect on work attitudes. This effect varies over time, and the initial impact, as a bare minimum, is generally negative. Results do suggest that after a longer period of time (1 year or more) attitudes may begin returning to their pre-downsizing level, but that could be said for any adverse situation. No matter how well-meaning management's actions were, I'm still going to quit as soon as I get a better offer. Finally, there is evidence that the very people you prize the most, the highly involved who love their work, are most at risk. So, take care of your brightest and best.

Leaks occur during the downsizing process. In a survey of 909 organizations that had experienced a downsizing, 43% reported that employees learned about the downsizing prior to any official communication (Raber, Hawkins, & Hawkins, 1995)

Justice

Downsizing can have a dramatic influence on all employees in an organization. Reasons given are: efforts to gain a more competitive advantage, to manage or reduce cost expenditures, and to streamline the way in which work is conducted (Hopkins & Weathington, 2006) The reactions of those who survive the downsizing determine the future success of the organization (Brockner J. , Wiesenfeld, Stephan, & Hurley, 1997).

It seems that employees left behind also suffer from the downsizing effort. Some studies indicate that they suffer as much as those let go. (Baruch & P., 1999). There is little doubt that life is tougher for those left behind. They have more work to do to make up the slack for those let go, the atmosphere is miserable because they are always looking over their shoulder waiting for the other shoe to fall. Other negative factors found were increased stress, burnout, job involvement, citizenship behaviors, effort, and productivity (Mishra & Spreitzer, 1998). Downsizing caused employees to become more cynical, demotivated, demoralized, and fearful of future downsizing. It was also found that decreased perceptions of organizational justice and trust can adversely impact an employee's level of commitment and satisfaction with the organization (Cohen-Charash & Spector, 2001), (Mishra & Spreitzer, 1998). Survivors often find themselves with new responsibilities and duties. The new work could be more difficult and/or uninteresting. (Brockner, Wiesenfeld, & Martin, 1995). To expand on the fear factor, there is also the general attitude incurred by these employees who have seen friends get sacked. It is very likely that they don't have the same love for the company anymore.

One of the more glaring and less obvious effects of all these various symptoms and attitudes is an increase in turnover. (Aryee, Budhwar, & Chen, 2002). One can't imagine in a downsizing world that there would be much available in the way of opportunity to jump ship. However, should that be the case, it is a significant expense. The cost to replace (interviewing, retraining, etc., is enormous. Therefore, the whole purpose of downsizing, to save money, would be undermined. (Brockner, Wiesenfeld, & Martin, 1995). "The layoff process consists of a series of events in which victims and survivors evaluate the fairness of the layoff procedures" (Konovsky & Brockner, 1993). If left with a feeling of unfairness, survivors could be destructive to the company.

Equity Theory as a way to determine justice is the belief that the distribution of rewards should rely on individual contributions (Adams, 1965). Capitalism at its best as opposed to Communism. In an organizational setting, equity refers to a give and take between an organization and an employee and its fairness (Hendrix, T., Miller, & Summers, 1998). If an employee suspects a discrepancy in the relationship, he/she may attempt to change it by slacking off, or by leaving the organization (Cowherd & Levine, 1992).

Unfairness could come in either the process (Hendrix, T., Miller, & Summers, 1998) or the outcome (Greenberg. J., 2005).

Organizational commitment is defined as "acceptance of organizational goals and values, willingness to exert effort on behalf of the organization, and desire to be a part of the organization" Commitment can be exemplified by a sense of responsibility (Meyer & N., 1991), acceptance of the organization's values (Somers, 1995), could be based on the costliness of leaving due to investments made (Brown R. , 1996).

Commitment, like justice, also affects turnover (Meyer & N., 1991) and Absenteeism (Hendrix, T., Miller, & Summers, 1998).

Job Satisfaction is made up of many things, like: pay, promotion, coworker admiration, supervisor respect and praise, interesting and/or fun work, and decent working conditions. How hard is that?

One would think that after the axe has fallen, those left behind would be feeling pretty good. Not true. Turnover actually increases after downsizing. Some people simply don't like change. New ideas scare or make them uncomfortable. An unstable environment is all it takes for people to leave. (Spreitzer & Mishra, 2002). All it takes is one departure to open the flood gates. (Krausz, Yaakobovitz., N., & Caspi, 1999). Turnover is expensive, both because of the time and money invested in those who left, and the time and money needed to replace them (Spreitzer & Mishra).

"The relationship an employee has with his/her

company is often described as a *psychological contract,* an unspoken agreement between the employer and the employee (Robinson, 1996). When one of the parties breaches this contract, it creates a lack of trust. In the downsizing process, as more work occurs and there is more job insecurity, trust commonly declines (Mishra & Spreitzer, 1998). Consequences would be engagement in destructive or withdrawal behaviors (Mishra & Spreitzer). Advanced notification may help in some small way. A lack of trust brought on by the company breaching a contract can cause an employee to shirk his/her obligations, good citizenship practices and commitment (Robinson)

Who Cares Why

Victims of downsizing very often believe their layoff to be unfair. Wouldn't you? And, of course it is! How can it be fair for an executive to fire someone making $40,000 per year who needs every penny of it, just to increase his/her compensation from 20 million to 25 million dollars? What? Couldn't squeeze out enough for the third house in the Hamptons and a fourth diamond ring this month? Why is it that whenever the management side is illustrating a point they describe the worker as a worthless wastrel who is lazy and only wants to game the system? Certainly there are those people who have learned to live off welfare, subsidized housing and food stamps. And there is no excuse for that. But that's not the normal average worker. Then there is the little old lady who can't seem to get the hang of these pesky computers, gets sick a lot, and gossips all day long. Give me a break! Anytime the young work over three hours a day they think they're being abused. I'm not sure whether the texting time is included in the three hours or not.

Assuming one cannot avoid the practice of downsizing, the questions is "can unpleasantness be avoided by providing information in a timely manner to both those let go and those left behind? If so, what method would work best to avoid any retaliation or destructive actions? Research found that it depended on the trust level the workers perceived that management had (Skarlicki, Barclay, & Pugh, 2008).

When employer's integrity was thought to be low, retaliation increased. The perceived sincerity of management also played a part in the attitudes of the workers (Skarlicki & Folger, 1997). This perception can be exacerbated if the layoff victims were loyal and hardworking but got canned anyway. Retaliation can be a way to restore the balance of justice, and help them deal with their strong negative emotions (Allred, 1999), (Bies & Tripp, 2002). Even though laid off employees are no longer around, they can affect the company through retaliating by bad-mouthing the organization (Konovsky & Folger, 1991), initiating law suits which consume time for the company and engaging in sabotage or violence against the company (Folger & Baron, 1996), (Wilkinson, 1998). The end result from a number of studies is that retaliation can be cushioned by advancing decent information up front in a timely manner (Greenberg J. , 1990) (Greenberg & Lind, 2000). But not always. (Bobocel & Zdaniuk, 2005); (Folger & Skarlicki, 1998). There is also the potential for managers to appear to be fair without actually being fair – a condition that Greenberg labeled 'hollow justice'. If employees see through this fakery it could make workers even madder.

If we didn't believe you before, why should we believe you now? 'Actions speak louder than words'. 'cheap talk' (Bottom, Gibson, Daniels, & Murnighan, 2002).

Explanations that are adequate (clear, reasonable and appropriately detailed) and provided in a timely manner contribute to perceptions of fairness because they help layoff victims make sense of their predicament. Moreover, explanations can signal to employees that they are worthy of dignity and respect (Bies & Moag, 1986).

Employees who have been laid off, often question whether they should have trusted their employer's integrity in the first place (Uchitelle, 2006). We all understand that layoffs by management who have high integrity are more likely to be deemed legitimate and credible than those done by management with perceived low integrity (Bies, 1987) More importantly, the ones who are perceived as having high integrity are likely to be given a bit of slack, or the benefit of the doubt (Robinson, 1996).

Being laid off by a company deemed to have high integrity could result in a heightened sense of unfairness. Viewing one's employer as having high integrity creates expectations for fair treatment that can be violated by being laid off, resulting in stronger negative reactions than had the employee had low expectations in the first place. (Rousseau & Wade-Benzoni, 1995) Muddying the water somewhat is that, over time, employees develop feelings of entitlement.

Many employees truly do love their work, and contribute much of their resources and themselves to their jobs. It can be a very positive and rewarding experience. However, when that much effort is put into something, the risk of disappointment is also great. It's like a strong romance that goes wrong. Emotions run high because you put yourself into it wholeheartedly. You become vulnerable to exploitation and threats to self-identity (Lind, 2001). The thought process required in these relationships to determine fairness consumes a lot of energy. When the employer has not always acted with integrity in the past, employees are more likely to question the employer's motives and the accuracy of the information being provided (McGill, 1989), (Van den Bos, Vermunt, & Wilke, 1997), (Tyler, Casper, & Fisher, 1989), (Lewis & Weigert, 1985).

Always remember that many studies are biased or simply inaccurate. Transferability of the data to general situations can be a problem. Different companies used different methods and explanations to announce the layoff. As to who responds to a survey request, it can also go either way. Maybe more positive respondents would answer, and they would be brown-nosing in their answer, or, angry workers might use the survey to vent their anger. Another problem-assessment of integrity can be very subjective.

Once again we find that it would help if the company had given a favorable severance package, given help in finding new employment, given counseling, given plenty of information and been fair, and treated their employees with dignity and respect. (Brockner, 1990), (Brockner, et al., 1994), (Konovsky & Folger, 1991),

Since a lack of prior sincerity seems to lessen the impact of a reasonable explanation program, the easy solution would be, then, to behave like a decent civilized human being all of the time so that, heaven forbid, there would ever be a legitimate reason to downsize, it would flow as smoothly as possible in a bad situation, limiting the bad feelings and therefore the retaliation. To not do this would pretty much negate the "fairness card" you might chose to play. This does not lessen the importance of being sincere in the explanations. It goes without saying that not providing any information at all is still worse than anything and will lead to the most retaliation.

A great strategy is having employee representatives participate in discussions and opening the books to them. It is very difficult to get mad at a decision when you were a part of that decision. Also, make every effort to build trust and integrity all the time so that employees have the right feelings if and when a downsizing situation becomes necessary.

Positives for the Let Go

As to the suggestion that downsizing creates an opportunity for improving their lives mentioned in the Literature Review, what are the odds, and thanks for the favor? This logic rings hollow, with little support and even then with an extremely small percentage receiving or taking advantage of the benefit. Easy for the postulators to say, they have a job. That may be true but there has to be a security blanket during an indefinite transition period. Reasonable severance packages could be offered to help until a new position is found.

Negatives for the Let Go

Record layoffs have been amassed (Hickok T., 1995). The only result of which appears to have been burnout, depression, anger, illness and a sense of betrayal by both those made redundant and those left behind to take up the slack. Hickok argues that the biggest effect will be culture change, not financial profit. Employees become paranoid, self-absorbed and their top priority is their own career rather than the bottom line of their employer. After a large percentage of downsizing, few of the remaining workforce easily adapted to change, while others never adapted. Many eventually quit. Noer (1993) and Brockner et al (1992) agree. Hickok also states that power has shifted away from the rank and file employees to top management and stockholders. The attitude seems to be swinging away from the well-being of individuals to corporate predominance; working relationships have become competitive instead of familial; and relationships have moved away from long term and stable to short term and contingent Robinson et al (1995). The negative effects of underemployment seem to be as detrimental as unemployment. Leana & Feldman (1994), O'Brien & Feather (1990). Crosby (1976); Martin (1991) suggest that negative effects occur because laid off workers desire and feel entitled to better jobs. The violation of psychological contracts may have a negative effect on the individual's long term attitude toward work in general and their careers.

Granting that some companies are not suited to the task, they may have to initiate drastic steps. Those who are able to compete effectively should have an obligation to care for their workers and have everyone-executives, investors and employees share the risk and reward of doing business. Over the years the senior executives claim that the huge layoffs were necessary to improve efficiency led to the initial assumption that the employee's loss was the firms gain. Boone (2004) indicated that now it appears that it is not an equal trade off but that the cost far outweighs the gain due to unemployment and reduction of economy wide growth. John Kay of the London Business School called the practice philistine individualism and claimed that free markets could exist without that level of aggression. He urged the private sector to stop trying to please Wall Street at the expense of employees and long term investment. There is a small ray of hope as Proctor and Gamble replaced their chief executive for eliminating too many too fast.

Feldman et al (2002) has addressed short term effects of job loss on individuals who have been downsized. No questions that these effects are immediate and strongly negative. Underemployment is conceptualized as laid off employees, re-employed in lesser paying jobs, with a demotion in title and not fully utilizing their skills. Any and all of these have consistently lower job attitudes. This study was more interested in long term effect on careers as opposed to the supposed short term end goal of simply getting reemployed. The quality of the re-employment is a major determinant of future career paths. Feldman's five hypotheses were: Underemployment will be negatively related to job satisfaction, organizational commitment and trust while positively related to careerist attitudes and continued job searching. The study builds on existing info in 3 ways. First, it examines effects of underemployment on job attitudes and work attachment. Second, it examines relative deprivation in order to try and understand how underemployment leads to negative job attitudes. Third, they concentrated on executives to get a perhaps more thorough investigation of the psychological as well as the financial problems. Some of the negative job attitudes are: job dissatisfaction, disappointment with pay, lower organizational commitment (psychologically distancing and lowering contributions), lack of trust as to unmet expectations, continued job searching. Why would anyone think otherwise? Picture an atmosphere in which you are cynical, disillusioned, frustrated, worried, and experience a lack of excitement. Relative deprivation satisfaction is a result not only of the actual job conditions but what people believe the conditions should be. Also, how it indicates how well a job satisfied the individual's values. Adams "equity theory" stated that individual satisfaction with rewards depended on how the rewards stacked up compared to co-workers (Adams & Freeman, 1976). Relative deprivation has to do with a sense of social injustice. Relative deprivation may be appropriate because much of the dissatisfaction comes from experiences with the previous employer and their future hopes as opposed to the present one. Equity Theory has to do with the present comparisons. This can be very subjective depending on how much an individual wants or needs certain rewards. A 60 year old with accumulated savings may not have needs at all. Workers with a graduate degree may have higher expectations of entitlements than a person, without a high school degree, who may care less about self-actualization. It is also the old ""Catch 22". If you, as an executive, compare yourself against a factory worker with few prospects, you might feel lucky; but if your comparison standard is against those who are at your level and not let go, you consider yourself unlucky. To be fair, Adam's study was only of executives with an average age of 46 and there was a standard deviation of +/- 7.75. The study concludes that underemployment is associated with a number of

negative attitudes toward jobs and careers. The greater
the discrepancy (relative deprivation) the more negative
the job attitudes. Skill utilization pays the greatest role.
The effects of underemployment on outcomes are
significantly mediated by relative deprivation.
Downsizing does affect everyone, executive as well as
lower paid workers and employee reactions to their jobs
may be based on previous job treatment. The study
concluded that taking care of employees may mitigate the
relative deprivation but more research is needed to
separate the economic from the psychological aspect of
downsizing.

Schumpeter (1942) wrote, "Downsizing may not
be pretty to watch and people will get hurt but that is
the way Capitalism takes care of the market. One might
get the idea that Schumpeter was against Capitalism
like Marx. This was not the case as Marx believed that
Capitalism's enemies (The Proletariat) would destroy it
because of what it did to them, while Schumpeter
believed that Capitalism would destroy itself from
within by its own successes. He believed that
Capitalism would create a large intellectual class that
would complain of, and ultimately ruin, the very system
of private property and freedom that allowed them to
exist. He wrote: "If a doctor predicts that his patient
will die presently, this does not mean that he desires it."
Schumpeter said that capitalism encouraged
entrepreneurship and innovation as a way of creating
new means of production, new products, and new forms
of organization. He did concede, however, his famous
phrase that capitalism led to "creative destruction" as
innovations caused old inventories, ideas, technologies,
skills, and equipment to become obsolete. He felt that
this creative destruction caused progress and improved

standards of living for everyone. Perhaps, but he stopped short of addressing the consequences of that action to those unable to compete. Schumpeter did not agree that "perfect" competition, where everyone produced the same thing for the same price, was the way to maximize economic well-being. He wrote: "What counts is competition from the new commodity, the new technology, the new source of supply, the new type of organization... competition which... strikes not at the margins of the profits and the outputs of the existing firms but at their foundations and their very lives." Again; this emphasis on creative destruction. He did go on to say that some degree of monopoly was preferable to perfect competition. Schumpeter never made completely clear whether he believed innovation was sparked by monopoly per se or, rather, by the prospect of getting a monopoly as the reward for innovation. Most economists accept the latter argument and, on that basis, believe that companies should be able to keep their production processes secret, have their trademarks protected from infringement, and obtain patents. As it now stands, there is no job entitlement. Fine, let us concede that and move along in our effort to deal with it. That kind of attitude lends credence to capitalism not being the ultimate system for Humanity. Again, are we here to work (a recent puritan ethic since the rich did nothing until a few hundred years ago)? There is an assumption that the first order of business is to thrive and be competitive. It is hard to disagree with this, for; if there is no business there is no job for the employee. This requires further debate as to the fundamental purpose of human beings. We should look to the animal kingdom for examples. Do they live to work or work to live? American culture rewards winners, not losers and number one above all others; thereby encouraging employees to hide failures rather than admit and correct them. Where is the happy medium here?

Downsizing creates the appearance of doing something to correct a bad situation. The costs might not bear this out if the cost of hiring outside contractors is more than the savings from employee elimination. There is a lack of empirical data on this aspect of downsizing (Cameron K. , 1994). The General Electric study, Tichy and Sherman (1994) was filled with a nightmare of examples as to the attitudes surrounding downsizing; such as "the intentional infliction of pain is good". This sounds like "Greed is good". Terms like necessary evil come to mind. It also give the usual credit to Jack Welch for accomplishing great things by merely canning 170,000 people while getting obscenely rich in the process. People do bad things under the guise of a good slogan. In this case it was "the ultimate test of leadership is enhancing the long term value of the organization". Profits should be viewed as a means to an end (Handy, 2002). Employees, suppliers, the environment and the community should also be considered. Remember, these shareholders are probably employees somewhere also. If not, and they are only wealthy non workers, then all the more reason to resent and restrict their profits at the expense on the thousands of workers laid off.

Cultural reinforcing is a term used for voluntary reducing by buyouts, job sharing, and attrition. Advanced notice, shared pain (management suffers also), explicit written criteria as to who stays and who goes, transition assistance-long term, participation in decisions. These are all alternatives to downsizing worthy of study.

Winefield (2002), in addressing unemployment, underemployment,   occupational   stress   and psychological well-being touched on an interesting subject-which he called the "official" rate of unemployment. It is possible, like the CPI, that this rate is not accurate due to those who have been dropped from the calculating surveys or are underemployed. Winfield et al (1991) demonstrated that there are substantial costs to the individual and the family not only in economic deprivation but psychological as well. First it was demonstrated that there is a causal link between employment and psychological well-being and second, that the psychological effects suffered cannot be attributed to economic causes alone. The inference is that they feel bad about themselves, are ashamed and feel lost even if they are little affected monetarily. Are employed individuals less depressed and have more self- esteem because they are employed (exposure) or do depressed people with low self-esteem not have a job (selection)?

When jobs are plentiful, unemployed people tend to be unemployable or work shy, suggesting the selection hypothesis. When jobs were scarce, evidence supported the exposure hypothesis. This is reinforced by the psychological theories of unemployment. The Learned Helplessness Theory states that those who attribute negative outcomes to internal, stable and global causes are more likely to become helpless and lose self-esteem and encounter depression if confronted with unemployment (an uncontrollable event). The Life Span Development Theory suggests that during one of the eight stages of development (identity conflict that occurs during adolescence), unemployment retards healthy psychological development. The Deprivation theory (Freud) states that any work was better than none; but that is not substantiated. There are as usual, plenty of conflicting theories (Jahoda, 1982), (O'Brien & Feather, 1990), and (Winefield A. H., 2002). Fryer (1986)rips apart Jahoda and his five latent benefits as not being benefits at all. Winefield assumes people to be proactive and independent. People work to earn money in order to be able to plan leisure activities and save for a satisfying retirement. That is only one theory and possible applies only to a minority of people. Recommended further research would be to compare the research carried out to that in the 1930's. It is not what you have but what you perceive you have in relation to what you feel you are entitled. (Feldman, Leana, & Turnley, A relative deprivation approach to understanding underemployment, 1997). This could apply to executives if I had any sympathy for them.

Wilkinson (1998) argues that increased income inequality has negative health consequences for all of society. This causes a breakdown of social cohesion which characterizes healthy egalitarian societies. These theories do not address the critical issue of keeping people at work, with the exception of Wilkinson.

Employees who have been let off may feel they have let others like their family down. They may also feel unqualified due to the blow to their self-image. The underemployment that sometimes follows may leave them feeling depressed, hopeless, bored and hating the new job. The financial strain caused can result in marital and other family problems (Lohr, 1996). Even if the breadwinner gets another job it may be in another state and force the spouse to sacrifice his or her career. Children would be uprooted from school and friends

Older unemployed people experience greater psychological distress that the young. There are a number of reasons for this. First, they have less time to recover from adversity financially. Second, same goes for emotionally. At twenty you are immortal. Or so you think. There may be an underlying cognizance that the elderly have, due to gaining maturity. Sort of an "it's not fair" realization. Stress begins even before the job loss if you know or suspect it is coming. New technology has added the burden of information overload as well as demands for greater immediacy of response. Karasek (1979) suggested high demands combined with low control led to greater stress. He acknowledged that there is a set of underemployed people who are involuntary, low paid, low status, insecure, public service workers with persistent hopeless search for a job that doesn't exist, managing households on inadequate resources and participating in humiliating bureaucratic rituals. Just because those left behind experience stress there should be no implication that it is ok to fire people because they will have stress either way. Winefield stated that it would be increasingly difficult to prove that unemployment has negative effects. (Winefield A. H., 2002). Another question for further research. Further research is needed as to mature worker employment because they will be needed in the future. It will perhaps be just the opposite of the current downsizing situation as the baby boomers retire.

The Social Costs

Worker displacement occurs when workers lose their jobs through no fault of their own. Another word for downsizing in other words. Usually, this occurs for reasons business leaders say is "beyond their control," such as foreign competition or declining worker productivity. Welcome to Neverland! In reality, it's because the business leaders are greedy, aggressive,

uncaring, dredges of the community, whose obscene
bonus and other perks are based on little more than
short term profits, (quarterly earnings); many of which
are either fudged, completely lied about, misleading or
just short sighted at the expense of the long term well-
being of the employees and the company. I just watched
a movie last night which took place during the Second
World War. The guy said that war was unimportant,
business was all that mattered. And if you believe that
isn't exactly how business people think you are living in
a mud hut.

When a major employer decides to close up
shop, not only the individual workers let go are effected
but there is a ripple effect into the community also. Not
only are laid off employees miserable but there is a
reduced tax base from the company leaving and the
workers having less money to spend in the community.

Eight million workers—one in sixteen working
Americans—became unemployed between January
1995 and December 1997. The elderly that were let go
were the least likely to find new jobs. Earnings of
displaced workers always seem to be less. During the 7
or more years following job loss, their average annual
earnings were 6 to 12 percent below expected levels
(Stevens, 1997). Studies indicate that the number of
workers displaced has been increasing over the
downturns studied from the 1970 thru 1990 (when 5.4
million people lost their jobs) (Gardner, 1995).

No matter how much credit is given to the
young, job insecurity is a terrible feeling for some
workers. Unfortunately, apparently the people doing
analysis for the Department of Labor don't hang around
Main Street very much or they would know that we
don't have many well trained, highly skilled and mobile

workers in this country.

In June of 2001 Bridgestone/Firestone closed their plant in Decatur, Illinois. This involved around 1200-1600 employees depending on the time frame counted. "Rounding up all the usual suspects," they cited declining consumer demand, economic downturn, and excess pre-production capacity in the US. Sound familiar? The last thing management said was "We want to assure our employees that we recognize, and will try to deal with, the serous toll this may take on them, their families, and the community." What a load of crap. A survey was conducted on this closing by Robert J. Hironimus-Wendt and Fred Spannaus ending in 2007. Their survey consisted of 3 mailed surveys questioning the effects on personal, familial and community costs. (Hironimus-Wendt & Spannaus, 2007)

After one year, only a little over half of the respondents had new jobs. It is difficult to determine what effort, if any, the remainder of the respondents had exercised. Whether those that retired needed to, or wanted to, is unknown. As for those drawing unemployment, it cannot be determined if they were being forced to because they can't find work or whether they are just living off the dole. Another group elected to take some kind of education or training. Same thing goes for them as to being forced or were they doing it because they wanted to. In this case, because the plant closing was attributed to international competition, workers were eligible to receive Unemployment compensation, Trade Adjustment Assistance (T.A.A.) and educational benefits all at the same time. Wow. That's like being able to retire from the government after twenty years and then go get another government job and retire from that one after another twenty years, drawing full benefits from both. It is sometimes hard to pity the workers over management after being made aware of these kinds of shenanigans.

The average salaries for those rehired within a year were only 55% of their previous salaries. That would be alright if all the costs of living had gone down also. Good luck. There was no evidence that those remaining unemployed had unrealistic wage expectations (Hironimus-Wendt & Spannaus, 2007)

Income figures are always hard to quantify because one never knows whether the average household income is from just one earner or two.

Bankruptcy and foreclosures are just words on paper unless it is happening to you. You are either a burden on the local community or you have to leave and are no longer a tax provider and shopper. The depression surrounding all this to the let go individual and his/her family is the stuff of suicides. The drag on the community from the additional number of houses hitting the market will likely depress prices for everyone. And finally, the loss of tax revenue to the city or county from having vacant property off the tax rolls substantially affect schools, protective services, parks and recreation, and infrastructure. Ironically, just when people are out of work and need every penny, the local government, in trouble also, raises taxes on those individuals. It's just as ironic for local governing bodies who create tax-free enterprise zones and tax abatement programs to get corporations to come to town just when they need more revenue from taxes. Clearly, there is a problem here to fix.

I am guessing that divorce would increase also. No question there won't be any vacations,

eating out, or new cars. But there will also be less cable
TV, more buying generic foods, less junk food, fewer
new clothes, cutting back on heating and air
conditioning, less home repairs, less tithes at church,
not going to the dentist, doctor, or hospital and
prescription medicines, letting health and life insurance
policies lapse and fewer gifts for family members. The
services on the receiving end of all that reduction would
then suffer as well. Other crummy circumstances
include: trying to sell cars, trucks and recreation
vehicles, trying to sell furniture, antiques, collectibles,
computers, tools, and/or lawn equipment. Overall, it is
not the atmosphere of a thriving growing, happy and
healthy first world society. The personal effects on the
people were very alarming. They included anger,
anxiety, depression, sleeplessness, emotional stress,
financial stress, feelings of worthlessness, and health
problems. Some of the more critical situations were
cutting back on extracurricular activities for their
children or no longer being able to help their older
children financially. A respondent wrote "My high
school son joined the National Guard because he did
not think I would be able to put him through college."
One wrote about not being able to help his elderly
parents with their bills (Hironimus-Wendt & Spannaus,
2007) In order to let a greedy SOB of a CEO increase
his already bloated income from 10 million to 15
million dollars by sending jobs somewhere else, a son
dies in some faraway place and a parent dies in some
rest home. Talk about misplaced dollars.

One relocated worker wrote "Had to move to
another state and leave behind my elderly parents who
are in poor health. My daughter and I miss them a great
deal and feel cut off and alone." Several reported that

they had relocated but left their wives and children behind. (Hironimus-Wendt & Spannaus, 2007).

It is noteworthy here to clarify one thing regarding the time line of all this downsizing. By studying history many of us feel that what goes up must come down. In other words, all those lovely jobs will come roaring back just as they always have, Well, let me tell you bubby, this ain't your Grand Dad's recession. As of 2013 we have had over 30 years of downsizing and a loss of our standard of living. The expression "Don't bet against America" may have seen its day. No problem. Just so the CEO's got their bonuses and another Rolls Royce to drive.

What are, or should be the stated goals of any advanced society? Workers need lifelong economic security. They need the opportunity to obtain skills that will guarantee them high wages. Workers should be able to use technology to their advantage, without fearing that it will make them "obsolete." Workers need to be able to balance work with caring for their families. Workers need workplaces that are fair—free from discrimination and other unfair employment practices.

No one seems to have a way to get greedy decision makers to cooperate Retraining people in a dying local market may be shutting the barn door after the horse has escaped. For this to work, there has to be a decent supply of good jobs in each labor market. It also assumes that those people can be retrained. Instead of complaining that many workers can't handle the "new" economy" full of computers and advanced technical gadgetry (which possibly they can't), the government might do well to re think their economy and society in general. Meaning, if technology is destroying the family and communities with no end in sight, the powers that be need a more macro approach to the direction of society. The topic to be approached seems to be local labor markets transitioning from well-paying, manufacturing jobs to low wage service sector jobs. So, what do you do? Go back to manufacturing and stop outsourcing? Figure a way to make the service jobs more viable? Big questions. Not many answers.

A response management always gives when destroying personal lives and entire local cultures is "We are a profit motivated business and it is our responsibility to make money for our shareholders." It is far more appropriate to think in terms of stakeholders, not just shareholders, of whom, workers are a major factor. Also in this group is the community. The big question then is "Does a corporation have Corporate Responsibility to a community and its workers? If one believes even a little bit that we have some "Noblesse Oblige" or obligation to our fellow man, then we have to at least visit the issue. If you don't believe that, I foresee a long, lonely winter ahead. Corporate welfare through local tax breaks and business subsidies must be made conditional upon ongoing, explicit corporate investments in local economic development. In exchange for tax breaks, businesses should be expected to hire and train local workers, and invest in locally-based training and skills development programs. In other words, give back-- or get out! The system today is just unfair, skewed toward those at the top and paid for by workers and their communities (Hironimus-Wendt & Spannaus, 2007).

It's All Relative

Most research has consistently found that layoffs have immediate, and often strong, negative consequences for employees' psychological and physiological well-being (Leana & Feldman, 1995). But what about after some of them have been rehired? Has there been any negative long term effects on the careers of downsized employees? When laid-off workers get new jobs, it is felt that the problems cease. Not true for the walking underemployed. The results suggest that the quality of replacement jobs (type, level, pay, responsibilities etc.), and not just being rehired is a major determinant to laid-off employees' subsequent career trajectories. Many downsized employees end up underemployed' in jobs which require less education and experience than they possess, in positions which pay considerably less than the jobs from which they were laid off, or in positions at lower levels of the organizational hierarchy (Feldman D. , 1996), (Kuttner, 1994). What are the effects of underemployment on the job attitudes and work attachment of employees? Initial studies of underemployment suggest that laid-off workers re-employed in lower quality jobs have more negative job attitudes towards their new employers, invest less energy in their new jobs and are more likely to keep searching for different jobs even after accepting those new positions. The negative effects of underemployment have been found to be as detrimental to psychological well-being as unemployment itself (Kuhnert K. , 1989), (Leana & Feldman, 1995), (O'Brien & Feather, 1990). Why would that be so? The answer. Relative Deprivation. In the past it has been accepted that obtaining a lesser job after being laid off would lead to a poor job attitude. But why? Because laid-off workers both desire and feel entitled to better jobs than the one they got. This psychological attitude is what leads to a bad job attitude (Crosby, 1982).

Whether right or wrong, most of the research on underemployment has been on two groups of workers: laid-off blue-collar workers (Leana & Feldman, 1995), (Liem., R., & Liem, 1988) and underemployed high school or college graduates (Feldman & Turnley, 1995), (Winefield, Winefield, & Tiggemann, 1991) (Winefield & Tiggemann, 1990). Probably because these workers suffer more harsh financial difficulties since every penny is more important to them. They have less disposable income. In the case of the laid-off managers the psychological trauma is probably more prevalent and more harming.

Feldman (1996) said, underemployment can be defined in a number of ways. All definitions, however, agree that underemployment means jobs which are lower in quality somehow. First, in terms of the "pecking order". Very often employees laid off from 'permanent' full-time jobs find themselves working in part-time or temporary jobs or, particularly in the case of managers, at lower hierarchical levels of organizations (Buss & Redbum, 1983). The managers are also paid less. Zvonkovic (1988) defined underemployment as 'current earnings at least 20% less than earnings in the previous job. It has been even more. I never could figure out what standards to use. Like the old expression, "If your neighbor is out of work, it's a recession. If you are, it's a Depression." The level of skills being utilized is critical also (Clogg & Shockey, 1984), (Clogg, Sullivan, & Mutchler, 1986),

(Humphrys & O'Brien, 1986). Previously the issue of skills utilization has been researched on the other, more financially stressed groups-teenaged 'school leavers' (O'Brien & Feather, 1990), (Winefield, Winefield, & Tiggemann, 1991) and college graduates (Feldman, Leana, & Turnley, 1997) in which the skills and abilities they learned in school were not fully utilized. In their research on underemployment among contingent workers, (Feldman & Doerpinghaus, 1992) actually asked individuals to report whether their jobs could be performed adequately by people with considerably less education and work experience than they themselves possessed. How one could obtain a reasonable answer to that question from such a group is beyond my wildest dreams. As usual, people do not think ahead as to the consequences of their actions, either for those they are hurting or even for themselves. Borgen et al (1988) found job dissatisfaction to be the number one issue, or problem. Dissatisfaction with the work itself has a strong impact on all other aspects of one's life. Following closely behind would be disappointments with pay and promotional opportunities. If either of the first two are present then lower organizational commitment is likely to follow. When employees feel they are not getting a fair shake compared to previously they will psychologically distance themselves from their employers and lower their contributions to their organizations (Borgen, Amundson, & Harder, 1988), (Leana & Feldman, 1995). Trust is always an important issue, and is now lacking. Trust is an individual's expectations of goodwill, willingness to reciprocate, and honoring of commitments. This is lost as many downsized employees feel the organization has violated the implicit agreements they have with them about job security and procedural fairness (Rousseau & Wade-Benzoni, 1995).

One of the outcomes of this loss of trust is the employee in the new job environment may have a chip on their shoulder (or just be more practically aware and realistic) in the new job, will then react more negatively to those unmet expectations, and may have less faith in their new employers in general (Rousseau, Sitkin, Burt, & Camerer, 1998). There is a certain amount of unfairness in all this as the new employer is paying for the sins of the previous employer.

Another consequence of the issue is that underemployed employees will more than likely be job-searching more now (Leana & Feldman, 1995). "What's good for the Goose is good for the Gander." Burris (1983) found that underemployed workers were giving the new employer less time to improve before leaving, and no notice was more the norm (Robinson, Kraatz, & & Rousseau, 1994).

Even those looking for work, in general were more cynical. Borgan et al (1988) found that underemployed college graduates were more disillusioned. The excitement was definitely gone along with any career investment. (Leana & Feldman, 1992). Whether or not it is for the better of not, this is no longer AT&T taking care of their own for life- and "the sword cuts both ways." Feldman (1996) suggests that underemployment may lead to an increased reliance on nonperformance-based tactics (such as networking and impression management) to get ahead. One more step for a nasty society.

Research regarding job satisfaction has been going on for a long time. Probably since before

downsizing became fashionable. In the 1970's much
was written about the discrepancy between what you
were paid, and what you thought you should be paid.
Lawler (1973) suggested that workers' satisfaction with
their jobs was not only a function of how positive
actual job conditions were (e.g. pay, work itself,
supervision) but also a function of what job conditions
employees felt *should* exist. To be fair, this attitude isn't
entirely one sided. Many of have a bloated opinion of
ourselves. Equity Theory plays a part in the situation
also. It proposes that individuals' satisfaction with job
rewards was influenced by comparisons with coworkers (Adams & Freeman, 1976). It manifests itself
starkly in the A- student who commits suicide because
they can't live with being number two. Recall Colonial
Cathcart in Catch 22 who was ahead on 98% of all his
contemporaries but fixated on being behind that one
person. Better to be fat, dumb and happy? Locke (1976)
touched on this briefly also. Similar to "beauty is in the
eyes of the beholder." Perception is everything.

     As a summary for reference, equity theory
examines how employees assess the fairness of their job
rewards relative to their present colleagues, whereas
relative deprivation theory examines the comparisons
underemployed workers make between past and present
jobs. Underemployment refers to 'objective' job quality
(such as lower pay, lower hierarchical level or lower
skill utilization), while relative deprivation refers to
individuals' 'subjective' reactions to those job qualities.
Relative deprivation theory depends on the personality
of the worker and can therefore be different. Executives
in their 40s who have lost their jobs may be more
demanding of similar replacement jobs at equally high
levels of pay, whereas executives in their late 60s may

not have high needs for replacement jobs at all so will settle for less. MBA types, being the snot noses they are, will feel more entitled to jobs that utilize their extensive education, while workers without high-school diplomas may have lesser expectations. They don't think in terms of self-actualization.

Relative Deprivation Theory comes more from the social psychology literature and focuses on an individuals' sense of injustice (Stouffer, Suchman, DeVinney, & Williams, 1949). It is only recently that researchers in the organizational sciences have used relative deprivation theory to explain individuals' reactions to work-related problems such as inequities in pay rises and promotion decisions (Bunk & Janssen, 1992), (Sweeney, McFarlin, & Inderrieden, 1990)

Much of the research and information from the management side is obtained from Feldman et al, (2002), where 1700 surveys were sent out and 500 responded. Although a reasonable sample size, the credibility of the response is questionable because it is a bit one sided. All of the respondents had other jobs already so unless that was the only group of concern, which it may have been, it is a bit narrow in scope. It is also only regarding managers and not blue collar workers. The results do suggest however, that relative deprivation is an important mediator in explaining how underemployment leads to poorer psychological well-being in those replacement jobs. Some of the statistics as related to that survey might be useful to the reader as a gauge of what to expect from a reasonable survey. Remembering that this dissertation is a Meta analysis for the very reason that it is felt that larger sample sizes and a variety of information is more valid. Names and mailing addresses were provided to the researchers by an outplacement organization. Surveys (along with self-addressed, stamped return envelopes to the researchers) were sent to a total of 1700 individuals who had used the services of the outplacement firm in the past year. The response rate was 30%. The average age of the participants in the study was 46. The sample was 74% male and 26% female. Seventy-seven percent of the respondents were married. On average, respondents had worked for the organization from which they were laid off for 12 years. The average respondent received six weeks' advance notice of his/her termination. Following their layoffs, it took the participants in the study an average of five months to transition into their current positions. The average respondent in the study had been working for his/her current organization for eight months at the time of the survey. On their replacement jobs, 33% earned over $100,000 per year. 50% earned between $50,000 and $99,000 and 17% earned annual salaries of less than $50,000. In terms of job functions, 28% were re-employed in marketing and sales, 14% in finance and accounting, 19% in engineering, operations and information technology, 27% in corporate and general management and 12% in other functional areas such as business law. In that study they measured the three most common ways that underemployment has been assessed; by measuring how the hierarchical level of respondents' current jobs compared with that of the previous jobs, by measuring how great a pay difference there is between respondents' current jobs and those from the previous jobs, and by examining both respondents' skill utilization on their current jobs compared with that on their previous job. Skill utilization was broken down into nine areas; supervisory skills (managing people), administrative skills (managing projects), industry knowledge, technical/ functional skills, knowledge of markets and competitors, communication skills, negotiation skills, complex decision-making skills, and financial and budgeting skills. This study had the following results: Underemployment will be negatively related to job satisfaction, Underemployment will be negatively related to organizational commitment, Underemployment will be negatively related to trust in the organization, Underemployment will be positively related to careerist attitudes towards work, and Underemployment will be positively related to continued job searching. Of the three underemployment indicators (skill utilization, pay difference and hierarchical level) effect on each of the five outcome variables (job satisfaction, commitment, trust, job searching and careerism), skill utilization effected all the outcome variables greatly, the pay difference variable was not significantly related to any of the five outcome variables and hierarchical level was only significantly related to the organizational commitment variable. As to the statistics involved, Baron and Kenny (1986) indicate that three conditions are necessary to demonstrate mediation: (1) the independent variable must be significantly related to the dependent variable; (2) the independent variable must be significantly related to the mediator variable (relative deprivation); and (3) the mediating variable (relative deprivation) must be significantly related to the dependent variable. The study also looked at whether Relative Deprivation moderated or mediated the relationship between underemployment and job outcomes. Relative deprivation literature has typically viewed relative deprivation as a mediating variable which precedes affective outcomes (Crosby, 1982). The underemployment literature has typically viewed relative deprivation as a moderating variable between underemployment and job outcomes (Feldman D. , 1996), (Feldman, Leana, & Turnley, 1997). In this study Relative Deprivation appears to play a mediating role rather than a moderating role in explaining reactions to underemployment. More could be established on this difference in future theory development but is beyond the scope of this paper.

The results of this study suggest several important conclusions. First, underemployment – regardless, is associated with a number of negative attitudes toward jobs and careers. This is true for all three different measures of underemployment. Thus, the negative consequences of underemployment for job attitudes are robust. Second, the results of this research suggest that declines in skill utilization, rather than pay cuts or demotions, are more important and cause more negative reactions to under- employment. This information could be useful to outplacement personnel and for the actual downsized manager looking for a position. Apparently, this is not known at outplacement firms who use the traditional measures of salary and hierarchical level instead. Third, the effects of underemployment on outcomes are significantly mediated by relative deprivation. Underemployment generates feelings of relative deprivation which, in turn, adversely affect individuals' attitudes toward both their present jobs and their careers in general. Fourth, underemployment is a problem that affects executives as well as lower paid employees. It is possible that the quality of outplacement assistance may influence how quickly laid-off managers find new jobs, how underemployed they become, and how negatively they react to that underemployment. It is possible that underemployment may not strongly influence certain individuals' behaviors because they can be caught and punished for failure to perform in tasks that can be quantified (Feldman D. , 1996). However, underemployment may have a longer-term negative impact on organizational citizenship behaviors because the performance of these behaviors can be disguised easier. Giving downsized workers extensive severance pay and outplacement support may sooth a lot of hurt feelings (Olson & Hafer, 1996). Nevertheless, even among downsized executives with significant financial resources, feelings are important and can be hurt.

Unemployed Longer?

What this country needs is more unemployed politicians. -- Edward Langley, Artist (1928-1995)
Unemployment duration is defined as the length of time that workers are unemployed. There is much to debate as to the relative significance comparing duration and actual rate of employment. The most recent recession that began somewhere in 2009 (or sooner) had the worst duration on record. In fact, as of 2011 it seemed to be getting worse. Even in the recession of 1981-82, although the peak rate was higher, the duration was not. To be clear, that statement is meaningless unless you know that the "higher" rate was 10.8% versus 10.1%, (U.S. Department of Labor. Bureau of Labor Statistics, 2011), so not earthshaking. The duration can be attributed to many things. To a lesser extent the survey parameters might change. Sort of like the government changing the way they calculate inflation and the Consumer Price Index (CPI), one of

the most blatant examples of government manipulation. This data is distorted in every conceivable way possible to make it appear there is no inflation. "The 'core rate' is a fictional concept designed to soothe the financial markets and distract them from the reality of rising inflation. The core rate does not exist anywhere in our economy. It is a fictional concept designed to conceal inflation" (Puplava, 2005)

Those let go

It would appear that Downsizing has created considerable economic hardship for a significant number of employees in the Western civilizations.

Lack of Safety Net

Maybe we wouldn't need all those social programs if workers could get jobs.

The government loves to tweak and change things. Just think of your IRS Tax forms. Well, that's true in the downsizing game also. I have yet to figure out how things get so screwed up. I really don't believe these people start out with malice in their hearts. If so, there wouldn't be some of the, at least intended, good programs to help people. Going from the old Aid to Families with Dependent Children (AFDC) to the Temporary Assistance for Needy Families (TANF) programs has tightened eligibility requirements for food stamp and Supplemental Security Income (SSI) recipients (Hagen, 1999). Doesn't the government know that to give something and then take it away is committing the cardinal sin? Better to never have given it in the first place. Are there deadbeats and the undeserving? Of course. But is that justification for punishing millions of others while stuffing your face with pork contributions from your rich buddies? How come we always pick on the poor people? Why not tax the rich and reduce defense spending? Ah, but I digress. These changes have definitely weakened the income supports for poor populations traditionally serviced by social workers (Hagen, 1999). There is also a legitimate question as to the inequality of services when programs are turned over from the Federal to the State governments. It never ends, does it?

Are the downsizers the only bad guys? Not likely. It is noteworthy to indicate that the stereotype applicant for those who do qualify for assistance is a young, male, urban African American. Correct me if I'm wrong, but doesn't downsizing affect all workers? "Say it ain't so, Joe" Empirical evidence suggests that there is room for everyone on the poverty lines, regardless of gender, age, families or single, disabled, race or simply regular folks who can't find a job (Halter, 1992), (Gallagher, Uccello, Pierce, & Reidy, 1999).

Are the recipients deserving? Are these people employable after a little help or are they terminally unemployable? Critics contended that some GA recipients were able to work and should be subject to stringent work requirements (Commonwealth of Pennsylvania, 1982). Others countered that many recipients had disabilities sufficient to exempt them from work (Halter, 1992). Pennsylvania split the difference by establishing two categories, one for those with disabilities of a long term nature and the other, those who only needed temporary assistance. The latter group received only 90 days of assistance in a 12 month period (Halter, 1989).

Bear in mind that these GA recipients only received around 40% of the poverty level (in 1996) (Gallagher, Uccello, Pierce, & Reidy, 1999).

As always, the governmental policies and implementation are amazingly laughable at best. Inconsistency is the watchword of the day. Social workers, on the one hand, are tasked with improving social conditions in order to meet basic human needs and promote social justice, while on the other hand, being asked to find ways to cut costs (by reducing services). Reminds me of working for a bank that advocates "relationship banking" in which the customers' needs are uppermost, while on the other hand, pushing to sell, sell, and sell all the time regardless. Damned if you do and damned if you don't.

It would be naive at best to think that these issues will be resolved positively on their own. Good advocacy is needed on behalf of the poor. This can be illustrated best with the example of the News media. Reporters seem to be right down there at the bottom of the ocean with lawyers, insurance salesmen, real estate agents and car salesmen. And yet, they clearly provide some form of deterrent of bad actions by the powers that be. I.E. downsizers, to keep us on track. Let's not kid ourselves, if left to their own devices, people do bad things to little furry animals. All it takes is "A few good men." Do the "Do Gooders" over react? Sure. Just like the reporters who shove a mike in someone's face or invade their privacy. Very often those protectors end up doing the very thing they are fighting against. Think the French Revolution. Can you picture the crowd cheering on as the aristocracy is being beheaded? No question the aristocracy is always in need of reining in. I'm just not sure where you draw the line. Certainly somewhere to the left of killing a little child.

Strategic Management textbooks are loaded with the statement that if you take care of the people in your organization the profits will follow. Gee, how does that tie into downsizing?

It's one thing to be provided educational opportunity, but quite another if you are incapable of availing yourself of it. Regardless, we need to use all available options such as shelters, emergency services, medical services etc., as a safety net of last resort if we have any intention of continuing the downsizing ruse.

Career Development

Unlike the duration of unemployment, the impact on both laid off workers and those left behind as to their career development is varied but usually ugly. Much depends on the size/scope, reasons for, strategy, how it was handled and number of times the downsizing occurs. Is there a way to tell which employees will have the most difficulty with a deteriorating career development?

Downsizing has been going on now for a quarter of a century in earnest. This as a new found toy for the rich to further exploit the poor. Sounds like Marxism, huh? The documentation has covered both blue collar workers in manufacturing and white collar workers in service organizations. The management tool has led to the elimination of millions of positions, prolonged unemployment among laid-off workers, and heavy workloads and anxiety for survivors (Baumohl, 1993), (Bennett, 1991), (Lublin J. S., 1991), Usually the excuse is given that there is a crisis in which management needs to act to cut labor costs in order to survive (Harrigan, 1980). A majority of this literature on the topic has focused on the short-term results and reactions of organizations, laid-off workers and survivors (Brockner, Grover, & Blonder, 1988), (Greenhalgh & Rosenblatt, 1984), (Leana & Feldman, 1992). Researchers have examined organizational strategies for announcing and implementing layoffs (Schweiger, Ivancevich, & Power, 1987), organizational strategies for providing effective assistance to employees at the time of their layoffs (Cameron, Freeman, & Mishra, 1993), employees' reactions and coping behaviors in the aftermath of job loss (Leana & Feldman, 1992), and survivors' feelings of guilt or anger as they see their coworkers depart (Greenhalgh & Lawrence, 1988). Very little, however, has been written as to the effects long term on career development.

Unfortunately, what starts out as a necessary evil to "hold the wolf at bay" quickly evolves into a pure financial play to improve an already profitable bottom line, gain a competitive advantage or really push the envelope of productivity so the executives can get a quarterly bonus (Cameron K. , 1994), (Feldman & Leana, 1994). Lot more of that going on today, in spite of the fact that we as a nation are falling behind in work ethic and productivity.

Scholars usually write as to strategy and theory but not so much on career development. Also there is the question of Macro versus Micro effects. Macro researchers think in terms of the environment and the company as a whole (Hambrick & D'Aveni, 1988), (Hambrick D. C., 1983) , (Kimberly & Miles, 1980), while Micro research concentrates on the individual,

their vulnerability to job loss, and the negative effects on employee performance and job attitudes (Cook & Ferris, 1986), (Markham & McKee, 1991), (Mone M. A., 1997). It is possible that coordination of these different viewpoints would be helpful, and very little coordination has occurred.
(Cameron, Whetten, & Kim, 1987), (Schuler & Jackson, 1987), (Staw, Sandelands, & Dutton, 1981).

How do we understand the impact of downsizing on career development? It would appear that both environmental factors and organizational factors can cause an organization's decision to downsize (Cameron & Kim, 1987) (Cameron & Kim, 1987), (Kimberly & Miles, 1980). Environmental factors generally mean turbulence in either the industry, the sector or the country as a whole (Cameron & Zammuto, 1983), (Murray & Jick, 1985), (Tushman & Newman, 1986). The factors within the organization would be age and life cycle of the firm e.g. turning around your business (doesn't seem to be effecting Coca Cola any), culture of the firm (meaning do they have any respect for workers and job security), and probably the main reason-the profitability of the firm (how greedy the CEO and executives are vs. are they really not making any money and are there structural problems to address), (Ford, 1980), (Weitzel & Jonsson, 1989), Strategic errors and/or operational inefficiencies (Cameron, Whetten, & Kim, 1987). There are a host of cute names for this last effort like the newest buzzword "Harvest Your Profits", or get ready to sell the business and putting on new lipstick, or even potentially killing the business (Harrigan, 1980). As Harrigan points out, when customers are loyal, industry demand is high, and suppliers are willing to help the struggling firm out, the organization is more likely to pursue goals of turnaround or harvesting troubled units. Duh! Wouldn't that be nice?

I suspect that there is a big and critical difference between a declining rate of profitability and a reversal between profitability and a loss. The methodology of the downsizing may differ because of that. The rate of decline (quick, gradual or even lingering slow death) should also effect the methodology. The above reasons lead to the implementation severity as to number of people to be let go and from which units of the company. Lump it all together and stir and you may be able to see a pattern of career development, but not always. Greenhalgh et al (1988) and Perry (1986) suggest that organizations can implement a wide variety of tactics to downsize the workforce, and that these tactics differ considerably in severity and scope. If you must perform the dastardly deed, are you in a position to just allow the downsizing by attrition, simply do not fill slots as they become vacant? How about redeployment to other areas of the company, or even into other job titles? Certainly stop the overtime. Maybe early retirement with a nice severance. Answer. Because, limiting the inflow of new employees, giving early retirement incentives, and redeploying current personnel are tactics which are much slower in generating cost savings and which have a less dramatic, immediate impact on corporate profitability. Large-scale layoffs of personnel, plant closings of now-peripheral facilities, and outsourcing of routine, generic service activities to outside contractors can generate significant cost savings and can be implemented reasonably quickly (Greenhalgh, McKersie, & Gilkey, 1986).

The dirty end of the methodology starts by using temporary help or outsourcing so you can avoid paying benefits (Davis-Blake & Uzzi, 1993), (Feldman & Doerpinghaus, 1992), (Pearce, 1993). Even this might be preferable to the plant closings although it seems to be splitting hairs. When outsourcing, there may be some short-run dislocations in the quality of the service provided, as outside contractors learn their jobs and as external stakeholders have to adjust to dealing with new faces (Feldman & Doerpinghaus, 1992). Then there is the union potential to resist, (Hecksher, 1988), and from regulatory agencies concerned with quality assurance and liability issues (Davis-Blake & Uzzi, 1993).

The two organizational characteristics we think of most are age and size of the firm (Kimberly & Miles, 1980), (Miller & Friesen, 1983). The "liability of newness" has been frequently cited as a contributing factor to organizational decline (Stinchcombe, 1965). What a great phrase. Newer, smaller firms have less cushion to fall back on as well as less experience with doing so. Therefore, they have no staying power, make major errors and don't correct those errors in a timely fashion. Older, larger firms are (or should be) more likely to perceive their problems as operational rather than strategic in nature, to experience decline in terms of stagnation rather than absolute losses, and to downsize slowly (Starbuck, Greve, & Hedberg, 1978). Knowing human nature as we do, it isn't far-fetched to believe organizations often try to hide their business reverses both from the public and from important stakeholders. Long-tenured top management teams may be less likely to perceive the need for strategic change, and to pursue "efficiency actions" rather than strategic redirection in trying to turn around their corporations (Ford, 1980), (Staw, Sandelands, & Dutton, 1981).

There is another side to this argument though. Some say that old, established firms are also quite vulnerable to business reverses, but in a different way (Lorange & Nelson, 1987). These firms may become inflexible, may not be quick to see problems which are different in type (rather than degree), and consequently, may lose their ability to adapt quickly and effectively to business downturns (Nystrom & Starbuck, 1984). They can't turn on a dime either so even if they see the problem they may not be able to change and correct as quickly as a smaller company. Harrigan (1980) agrees with the former theory of the importance of the financial resources of the downsizing firm in responding to environmental turbulence. The worse the problems like declining revenues, profitability, market share, the more likely the firm is to liquidate poor performing units and to implement large-scale downsizing quickly to generate needed cash In contrast, organizations with greater slack resources will be better able to consider pursuing a turnaround strategy and to implementing downsizing actions more slowly and selectively.

Firms vary in their corporate cultures, especially when it comes to belief in a "psychological contract" (Rousseau D. M., 1990). When firms have long prided themselves on benevolent/paternalistic treatment of employees and have viewed job security as an important corporate value, they are more likely to pursue a turnaround strategy and to downsize slowly and selectively if downsizing has to happen. They will genuinely try to minimize the number of employees affected. Last I remember this being the case was IBM in the 1960's. Again, this isn't your Grand Dad's AT&T.

With all that in mind we get to the Career Development question. The extent to which a firm downsizes will influence what career development the company considers. In the case of the laid off workers, depending on the company, there could be severance pay, outplacement assistance for job searching and retraining. In the case of the "survivors", those who were not laid off, there should be social support, reassurance, monitoring of the "reasonable" workload and monitoring of stress load with help if needed (Leana & Feldman, 1992). One must be careful that the quality of career guidance does not deteriorate. Overworked supervisors may have less time and energy for socializing, mentoring, and counseling employees- and, even if they do provide such guidance, may do so with less enthusiasm and supportiveness (Cameron & Zammuto, 1983).

How the company downsizes and any changes they make in their career development programs can make employees vulnerable to what is called career deterioration. Meaning they can't get another job, can't get as good a job, can't get the necessary training to stay current and will experience an attitude of desperation because of all that plus a feeling of hopelessness and lack of confidence. Although there is some question as to the validity of a nation's necessity to grow, most will agree that growth in an individual makes for a happier individual. This vulnerability comes in all shapes and sizes and effects people differently. At 22, you feel you can conquer the world so no big deal if you get laid off. At 45 with kids in college and a mortgage you may be a bit more apprehensive. At 55 or above there is no time for a mistake as retirement loams ahead. This observation does not pretend to address the subject that says you should have been more prepared with more savings at 55. These vulnerabilities may fall in an inequitable fashion also depending on race and gender. Women generally have a more difficult time obtaining satisfactory reemployment than their male counterparts and, once women are laid off, they are twice as likely to be unemployed for long periods of time (Bartell & Bartell, 1985), (Nowak & Snyder, 1983). Likewise, the average time spent before reemployment is significantly greater for minorities than for whites (Ullah, 1987). Women and minorities are more vulnerable to career deterioration in firms using tenure-based criteria, because their representation has only increased recently. Although with all the "quotas" and equal opportunity laws I fail to see the likelihood. I would rather be anything other than a middle aged white Anglo Saxon protestant male looking for work or anything else. But that's another story.

Skill levels (or lack thereof) such as formal education, cross-functional training, and organization-specific skills) may influence career deterioration as well. And so they should. Some would say that certain job titles and levels are affected more, and that may be true. The question is, "Who cares? There seems to be enough misery to go around. Blue collar workers because they can be easily replaced and are (by robots and computers), older workers because they are paid more, which is true. Whether they are worth more, the same or are becoming a drag has many supporters and detractors. Staff workers because they are not functionally necessary yet line workers because they can be replaced (see above blue collars). Even factors such as job tenure, mobility, having children and driving a Chevy may play a part. Don't need much of an excuse, do they? Finally, individual personality characteristics (e.g., self-esteem, hardiness, or tolerance for ambiguity) may buffer or exacerbate employee's reactions to negative career events (Shahani, Dipboye, & Phillips, 1990).

And yet, organizations then wonder why there are changes in employees' job attitudes, job performance, and role behaviors. Research suggests that individuals facing layoffs, underemployment, or fewer career development opportunities are more likely to experience poorer job attitudes. Another genius is born! Probably this career deterioration may be correlated with turnover and absenteeism as well (Markham & McKee, 1991). I just love it!

Additionally, job performance and decision making would be effected (Carroll G. R., 1984), (Hershey, 1972). There is a difference of opinion. One school of thought says that performance deteriorates among both workers laid off and survivors, while others say performance/productivity increases (Brockner J. , Grover, O'Malley, Reed, & M.A., 1993). At the risk of repeating myself (which others seem to have no problem doing) I will reiterate that "Gee, wouldn't it occur to you to do a little brown nosing in order to keep your job? Decision making does seem to fall into the one camp though, that says it becomes more standard, stoic and rigid- sort of by the book, and innovation goes by the wayside (Whetten, 1980). This despite the fact that innovation is probably exactly what is needed at the time. It does appear then that there is a strong link between downsizing and citizenship behaviors (Organ, 1988). What is not in much dispute is that increased conflict is a likely outcome of downsizing in those left behind (survivors). Consider; you have lost some of your friends, you are being asked to do their work as well as yours, and you don't know if/when you will get the ax. I'm thinking, protect my turf, lay the blame on someone else, find scapegoats and be a jerk to everyone (Cameron & Kim, 1987), (Cameron & Zammuto, 1983). Let's not forget to blame the unions, the government and regulatory agencies. Of course, this does no good, even if it has a grain of truth. We're not dealing much with truth here.

If the environment is relatively prosperous, stable or business friendly then management will usually believe that their business problems are operational rather than strategic in nature and acting accordingly, will more than likely implement a reduction slowly, on a small scale, and focused on just the specific units having business problems. If, on the contrary, environmental turbulence exists (Cameron & Kim, 1987), and real losses are occurring, not just less profits, then management will be their problems to be strategic in nature and act accordingly by either divestiture or dissolution or downsize on a large scale quickly. Interestingly, one would think that those firms that operate in multiple industries would have the staying power to "do the right thing" and slowly try to fix the problem. Not so. Apparently, because they have spread their risk more widely, they are more likely to quickly kill the ailing unit in the troubled industry. As expected, public sector organizations respond more slowly because; they are lazy and poorly managed, they have political ramifications if they don't care for their constituencies

This brings up one of the more serious evolutionary paths of business downsizing problems. Once top management loses credibility and is scapegoated for failure, a new executive team is usually brought in to deal with the problems (Cameron, Whetten, & Kim, 1987). Unfortunately, by this time, everyone is screaming for solutions which is always the easy way out-change and quickly. (Greenhalgh & Rosenblatt, 1984). It seems that all newly hired top management thinks everything is strategic, or at least that the solution to everything is to lay off people and divest units. And we're back to glorifying the likes of Jack Welch at General Electric, who gets all the credit for any turnaround merely because he fired 175,000 employees.

Seems like firms should be seeking to increase their cash flow without gutting the basic human resource capital of the business (Harrigan, 1980). Most will regret it later when they need that human capital to grow. That does not mean that firms with truly inept or incorrigible employees or really doomed and outdated business units or models shouldn't be eliminated. In this case they should "rip off the Band-Aid quickly" and drastically reduce the bad apple workforce.

There are several potential problems firms may encounter in conducting the downsizing exercise. Downsizing firms which are currently profitable may not wish to use severe strategies, because of the morale problems they may cause and because of the negative public relations backlash they could create. In contrast, firms facing absolute losses cannot afford to tackle their financial problems gingerly and incrementally. For these firms, layoffs, plant closings, and increased outsourcing are more likely to be imperative to stem the loss of cash.

Firms pursuing rapid, large-scale, firm-wide downsizings can more easily lay off employees and limit the inflow of new employees. That's because these two tactics are more easily and quickly implementable on an organization-wide basis by top management. In contrast, firms pursuing gradual, smaller-scale, selective downsizings are more likely to pursue outsourcing, redeploying current employees, and early retirement incentives as tactics to shrink the workforce. Redeployment is usually a piecemeal process which takes place over a long period of time and is generally not meant to achieve fast, massive relocation of employees.

As to how determination is made regarding those to be let go. Are organizations likely to use evaluations of individual competence and meritorious performance, job-based importance, or tenure-based criteria for shrinking the workforce?

Newer, smaller firms, firms operating in turbulent environments, and firms downsizing for strategic purposes are more likely to use performance-based criteria or job-based criteria as grounds for layoffs. That's because the whole notion of strategically-driven downsizings is selectivity; we are doing this in order to make changes in dramatic ways. By firing you we can make more money. Because of this mandate, these firms will seek to get rid of the deficient and those whose jobs are no longer essential (Feldman & Turnley, 1995).

Large established firms are more likely to use tenure based criteria (seniority), not only because they have the staying power but because they are bureaucratized and governed by lots of rules, while newer smaller firms operating in a turbulent environment who don't have the staying power will likely act quickly to chop workforce and base it on performance. This plays right into any changes in the organization's career development activities. Firms pursuing a turnaround strategy will be more likely to sustain long-term career development programs than firms pursuing harvest, divest, or dissolution strategies. They are in it for the long haul and are thinking long term. These firms will want to keep their human resources well trained and committed to their employers, knowing that the employees will be needed later. The firms pursuing a harvest strategy and thinking short term will want to eliminate most non-essential costs to generate more short-term cash, and of course the firms intending to divest or dissolve troubled units won't have any need for or incentive to invest in, long-term career development activities. As mentioned above, stagnating firms are likely to be larger, more established, and to have more slack resources at the time downsizing begins. As a result, these downsizing firms are more likely to have both the human resource management staff to provide such assistance and the financial resources to provide severance pay, extended benefits, and outplacement for laid-off workers (Cook & Ferris, 1986), (Leana & Feldman, 1992). A point worth mentioning; the gradual nature of the downsizing in this case helps to offset the work loan invariably associated with the survivors.

Those declining firms who are rapidly and large scale downsizing are much less likely to address the long-term career development programs because anything thought to be non-essential is likely to be cut and unfortunately career development is high on that list (Ferris, Schellenberg, & Zammuto, 1984).

It goes without saying (but I will anyway) that downsizing has a negative effect on career development because; you are at risk of being laid off (bummer), you are less likely to be promoted, and the job prospects in the industry as a whole will be bleak. Less obvious is that what might appear to be the better method to downsize will still hurt some vulnerable groups more than others. For example, downsizings achieved through less hiring and therefore attrition will have the greatest negative impact on young workers since they are the new entrants in the job market. These job seekers (new college graduates) then are forced to take a job which does not require as much education as they possess (Morrow, 1993), (Tilly, 1991). Underemployment is becoming worse and worse (Newman K. S., 1988). This is exacerbated by the fact that older workers, with better skills, better education and usually better customer service skills, who have been let go are taking up some of these jobs. I see a lot of gray hair and wrinkles serving at McDonalds. The dilemma hold true for the less educated and less trained. (Harrison & Bluestone, 1988); (Winefield, Winefield, & Tiggemann, 1991). Worth mentioning here is the fact that these very workers- young or less educated- are the easiest to replace also. But, middle management is expensive so therein lies a great deal of temptation.

When layoffs are done through redeployment it will harm a different set of workers. This is where the negative effect is felt by staff positions (lawyers, accountants, engineers, receptionists) rather than line employees and middle management, middle-aged workers, and employees with little or no cross-training. In other words, those who do seem to contribute to the bottom line (Baumohl, 1993). Even if these workers don't get laid off, they are often forced to take new positions either of a lesser stature, or that they don't like or for which they are unqualified. Redeployed workers are likely to experience more job dissatisfaction, both because their psychological contracts with their employers have been violated (Rousseau D. M., 1990), and because these workers are often redeployed to jobs which are poor fits for their abilities and interests. Because they are new to their jobs and may not be as well trained for them, their job performance may decrease as well. Lastly, redeployed workers may be more likely to quit because they think they see the handwriting on the wall and they are next! Many times the older worker gets the most set in the position, and it's even worse if the new position requires a physical move to a different community (Folkman & Lazarus, 1980), (Dunn, 1979). On a slightly less sympathetic note for the worker, they often are not willing or able to retrain, either because they don't want to, can't or think it will not do any good (Loomba, 1987).

According to the natural business pyramid, a substantial segment of the labor force is engaged in clerical or low-skill service jobs at the bottom of the pecking order, therefore a firm using outsourcing to downsize can easily outsource and get the same or even better results. The only risk is finding and training these outside workers in the organization specific skills, (Greenhalgh & Rosenblatt, 1984). If the worker does the job poorly from 10,000 miles away, what recourse do you have? (Davis-Blake & Uzzi, 1993).Sometimes there is a question of privacy or security involved. Look no further than the cultural differences between China and the United States regarding piracy of music properties. Notice I said cultural differences. We must all be careful to not judge others by our standards, by standards from the past or judge past actions by current standards.

It has probably always been true that higher mobility, especially of an international bent today, along with language skills and cross training would serve well in any work environment. I'm not sure there is any measurable difference in a downsizing firm versus one that is not, other than that it may be the difference between working and not working in the former. Suffice it to say, although it appears not to be the case with CEO's, at the normal level it wouldn't hurt to be a decent person with good communication skills (Loomba, 1987). Bear in mind, "in for a penny, in for a pound." Meaning, if you are unfortunate enough to possess one of the undesirable traits, management (and society in general) are pre disposed to believe you have other issues. Yes, we are nasty human beings.

Ah, the sword of Damocles hangs again in the halls of the less fortunate. Why is it that those who need the most get abused the most? Or so it seems. Financial well-being, just as in the organization, is a paramount problem for workers. Once a family unit is formed, expenses occur frequently and constantly. These financial burdens do not go away if you are laid off (Newman K. S., 1988). You are darned if you do and darned if you don't. It's like having to pay child care in order to go to work. In this case, you need a job to get money to pay the bills but you can't get a job because you don't have the money to get the training to get the job. Whew!

Need I say that severance pay and extended benefits are hyper critical for this group? A similar situation exists for the less educated who are unlikely to have accumulated any reserves but have the least possibility of obtaining decent work. They are also most likely to have low self-esteem (Brockner J. , Grover, O'Malley, Reed, & M.A., 1993), most likely to feel guilty about the layoffs, (Kobasa, 1979) and less able to absorb the negative disruptions and tolerance for adversity, flexibility and ambiguity (Cohn, 1978), in which they have trouble coping with new and uncertain environments. Being inflexible can be a terrible cross to bear and sometimes makes you your own worst enemy. This group definitely needs outplacement assistance and training (Leana & Ivancevich, 1987). Everybody needs training!

Due to career plateauing, which can occur at any time but usually does in middle age, decreases in the availability of formal career development programs will be most detrimental to mid-career employees (Alderfer & Guzzo, 1979). Of course this lack of formal career development will also be especially detrimental to employees who have relatively low levels of formal education and cross training to begin with.

It's the informal mentoring that is especially important to workers who are relatively young and new to the firm, (Kram, 1985). This mentoring is critical to making a worker feel at home and a part of the team. It can make the difference between learning their jobs, adjusting to new work groups, and learning the ropes or simply not. Females and minorities seem to have more difficulty in finding appropriate mentors anyway (Missirian, 1982).

By not replacing workers who leave or by

implementing a hiring freeze, firms increase the amount of stress due to work overload experienced by workers (Brief, Schuler, & Van Sell, 1981).Workers left behind may also be unsure as to who should be performing the duties previously done by others. Intergroup conflict may increase as members of other groups in the organization express anger or frustration with what they perceive as decreased quality of work or service from downsizing units (Greenhalgh & Rosenblatt, 1984). All of this while feeling greater job insecurity.

Downsizings achieved through layoffs and plant closings are associated with poorer job attitudes, decreases in the quality of decision making, increased conflict with external constituencies, and decreases in absenteeism and turnover among those who lose their jobs and those who remain (Warr, Jackson, & Banks, 1988). The decrease is due to a number of factors, from job insecurity to trying to look good to the employer in order not to be the next to go (Markham & McKee, 1991). Also, if there is a downsizing mentality in the entire community, jobs may be scarce so workers think twice about taking the risk of leaving (Ehrenberg & Jakubson, 1989). For every study that affirms this there is one that confirms the opposite viewpoint; that absenteeism and turnover go up. The threat and stress faced by employees in downsizing firms frequently results in rigid decision-making and loss of innovation and creativity (Staw, L. E. Sandelands, & Dutton, 1981). Ironically, this decreased quality of decision-making often occurs just as management needs to innovate and come up with new solutions to the major business problems they are facing (Lorange & Nelson, 1987). In addition, conflict arises with unions and regulatory agencies when layoffs occur. In an attempt to compensate for the lost employment, these entities often seek to construct exit barriers to protect current employment levels or to extract considerable assets from downsizing firms (Carroll A. B., 1985); (Harrison & Bluestone, 1988), (Sethi, 1975).

A lot depends on what kind of individual and worker I was to begin with! Couple of things are clear, however. Take away my job and I am unhappy. Don't offer me career development services and I will be unhappy. Be unfair about the process and I will be unhappy. If I feel cheated, it will affect my job performance and my attitude. If transferred somewhere else, it probably will not make me happy and I will be in conflict with the new surroundings, as they will be with me. There is, or should be a psychological contract between the worker and the employer. If you do any of the bad things above you violated it and that's not fair! If layoffs occur, some recompense should be provided (Kinicki, Bracker, Kreitner, Lockwood, & Lemak, 1987). Oh yeah, and if I feel there is inequity here I am going to sue you! I will get some help in my quest from external do good organizations and the government (Langley, 1984). Even if my performance can't be determined and may vary depending on how I react, you can bet that there will be trouble if I perceive that you didn't act in good faith and as a good corporate citizen.

The more positive way to look at this debacle would be to turn the situation around. Keeping the long -term formal career development programs and informal career guidance assistance during downsizing will bring positive benefits. If the worker perceives that the employer is making positive investments in their workers, then that will create a positive attitudes in the workers (London, 1988). It will increase worker commitment and loyalty which in turn will result in less turnover, less bad attitude, less trouble and less friction.

Notwithstanding the horror stories of workers laid off 6 months prior to retirement (where do they get these stories-from reality, of course.), most of the carnage is placed at the steps of the middle aged worker and consequently they have the propensity for the worst attitude and worst job performance.. He/she is not young enough to be easily retrained, geographically relocated or led around by the nose yet not old enough to afford early retirement or cut back their expenses significantly such as mortgages and children in college (Leana & Feldman, 1992).

Next in line for abuse would be those with less formal education and those with staff rather than line jobs. Regarding the less educated, they are susceptible to outsourcing, ease of replacement with either an equivalent worker later or a robot now. The staff worker finds himself/herself looking down the wrong end of the barrel on the specialist vs. generalist debate and the non-productive label. Here comes poorer job attitudes and job performance.

Add in those with little cross-training, inter firm mobility, and geographical mobility. All of which will have greater anxiety about the prospects of layoffs. This because they see their chances of successfully launching a job search and finding a decent new job to be slim to none. Toss in those with low self-esteem who are more likely to blame themselves for their predicament, to be confused about their present circumstances, and to have more difficulty adjusting to, and coping with, job insecurity and you have a fine mess. But oh those executive bonuses were necessary, right?

Still not convinced? The trend is becoming evident. There are two kinds of downsizing. The first because you are in trouble and need to save your neck. One can understand this, even if you have issues with it. Many ways have been recommended, some of which actually have merit. Plus, we sometimes have to do things we don't like. Or put another way, "good people do bad things." The second reason isn't so magnanimous. This is a pure play to increase profits for the sake, usually, of earning bonuses and high reward for the select few. But even in the latter case, those greedy managers could have us for lunch with just a little give and take. Why is it that "absolute power corrupts, absolutely", and there never seems to be enough money for most people? Using a number of the many techniques mentioned the executives could have their cake and eat it too. There is more than enough frame work here on how to do the deed in a responsible manner and still get rich and keep your company afloat. In this section we found that many environmental and organizational issues can be addressed responsibly for all participants concerned, even though some are effected more than others. With all this information (a veritable textbook of how to), what reason, other than sheer greed, would there be to not get this right? What's left? Is there real trouble or not- is it for the sake of survival or the sake of a bonus? Leaving behind my ranting and name calling; turbulence requires strategic head chopping on a large scale and quickly while in a more easy going atmosphere/environment (where the firm is down but not out), a slow less abrupt and severe exercise. In either case, do it right, with integrity and don't spare the horses (assistance) and you will have less trouble. More research is needed as to the appropriate pyramid for control. How many people would be reporting to whom (Ford, 1980). Perhaps a good combination of seniority coupled with merit would be in order. I personally suggest that individual cases might not provide the same comprehensive look see as a Meta-analysis. There is always the attitude that several different approaches would be beneficial. Whetten (1980) agrees that there can be problems with research based on one organization in one industry. There is a risk that the organization that invites you in or allows you to study them may not be representative of failures in general. Organizations don't like to document their "failures." Consequently by deduction, most of the research is done in happy surroundings (Harrigan, 1980). Again, not always possible to get a good sample group so you do what you can but it does seem logical that more is better-- in this case.

Job Declines

Life in the employment world has been so bad for so long, it's difficult to determine when it was at its worst. However, 2008 can certainly rank right up there. Eight years later it might seem like a broken record, but like the Holocaust, it never hurts to serve as a reminder. Both job openings and hires declined during 2008. Fewer job openings mean fewer opportunities for job-seekers to find employment. In that year the drop was dramatic, meaning if compared to the unemployment rate (which isn't an exact analogy, I know), the numbers would be the same, around a 25% drop. My point being that, if 25% unemployment was a catastrophe in 1930, then a 25% anything rate is also a catastrophe in 2008. These numbers also dropped in 2007 (Zhi Boon, 2007). Needless to say the layoff and discharge rates has similar results as did increasing unemployment and employment levels.

For reference, In December 2008, the National Bureau of Economic Research announced that the current recession had begun in December 2007 (National Bureau of Economic Research, 2008). In one year (from Dec 2007 to Dec 2008, the unemployment rate went from 4.9% to 7.2%. It ended up at about 10% a little later, then went back down to a little under 5% in 2016. That's an eight year drought from a job for someone! The net employment loss was 3 million over the same period (U.S. Department of Labor. Bureau of Labor Statistics, 2009)

Although discussing the 2008 period, the actual declines and recessionary trends started almost two years earlier in 2006. This includes unemployment claims.

Tabulation and things like hedonics (discussed elsewhere) should always be considered when viewing statistics due to changes in how to measure over time (as well as "Liars figure and figures lie").

In order to have an economic expansion you would need a rising number of job openings and falling unemployment. Even that definition doesn't seem to hold true in the supposed expansion of 2008-2016. If the separations exceed the hires we are in an economic contraction.

Here we are again discussing 2008 but as mentioned above, (and even worse), not only did separations exceed hires during all of 2008 but did so in 49 of the previous 53 months. That's going back all the way to 2003! (Stafford, 2008). Does anyone see a long term pattern here?

Separations include terminations from quits, layoffs and discharges (fired). Further research might separate out these three. There are also other reasons which are somehow excluded from the separation rate due to legitimacy such as retirement, transfer to other locations of the same firm, death, and disability. Other separation factors do affect the numbers. For example, we would find a decline in the separation numbers because people might put off retirement during a recession. The question however, is, "what good is that information?" The separation rate is determined by dividing the total separations by the average employment level times 100. So, low is good. Some research has determined that even if the separations increase, which is bad, there is a component issue in which the people quitting has decreased while those in the other two categories (fired and laid-off) have increased (Stafford, 2008). That makes sense. Why quit your job in hard times unless you have another one? Other auxiliary reason would be a housing market collapse and higher gas prices (Zieminski, 2008). Supposedly, here's how it works. When times are tough, people don't travel, the market drops taking away equity and people lose their jobs, thereby not spending a lot of money. As the economy gets better, all of those things turn around and gas producers see an excuse to raise prices. Upon raising prices, a key component of effects on the economy as mentioned above, the economy slows down again. Isn't that where we came in? Am I the only one that sees a never ending cycle here that we can never eliminate?

These studies found that the unemployed compared to the job openings was as high as 4 to 1 in some cases (U.S. Department of Labor. Bureau of Labor Statistics, 2009). A subset of this information again, for further research, is that job openings are not the same as hires. Many jobs go unfilled because of a mismatch of needs versus skills.

As in other research studied, all of these numbers depend on the industry. Although most of these figures were consistent across industries, as stated before, certain industries such as construction always seem to be more volatile during changing economic environments. Travel and entertainment would be another area more affected.

There is always an exception to the rule. In this case, there were industries that did quite well during the down turn. Meaning job openings exceeded hires. Lately, that has been the case in health care and information. Periodically finance has cropped up here also, but not always.

School is still out on education- no pun intended. Outrageously expensive yet we keep hearing how tough teachers have it and how poor the system is.

It's simple really, thanks to the government providing loans, the educators raise their prices since they know the government is footing the bill. Then the money goes to administrators, not faculty. In fact, faculty is now made up of adjuncts who don't get benefits and are paid little or nothing.

Buried in the research statistics is the amusing fact that Federal employment quits dropped to 0.1% of total employment in 2008. Seriously? If you were overpaid above and beyond the average private sector by 60% plus had 30 days of vacation, 30 days sick leave, personal business days and great benefits and pension, would you quit your job?

CHAPTER 5 SUMMARY

Much information has been supplied on how the process of downsizing has effected different parties. By now you should be feeling like there is a lot of Mickey Mouse going on here. Ultimately, one is supposed to narrow the focus so I suppose I must choose one of the parties for the final analysis. I chose Those Let Go. After all, there is little suffering in the management ranks, they're getting rich. As to those left behind? Sure, there is unhappiness, but your children can eat, so even though you are being abused and put upon and I sympathize, get over it.

It would appear that downsizing isn't any different than anything else. Lots of people are wrong and lots more are selfish, greedy and unfair. Human nature being what it is, I suspect it will take more than a few good men to correct it in the near future. The rich get richer, the mean go to the top, nice guys finish last and we would rather pay peddlers (salespeople) than Nuclear Physicists, Rocket Scientists and the better educated.

All that talk of stress and the psychological effect is making me hungry. If it seems a bit heavy handed and overdone in the context of downsizing that's because I feel that we need to address our human frailties. Time and time again throughout history we have complained about the same thing- a few doing nasty things to the masses in order to gain an extra few cents. Unless we address the human factor it is likely to keep rearing its ugly head. I didn't used to believe in "all that crap", but I stand corrected. I'm convinced it is not just the economic structure we need to fix, but our basic instincts. Maybe it is time to fool Mother Nature.

Conclusions

Human nature is at the bottom of all this. One can imagine that Mother Nature (or somebody's God) set this up to propagate the human race and strengthen the species. Actually make a lot of sense. Unfortunately, it also doesn't seem very fair. Especially when it seems hard to breed in beauty and brains in the same body. As mentioned before, entitlements is a bad word. However, there must be some word that describes a fairness method for how to care for those less fortunate. If not, I guess it will be business as usual but kind of sad, because it's not very humane. I suppose it depends on how important it is for us to be humane.

To be fair, we are not so bad. Europe is expensive, they are snooty, and even more socialistic (both good and bad). However, their colleges, corporations and government seem to work better together than we do.

The Austrian School was discussed because it addresses free market economics versus a more controlled environment- rules to live by for the corporate world. It addresses Deductive reasoning as a tool, speaks out against lab studies as a vehicle and for Meta-Analysis. It speaks to suggestions to actually solve this downsizing issue from a macro level and even illustrated the fact that there is always a different opinion on any subject. Increasing the minimum wage is not a cure all; but it would be a start. In the alternative, maybe we should address the income gap in another way instead. Older workers have much to offer but in a society that worships movie stars and youth it can be very difficult. Age discrimination is a huge issue in most every walk of life.

There is no question that we need to remain competitive, and that new roles will appear and be necessary. I have also addressed the danger of the various ploys being thrust upon unsuspecting employees, the necessity for reallocation, how to be a survivor and how to treat survivors, who gets designated redundant and the potential legacy of the act (of downsizing), communication and when explanations are not enough, unemployment and relative deprivation, why the duration is so long, hedonics and its silliness, eugenics and its flaws, inequality and redistribution.

Downsizing fails to consider the future resources needed (Hickok T. , 1995).
These findings also suggest that reductions in workforce resulted in a decrease in workplace performance.

We have studied the effects (Impact) on the company, those left behind and those let go. We have looked at short term and long term consequences, work overload, job insecurity, levels of commitment, loyalty, the effects of outsourcing, how to best handle the process e.g. retraining, redeployment, hiring freezes, allowing attrition to reduce personnel, early retirement, discrimination and who suffers, e.g. the aged, the new hires, the low skilled, organizational career development and more.

Justice and trust building have a strong influence on a workers organizational commitment and satisfaction. Surveys and their form of distribution may have less value due to follow-up problems and confidentiality. Also, generalization of information from case analysis might be a problem.

We have seen strong empirical evidence that the innovative capability of an organization is likely to be harmed by the adoption of downsizing.

Sometimes the corporations become the biggest losers because brainpower and experience is lost with downsizing of older workers (a loss of expertise) and a quick fix is usually the initial motivation and later the problem. We are still lemmings (followers). In America "Greed is still good."

Everyone needs a little help from time to time. When you have lost your job the need is especially acute. Any Safety net that can be provided would be helpful, whether it be formal education, retraining, shelters, emergency services, welfare, food assistance, housing etc. Naturally, all of the various programs, if they were available, need thorough cleansing

The financial bottom line is not the only benchmark of a successful firm. There are social costs. Corporations have or should have, a responsibility to the community and all stakeholders. Many outside forces are effected as well. Tax revenues, housing price decreases, divorces, uprooting of relationships (friends, elderly parents, school mates). Health issues, anger, anxiety, depression, sleeplessness, emotional stress, financial stress, feelings of worthlessness.

Survivors have difficulties as well. Their reaction counts. Perhaps not as distressing as those let go (and it certainly depends on the personalities involved), but critical nonetheless. In spite of a select few who somehow come out of the debacle stronger and also a few that seem to recover over a longer period of time, most workers left behind deal with a negative environment. Whether it be stress, overwork, mistrust, fear of being next or whatever, life could be a lot better. For the employer the above scenario may lead to destructive behavior and a less productive output.

The legal profession is a fickle mistress, sometimes turning on its owner like a rabid dog. Nothing's fair in life. But you had better be careful anyway, management, even though you appear to have all the cards. If the plaintiff can somehow struggle into court he/she has a good chance of beating you. And that is costly, in terms of money, time wasted, reputation and the risk that it will set a precedent for future suits and losses. Preparation begins long before the downsizing act. You would think corrupt upper management would know this.

What does productivity really mean? Is there a good and bad productivity? Perhaps not, but definitely there is a good and better. The old saying goes something like, "most of us are too busy working to really earn money." That's close enough. Creativity, along with its little pal innovation, is what makes a good company great. That excludes those that have a monopoly and/or an inelastic product, of course. The entire concept of downsizing would seem to be a complete anathema to a creative, therefore successful company. Getting rid of people does not breed creativity. It breeds mistrust and discomfort. Workers left behind in a downsizing atmosphere will in all likelihood gravitate toward simple achievable tasks so as to look good and not be the next on the chopping block. So, you go for the "lean and mean"; personally I'd rather be "big and bad".

How much effect does the inexpensive manufacturing in China have on United States workers and where are we in the cycle? It would just show our ignorance to believe that there is or has been no effect. Notwithstanding technological changes, those millions of manufacturing job went somewhere. So, they have destroyed our way of life for a generation; with the help of corporate America, of course. But, wait! That's all about to change. Our great technological expertise will soon allow us to do things cheaper and compete with them. Heard that broken record before. Manufacturing is coming home! My guess is, like the peace dividend after 1989 and the supposed technology benefit of more free time, it's just a lot of talk. Been there, done that and heard it all before. There will always be another nemesis (or excuse for one). Someone or something to give the powerful an excuse to abuse. Nothing has changed in the last 2000 years. Already, the Vietnamese and others are stepping in to undercut prices in China. Maybe we should join forces with China. No I won't, no I won't, no I won't-- oops! I had to.

There is no way to lay off personnel without morale suffering. If one's morale is lower, it is hard to imagine that you can be at your best with customers, or anyone else for that matter. This in addition to the fact that there are less people to care for customers. Upper management still doesn't get the fact that customers buying your product or service are what creates profit. No decent customer service- no customers. No customers-no buying of product. No buying of product-no earnings. And no earnings- no profit and no company. Employees are assets, not costs. Loyalty is meaningful. A major management philosophical turnaround would be to begin rewarding everyone (workers and management), through performance-based pay, for taking care of customers.

Some effort has been made to ease any transition by means of special envoys. These are the people tasked with doing the firing. The question remains, is the role beneficial and if so, how do you carry it out? Or have we just created another stress related group of individuals.

Mass layoffs are now practiced at random, affecting locations and groups in different manners and degrees. There has to be a better mousetrap.

CEO pay is out of control. From 20 times forty years ago to 400 times the average pay would make Andrew Carnegie role over in his grave.

In a recessionary environment job openings and hires decline anyway, exacerbated by the urge or need to downsize and layoffs and discharges increased while quits decreased. This has all the earmarks of a self-fulfilling prophecy and very self-evident. Nevertheless, we should at least be aware of the situation.

Is there a "Progressive" way to handle outsourcing? If you must outsource your insignificant tasks, why not do so to less fortunate workers in West Virginia or Des Moines, Iowa rather than go overseas and help other economies? My guess is that there are workers in this country who would be delighted to have a job at any pay, in spite of any thought that we are too lazy and spoiled. Notice I said the insignificant tasks. There is still good reason to keep a decent manufacturing base, even if only in case of another conventional war. If the profits were passed along to employees rather than end up in the pockets of a few executives then the system might be alright.

Outsourcing was addressed heavily because it is really a sister culprit to downsizing. Or more appropriately, a precursor to it. If you hadn't shipped all those jobs overseas, you wouldn't have to downsize dummy!

Government money should or would be better spent on retraining those who lost their jobs. Teach people correctly to do the radiology and engineering, and pay them more to do the gardening.

Many different situations are effecting downsizing. How about the fact that we never seem to have enough money for education, retraining, or providing a cushion for our people. Yes, we have some welfare, it's not enough, it's not as good as others and it's busted because the human beings on the other side (lazy, civil servants and even lazier, welfare cheats who should be working.) Maybe if we would keep out nose out of other peoples (nations) business we might have a little bit more to go around. Do I have to repeat that we spend 10 times as much in defense as anyone else? And we're not even that good at it. You know, I can understand the mighty British Army being defeated by a rag tag 19th century band of no bodies- there were millions of them. But we, the most powerful nation ever, get slapped around by a mere dozen men. When was the last time we had a resounding victory? Sure wasn't Korea, Vietnam, Afghanistan or Iraq.

Walmart, the company everybody loves to hate, but still shops there. Sure, we are our own worst enemy. But like the banks in the sub-prime debacle, you should know better and be held to a higher standard. I keep hearing how much you're worth and how smart you are; so how come I'm left holding the bag and it's my fault! This company is either a prime example of American business at its best or our worst nightmare due to their buying overseas, poor work ethic, low pay or long unpaid hours. Probably qualifies as both.

Is Walmart really a bad guy, or just a well-run organization that is getting prices down for all of us? First of all, you would have to concede that there is a way to treat customers well, employees well, and your shareholders (financial profit) well. Evidence exists that it can be done. As it stands Walmart treats their employees poorly in terms of wages and benefits. Time and time again I serve up the theory that most people would pay a little more to insure a decent job market.

Although many studies show that there isn't any long term financial gain (Return on Investment), or, the financial gain is debatable; assume for a moment that there is financial gain. Certainly one of the main necessities of a company is to make money. You won't be around to help anyone, yourself or your employees if you go broke. But how much is enough? Also, who are or should be the stakeholders? Do most employers think of employees as a cost or an asset? Now we must compare the carnage created for the sake of financial gain for a limited few at the top and determine if it's worth it. Finally we can try to minimize that destruction. The destruction consists of stress for those let go because they may encounter financial difficulties, lose a home, or have family problems; and those left behind who mistrust their employers now (seeing what happened to their friends), increasingly litigate against the corporation, take more sick days, have lower productivity, have higher turnover, create destruction (by disgruntled left behind employees and to a certain extent, those let go before they leave); all of which leads to lower stock prices and lower profitability. Several ways to counter that would be: high quality outplacement (counseling before, during and after, training, resume writing, coaching), ample severance packages, and communication before, during and after the process.

People want good health, good wages, job security, retirement pension plan, pleasant working conditions. I realize there are really no entitlements, but in a civilized world, isn't that what we should at least be striving for?

Is it a good or bad thing to preemptively downsize? This also appears to depend on your point of view. One burning question is; is downsizing being done to stay alive economically or strictly for extra profit? Why should you destroy lives if you are healthy and profitable just because you want more? As to whether or not there is a long term payoff to downsizing, studies cast serious doubt as to a positive answer to that question. Empirical evidence is still scant and mixed (Chalos & Chen, 2002), but that which does exist indicates that long term financial gain is not forthcoming. It is a critical and much used yet understudied phenomenon. Why does it continue to be viewed as a viable option? Firms downsize for short term gain at the expense of long term productivity. Is the quick fix worth potential long term negative consequences? Do we wish to live in a world that adheres to a philosophy of "the end justifies the mean"? Do we want to be a nation of temporary workers and do we realize the social cost? Should we ask ourselves, "Is an 80 hour week what we want"? Again, the top elite will answer yes to all of these questions, and therefore, the power gap continues to widen causing more downsizing. Would downsized companies have turned themselves around anyway and even quicker if they had not? If left unchecked, are we becoming a nation of depressed, mean, mad people whose health suffers because of it? We are like rats in a spinning wheel-running faster and faster just to stay in place. Even if you do hire back the people you fired as contract labor, you lose control and loyalty. Is the elimination of the benefits costs and ability to dump the contract workers at a moment's notice worth it? The question is; at what price do you hire them back? Care must be taken not to mimic the government that hires contract labor at far more than the cost they saved. Having certain functions outsourced may also have consequences on a national scale in case of a war. We will no longer have the plants and factories to provide the equipment that served us so well in past unfortunate crises.

A majority has come to agree that, in an increasingly competitive globalized world, downsizing is an unavoidable reality. Your next question should be, is the majority always right?

How can there be challenges along with commensurate pay increases and promotion in firms with fewer hierarchical levels and fewer promotional opportunities? With the exception of mergers and acquisitions (Ference, Stoner, & Warren, 1977), (Hirsch, 1987) Most of the policy and how-to manuals have been written assuming organizational growth and therefore individual development and growth as well. Unfortunately, those assumptions are obsolete. The point of all this whining is that, even if we were to concede that the laid off worker's plight has been addressed, much less attention has been given to career development for everyone in slow or no growth situations. (Cameron, Freeman, & Mishra, 1991), (Feldman & Leana, 1994)

Solutions

Writers commit errors. Many have a tendency to be long winded, academically highbrow and hard to understand. And many are also very repetitious throughout their papers. Some academic writers write on issues that seem to be nonsense and of little importance. Do the mating habits of a spotted owl really rank up there with losing your livelihood? So, what makes this writer any different? Maybe not much. However, seeing the problem through the eyes of a B plus person will make it easier to understand. Especially an older, and hopefully more mature one. Not to say there are not a lot of brilliant young people. Smart people can be common sense challenged and a little aloof and nasty as well. Because I didn't spend all of my career in academics and am more down to earth, I might have a broader perspective. Again, maybe more common sense.

My idea of focus also may be different. I have made an effort to start with a broad picture, because I feel it is important to see that overall picture. By first taking a look at the perspective of everyone involved, I have then, after analyzing all the players, attempted to focus on the critical ones. That would be the workers who no longer have the security of a job. Along the way I have digressed with topics that bear mentioning-again, for that broad perspective. I don't want to assume the reader knows about that topic and I inadvertently leave them behind. (Sill, 2016)

Figure out a way to care for the less fortunate at a level necessary to fill their basic needs and protect the unemployed temporarily without creating a nation of lazy welfare cheats.

Downsizing isn't likely to go away. It goes far beyond whether a corporation needs an extra few dollars for bonuses. Until we address basic human nature and figure out what we want and how to either get it or at least control it, we will continue to have problems.

Knowing that to be true, here is a summary of a few ideas to make the technique as painless as possible: Make it a last resort, communicate, no overtime, forced vacations, get employees involved, grant stock options, give bonuses, find employees jobs through farming them out, transferring them or simply getting them another job, shorten hours or cut pay, and encourage employees to innovate.

As a means of actual and perceived fairness, CEO pay should be caped. (Sill, 2016)

Stop outsourcing-especially overseas.

Why not perhaps think in terms of local economies again instead of globally?

Provide career transition assistance like career counseling, personal counseling, career/skill and career transition training, relocation assistance, outplacement assistance, resume writing assistance, access to office equipment, paid time off, child care, financial counseling, and access to job fairs and to Internet job placement sites. And provide these services for 3 years, at least. Have the severance (3years), shared between government, and corporation with individual requirements to study or seek work. Health care should be a given by government anyway but if not, then the corporation must provide it. Always offer a reduced salary first to those being considered for downsizing. All training is to be paid by the employer. Alternative work programs-job sharing, part time, flex schedules. Be kind but honest, sympathetic and understanding. Make sure cost to Downsize is not as much as cost to continue.

Real quick! Lower taxes, raise interest rates, break up big banks, reduced regulation, clean up Dodd-Frank, reinstate Glass-Steagall, ban most derivatives transactions, improve education, invest smartly in infrastructure, and reduced entitlements. (Sill, 2016)

At the educational level, let's concentrate on Technical high schools, especially if we keep whining that many people can't make the leap to any new technology. I wonder if things were really so bad "keeping it simple"? Likewise, more "Career Days". Let's make the available choices known for our young people. We must never stop attempting to educate and train human nature to be socially responsible.

Here's just one example: A solution to closing military bases. It was a dead expense anyway, so they should keep paying people while they are retrained or educated. This effort should be used whenever a transition occurs. In fact the expense should still go down during this time period because there will be no expense for the maintenance of the base, utilities for parts of it etc.

Following are a few reasons why you might not want to downsize:

It's morally wrong, especially when CEOs are getting bonuses and the gap in wages is so large.

There will be poor morale in those left behind which will sabotage your organization, even among the young as they see how you treat older loyal workers.

You will lose the experience found in those senior workers let go.

You will not have mentors available for your new employees.

Your customer service will deteriorate due to the poor attitude mentioned above.

All of the above will result in hidden costs you did not foresee so that even the very profit motive you initiated this for will not materialize.

In observing the effects of downsizing on those employees let go, data has been gathered and analyzed concerning the unemployment rate since it is a direct result of the downsizing process. Further research needs to be performed regarding the validity of this statistical data and whether it is accurate and takes into consideration all of the important aspects. It would appear that it does not, since there is no inclusion of underemployment statistics. It also may be lacking in validity because it does not fully account for those who have exhausted their unemployment benefits and have dropped from the radar. The benefits obtained from unemployment insurance may need to be extended.

It's almost impossible to create new products, improve existing ones and come up with new ideas when you are laying off people?

Some people postulate that manufacturing is coming back. Even if a renaissance is underway for manufacturing in America, it isn't your Grandfather's manufacturing. Today the robots do a lot of the work that employees used to do.

How about Socialism with incentive? Carrots for kindness, pay for kindness. There is a lack of incentive if paid anyway.

How do you correct the system e.g., better pay for workers and less for executives when you have to go through the executives? How are you going to change the budget and other political problems when your representatives will not vote as you dictate? When you vote them out for not doing it the next one in will just do the same.

Exporting only helps a small percentage of business here in the United States that are in that line of work. Maybe things are a little cheaper, but those who lost their jobs or are under employed can't buy anything.

Some studies contend that when people get downsized, they reinvent themselves into high tech. What a load of crap! The ratio of those who reinvented themselves must be miniscule. Not only that but now high tech is being transferred overseas.

There are tremendous skills required for some of the $30,000 jobs available. Winston Churchill once said, "Never in the field of human conflict was so much owed by so many to so few." He might also have inferred, "are there really so many people with so much skill willing to work for so little?"

No 50 year old man/woman with or without an education should be out of work.

Competitiveness is overrated. Not sure it is doing any good. It's only good if we believe we are here to work and not to simply enjoy life.

Draw your own conclusions.

GLOSSARY

<u>Downsizing</u>- loss of intellectual capital by reduction in personnel OR to make an organizational entity more competitive compared to its rivals (by reduction in personnel and to achieve bottom-line objectives. Downsizing is used today as a management tool in the United States (and elsewhere), to cut costs in the hope of creating a more efficient, productive and competitive firm. It has evolved from being used simply by those in danger of going out of business to those merely trying to squeeze an extra penny of profits.

<u>Deductive reasoning</u> from something known, general laws and principles of truths/statements to a specific conclusion. From the Meta-Analysis of others?

<u>Inductive reasoning</u> from evaluating specific actual experiences/ observations/propositions to making a new general principle/hypothesis. From facts and evidence.

<u>Declarative knowledge</u>- what I know

<u>Procedural knowledge</u>- how to apply it

<u>Descriptive</u> is quantitative

<u>Inferential</u> is qualitative

<u>Discursive</u>- proceeding by reason or logic

<u>Dialectic-</u> logic in investigating the truth of a theory or argument

<u>Didactic</u>- lecturing and textbooks vs. lab work and demonstration

<u>Epistemology</u>- knowledge or, the theory or science of the origin, nature and limits of knowledge

<u>Inductive reasoning</u> from evaluating specific actual experiences/ observations/ propositions to making a

new general principle/hypothesis. From facts and evidence.

Deductive reasoning from something known, general laws and principles of truths/statements to a specific conclusion.

Intuitive-comes naturally

Empirical-pragmatic. Based upon observation or experience or experiment,   not based on science or proven theory. Based on the experiments of others.

Theory is a general prediction of events or explains general principles. A theory comes from repeated observation and testing and incorporates facts, laws, predictions, and tested hypotheses that are widely accepted. Stronger than Hypotheses

Hypothesis is a specific, testable prediction about what you expect to happen in your study. For example, a study designed to look at the relationship between study habits and test anxiety might have a hypothesis that states, "Students with better study habits will suffer less test anxiety." Unless your study is exploratory in nature, your hypothesis should always explain what you expect to happen during the course of your experiment.

Paradigms- methods, accepted ways of doing things, standards, habits, rules, ways of thinking,

Propositions   An offering or suggestion of something to be considered, accepted, adopted, or done.

Quantitative-Positivism- more numbers oriented and measurements. Measures the external world objectively. It bases things on facts and is scientific. They claim to be independent, but they are influenced by outside power forces. It questions what, is it, how much, and does it, not why or how.

Qualitative -Phenomenology more meaning and perception. Researchers are more sympathetic and sensitive to human feelings, more in control but subject to interpretation mistakes. If a case study is undertaken it is hard to not be deceitful about your purpose, because when the study subjects find out they will change their reactions. Phenomenologists are not so much fact gatherers but address how and why people react to situations/ circumstances. Human beliefs, behaviors, perceptions and values are considered.

BIBLIOGRAPHY

Adams, J. S. (1965). *Inequity in social exchange. In L. Berkowitz (Ed.), Advances in experimental social psychology.* New York: : Academic Press.

Adams, J. S., & Freeman, S. (1976). *Equity theory revisited.* Academic Press.

Aiken, L. H., Clarke, S., & Sloane, D. (2001). *Hospital Restructuring: Does it Adversely Affect Care and Outcomes?* Journal of Health and Health Services Administration.

Alderfer, C. P., & Guzzo, R. A. (1979). Life Experiences and Adults' Enduring Strength of Desires in Organizations. *Administrative Science Quarterly* , 347-361.

Allen v. Diebold, I. 3., & Thomure v. Phillips Furniture Co., 3. F. (1994). Legal.

Allen, T. D., Freeman, D. M., Russell, J. E., Reizenstein, R. C., & Rentz, J. O. (2001). *Survivor reactions to organizational downsizing: Does time ease the pain?* . Journal of Occupational & Organizational Psychology.

Allred, K. G. (1999). *Anger and*

retaliation: Toward an
understanding of impassioned
conflict in organizations. In R.
J. Bies, R. J. Lewicki, & B. H.
Sheppard (Eds.), Research on
negotiations in organizations.
Greenwich, Ct: JAI Press.

Amabile, T. M. (1997).
Entrepreneurial creativity
through motivational synergy.
Journal of Creative Behavior,
31, 18-26.

Amabile, T. M., & Conti, R. (1999).
Changes in the work organization
for creativity during
downsizing. *Academy of*
Management Journal, 42, 630-640.

American Management Association .
(1996). Survey) on downsizing,
job elimination . *American*
Management Association.

Amundson, N. E., Borgen, W. A.,
Jordan, S., & Erlebach, A. C.
(2004). Survivors of Downsizing:
Helpful and Hindering
Experiences. *Career Development*
Quarterly, Mar, Vol. 52 Issue 3,
p256, 16p.

Anderson, G. L. (2004). Outsourcing
America. . *World and I*, Jan Vol
19, issue 1.

Armstrong-Stassen, M. (1993).
Survivors Reactions to a
Workforce Reduction: A

Comparison of Blue-collar
Workers and their Supervisors.
*Canadian Journal of
Administrative Sciences.*

Armstrong-Stassen, M. (1998).
Downsizing the federal
government: A longitudinal study
of managers' reactions. .
*Canadian Journal of
Administrative Sciences,,* 15,
310-322.

Armstrong-Stassen, M. (2002).
Designated redundant but
escaping lay-off: A special
group of lay-off survivors. .
*Journal of Occupational &
Organizational Psychology,,* Mar,
Vol. 75 Issue 1.

Armstrong-Stasson, M. (1997). The
effect of repeated management
downsizing and surplus
designation on remaining
managers: An exploratory study.
. *Anxiety, Stress, and Coping,,*
10, 377-384.

Armstrong-Strassen, M., Cameron, S.,
& Horsburgh, M. (1996). *The
Impact of Organizational
Downsizing on the Job
Satisfaction of Nurses.* .
Canadian Journal of Nursing
Administration.

Armstrong-Strassen, M., Cameron, S.,
& Horsburgh, M. (2001).

Downsizing-initiated Job Transfer of Hospital Nurses: How Do the Job Transferees Fare? . Journal of Health and Health Services Administration .

Arndt, E., & Duchemin, K. (1993). More than 'Bandaids'": Emotional Support and Education During the Downsizing Process. *Healthcare Management Forum* , 6 (3): 5-17.

Aryee, S., Budhwar, P., & Chen, Z. (2002). Trust as a mediator of the relationship between organizational justice and work outcomes: Test of a social exchange model. *Journal of Organizational Behavior.*, 267-285.

Ashford, S. J., Lee, C., & Bobko, P. (1989). Content, causes, and consequences of job insecurity: A theory-based measure and substantive test. *Academy of Management Journal*, J2. 803-829.

Ashman, I. (2012). A new role emerges in downsizing: Special envoys. *People Management*, Aug, p32- 35. 4p.

Auerbach, C., Rock, B., Goldstein, M., Kaminsky, P., & Heft-Laporte, H. (2000). A Department of Social Work Uses Data to Prove Its Case. . *Social Work in Health Care* , .32 (1): 9-23.

Bahk, B.-H., & Gort, M. (1993).
     Decomposing Learning by Doing at
     New Plants. . *Journal of
     Political Economy*, 101(4): 561-
     83.
Bailey, M., Bartelsman, E., &
     Haltiwanger, J. (1994).
     *Downsizing and Productivity
     Growth: Myth or Reality?* .
     National Bureau of Economic
     Research.
Baron, R. M., & Kenny, D. A. (1986).
     The moderator- mediator variable
     distinction in social
     psychological research:
     Conceptual, strategic, and
     statistical considerations.
     *Journal of Personality and
     Social Psychology,*, 1173-1182.
Bartel, A., & Sicherman, N. (1993).
     Technological change and
     retirement decisions of older
     workers. , . *Journal of Labor
     Economics*, 11(1), 162-168.
Bartell, M., & Bartell, R. (1985). An
     Integrative Perspective on the
     Psychological Response of Women
     and Men to Unemployment. *Journal
     of Economic Psychology*, 27-49.
Baruch, Y., & P., H. (1999).
     Perpetual motion in
     organizations: Effective
     management and the impact of the
     new psychological contracts on

survivor syndrome. *European Journal of Work and Organizational Psychology.*, 295-306.

Baumohl, B. (1993, March 15). When Downsizing Becomes Dumbsizing. *Time.*

Bay v. Times Mirror Magazines, 9. F. (1991). Legal.

Bazzoli, G., LoSasso, A., Arnould, R., & Shalowitz, M. (2002). *Hospital Reorganization and Restructuring Achieved Through Merger.* Health Care Management Review .

Bennett, A. (1991). Downsizing Doesn't Necessarily Bring an Upswing in Organizational.

Bergh, D. D. (1993). Watch the time carefully: The use and misuse of time effects in management research. *Journal of Management,* 19, 683—705.

Bergman, B. J. (2008). *Extended mass layoffs after 2001: a comparison of New York and the Nation.* . Monthly Labor Review.

Bialas v. Greyhound Lines, 5. F. (1995). Legal.

Bies, R. J. (1987). Beyond 'voice'. The influence of decision-maker justification and sincerity on procedural fairness judgments. Representative . *Research in*

Social Psychology,, 3-14.

Bies, R. J., & Moag, J. S. (1986). *Interactional justice: Communication criteria for fairness. In B. H. Sheppard (Ed.), Research on negotiation in organizations (Vol. 1, pp. 43-55).* . Greenwich, CT: JAI Press.

Bies, R. J., & Tripp, T. M. (2002). *Hot flashes and open wounds, Injustice and the tyranny of its emotions. In S. W. Gilliland, D. D. Steiner, & D. P. Skarlicki (Eds.), Emerging perspectives on managing organizational justice (pp. 203-221).* Greenwich,: Information Age Publishing.

Bobocel, D. R., & Zdaniuk, A. (2005). *How can explanations be used to foster organizational justice? In J. Greenberg & J. A. Colquitt (Eds.), Handbook of organizational justice (pp. 329-354).* . Mahwah, NJ:: Erlbaum.

Bommer, M., & Jalajas, D. (1999). *The threat of organizational downsizing on the innovative propensity of R&D professionals.* Blackwell.

Boone, J. (2000). Technological Progress, Downsizing and Unemployment. *Economic Journal.*

Boone, J. (2004). *Downsizing is bad*

for business. Royal Economic
Society Journal.

Borgen, W. A. (1997). People caught
in changing career
opportunities: A counseling
process. *Journal of Employment
Counseling*, 34, 133-143.

Borgen, W. A., Amundson, N. E., &
Harder, H. G. (1988). The
experience of underemployment.
*Journal of Employment
Counseling,*, 149-159.

Borgen, W. A., Amundson, N. E., &
Tench, E. (1996). Psychological
well-being throughout the
transition from adolescence to
adulthood. *The Career
Development Quarterly*, 45, 189-
199.

Bottom, W. P., Gibson, K., Daniels,
S. E., & Murnighan, J. K.
(2002). When talk is not cheap:
Substantive penance and
expressions of intent in
rebuilding cooperation.
Organization Science, 497- 513.

Bridges, W. (1986). Managing
organizational transitions.
Organizational Dynamics, 15(1),
24-33.

Bridges, W. (1994). *Organizational
Psychology: A Scientist-
Practitioner Approach.* John
Wiley and Sons.

Brief, A. P., Schuler, R. S., & Van
     Sell, M. A. (1981). *Managing Job
     Stress*. Boston: Little, Brown.
Brister, K. (2000). *Eastman Focusing
     on Improving its Earnings;
     Short-haul Results Fit with
     Long-term View.* . Knoxville News
     Sentinel.
Brockner, J. (1990). Scope of justice
     in the workplace: How survivors
     react to co-worker layoffs.
     Journal of Social Issues, 95-
     106.
Brockner, J., Grover, S. L., &
     Blonder, M. D. (1988).
     Predictors of survivor's job
     involvement following layoffs: A
     field study. *Journal of Applied
     Psychology*, 73, 436-442.
Brockner, J., Grover, S., O'Malley,
     M., Reed, T., & M.A., G. (1993).
     Threat of Future Layoffs, Self-
     Esteem, and Survivors'
     Reactions: Evidence From the
     Laboratory and the Field.
     Strategic Management Journal, .
     14: 153-166.
Brockner, J., Grover, S., Reed, T.
     F., & DeWitt, R. L. (1992).
     Layoffs, job insecurity, and
     survivors' work effort: Evidence
     of an inverted-U relationship .
     Academy of Management Journal,
     35, 413—425.

Brockner, J., Konovsky, M., Cooper-
    Schneider, R., Folger, R.,
    Martin, C., & Bies, R. J.
    (1994). Interactive effects of
    procedural justice and outcome
    negativity on victims and
    survivors of job loss. *Academy
    of Management Review*, 397-409.

Brockner, J., Wiesenfeld, B. M., &
    Martin, C. L. (1995). Decision
    frame, procedural justice, and
    survivors' reactions to job
    layoffs. *Organizational Behavior
    and Human Decision Processes,*,
    59-68.

Brockner, J., Wiesenfeld, B.,
    Stephan, J., & Hurley, R.
    (1997). The effects on layoff
    survivors of the fellow
    Survivors' reactions. *Journal of
    Applied Social Psychology,*, 27,
    835-863.

Brown, A. S. (2005). The China Road:
    The outsourcing option isn't as
    cheap or as easy as it looks. .
    Mechanical Engineering Magazine.

Brown, R. (1996). Organizational
    commitment: Clarifying the
    concept and simplifying the
    existing construct typology.
    Journal of Vocational Behavior,
    230-251.

Bruton, G. D., Keels, J. K., & Shook,
    C. L. (1996). *Downsizing the*

firm: *Answering the strategic question.* Academy of Management Executive;.

Bumbaugh, M. (1998). Moving beyond Survival after Downsizing. . *Nursing Management.*

Bunk, B. P., & Janssen, P. (1992). Bunk, B. P., & Janssen, P. (1992) Relative deprivation, career issues, and mental health among men in midlife. *Journal of Vocational Behavior,,* 338-350.

Bureau of Labor Statistics, U.S. Department of Labor. (2015). *The Economics Daily, Rising wage inequality, 2003-13.* Department of Labor.

Burke, R. J. (2001). *Hospital Restructuring and Downsizing: Taking Stock, A Symposium, Part 1.* . Journal of Health and Health Services Administration.

Burke, R. J., & Greenglass, E. (2000). *Hospital Restructuring and Downsizing in Canada: Are Less Experienced Nurses at Risk?* Psychological Reports.

Burke, R., & Cooper, C. E. (2000). *The Organization in Crisis: Downsizing, Restructuring, and Privatization.* Blackwell.

Burris, B. H. (1983). *No room at the top: Underemployment and alienation in the corporation.*

New York: : Praeger Press.

Burroughs, S. M., Bing, M. N., &
    James, L. R. (1998). *Employee
    Tenure in 1998, Effects of
    personality and job stressors on
    affective reactions and
    aggressive work.* Bureau of Labor
    Statistics.

Buss, T., & Redbum, F. (1983).
    *Shutdown at Youngstown: Public
    policy for mass unemployment.* .
    Albany, NY: State University of
    New York Press.

Byrne, J. (1994). *The Pain of
    Downsizing.* Business Week.

Cameron, K. (1994). *Strategies for
    Successful Organizational
    Downsizing.* Human Resource
    Management .

Cameron, K. S., & Kim, M. U. (1987).
    Organizational Effects of
    Decline and Turbulence.
    *Administrative Science
    Quarterly*.

Cameron, K. S., & Zammuto, R. (1983).
    Matching Managerial Strategies
    to Conditions of Decline. *Human
    Resource Management*, 359-375.

Cameron, K. S., Freeman, S. J., &
    Mishra, A. K. (1991). Best
    practices in white-collar
    downsizing: Managing
    contradictions. . *Academy of
    Management Executive*, 5, 57-73.

Cameron, K. S., Freeman, S. J., &
    Mishra, A. K. (1993).
    Organizational downsizing.
    Oxford University Press.
Cameron, K. S., Sutton, R. I., &
    Whetton, D. A. (1988). *Readings
    in organizational decline:
    Frameworks, research and
    prescriptions.* Cambridge, MA:
    Ballinger.
Cameron, K. S., Whetten, D. A., &
    Kim, M. U. (1987).
    Organizational Dysfunctions of
    Decline. *Academy of Management
    Journal* , 126-138.
Canaff, A. L. (2000). The Y2K
    employment counselor. *National
    Employment Counselors
    Association.* National Employment
    Counselors Association.
Canaff, A. L., & Wright, W. (2004).
    High anxiety: Counseling the
    job-insecure client . *Journal of
    Employment Counseling*, Mar, Vol.
    41 Issue 1, p2.
Carnevale, P. J., & Probst, T. M.
    (1998). Social values and social
    conflict in creative problem
    solving and categorization.
    *Journal of Personality and
    Social Psychology,*, 74, 1300-
    1309.
Carroll, A. B. (1985). When Business
    Closes Down: Social

Responsibilities and Management
Action. *California Management
Review*, 125-139.

Carroll, G. R. (1984). Dynamics of
Publisher Succession in
Newspaper Organizations,.
*Administrative scientific
Quarterly*.

Carter, M. E. (1998). *An Analysis of
the Operating Performance and
Financial Statement Disclosures
Associated with Corporate
Restructurings*. MIT.

Cascio, W. (1993). *Downsizing: What
Do We Know? What Have We
Learned?* . Academy of Management
Executive.

Cascio, W. (1995). *Guide to
Responsible Restructuring*.
Department of Labor, Office of
the American Workplace.

Cascio, W. (1998). *Managing Human
Resources: Productivity, Quality
of Work Life, Profits*. Irwin
McGraw Hill.

Cascio, W. F. (2002). *Strategies for
responsible restructuring*. .
Academy of Management Executive.

Cash, W. (1993). *A Consultant
Explodes Myths About Downsizing*.
National Undrwriter.

Challenger, J. (2005). *A Return on
investment of high-quality
outplacement programs*. Economic

Perspectives-2nd Quarter, Vol. 29 Issue 2, p86-93.

Chalos, P., & Chen, C. J. (2002). *Employee Downsizing Strategies: Market Reaction and Post Announcement Financial Performance. , .* Journal of Business Finance & Accounting.

Chan, S. H., Gau, G. W., & Wang, K. (1995). Stock Market Reaction to Capital Investment Decisions: Evidence from Business Relocations. *Journal of Financial and Quantitative Analysis.*

Charan, R., & Colvin, G. (2001). *Managing for the Slowdown: 13 Moves to Make Before Your Competitors Do, Plus 3 Rules Not to Forget.* Fortune.

Checkland, P. (1999). *Systems Thinking, Systems Practice.* John Wiley & Sons.

Chen, P. Y., & Spector, P. E. (1992). Relationships of work stressors with aggression, withdrawal, theft, and substance use: An exploratory study. *Journal of Occupational and Organizational Psychology*, 65, 177-184.

Chisholm, R. P., Kasl, S. V., & Eskanazi, B. (1983). The nature and prediction of job related tension in a crisis situation:

Reaction of nuclear workers to
the Three Mile Island accident.
Academy of Management Journal,,
26, 385-405.

Ciancio, J. (2000). Survivor's
Syndrome. *Nursing Management,* 31
(5): 43-45.

Clay, R. (1998). Downsizing backfires
on corporate America, APA
Monitor,. *America Psychological
Association.*

Clogg, C. C., & Shockey, J. W.
(1984). Mismatch between
occupation and schooling: A
prevalence measure, recent
trends, and demographic
analysis. *Demography,* 235-257.

Clogg, C. C., Sullivan, T., &
Mutchler, J. (1986). Measuring
underemployment and inequality
in the work force. *Social
Indicators Research,* 375-393.

Cobb, S., & Kasl, S. V. (1977).
*Termination: The consequences of
Job loss. Report No. 76-1261.*
Washington, DC:: National
Institute for Occupational
Safety and Health Research.

Cohen-Charash, Y., & Spector, P. E.
(2001). The role of justice in
organizations: A meta-analysis.
*Organizational Behavior and
Human Decision Processes,,* 86,
278-324.

Cohn, R. M. (1978). The Effect of
     Employment Status on Self-
     Attitudes . *Social Psychology* ,
     81-93.

Collins, A. L., & Noble, R. (1992).
     Hospital Rightsizing: In line
     with Long-Term Strategies and
     Economic Realities. *Healthcare
     Management Forum*, 5 (1): 4-10.

Cook, D. S., & Ferris, G. R. (1986).
     Strategic Human Resource
     Management and Firm
     Effectiveness in Industries
     Experiencing Decline. *Human
     Resource Management* , 441-458.

Cooper, C. L. (1999). Can we live
     with the changing nature of
     work? *Journal of Managerial
     Psychology*, 569-572. .

Corrado, C., Hulten, C., & Sichel, D.
     (2005). Measuring Capital and
     Technology: An Expanded
     Framework, in Measuring Capital
     in the New Economy. *NBER*.

Cowherd, D., & Levine, D. (1992).
     Product quality and pay equity
     between lower-level employees
     and top management: An
     investigation of distributive
     justice theory. *Administrative
     Science Quarterly.*, 302-320.

Crosby, F. (1976). A model of
     egoistical relative deprivation.
     . *Psychological Review*, 83, 85-

113.

Crosby, F. (1982). *Relative deprivation and working women. .* New York: : Oxford University Press.

Dalton, M. (1959). *Men who manage.* Wiley.

Davis, J., Savage, A., Stewart, G., & Thomas, R. (2003). Organizational Downsizing: A Review of Literature for Planning and Research. *Journal of Healthcare Management,* May/Jun, Vol. 48 Issue 3, p181, 21p .

Davis-Blake, A., & Uzzi, B. (1993). Determinants of Employment Externalization: A Study of Temporary Workers and Independent Contractors. *Administrative Science Quarterly,* 195-223.

Davy, J. A., Kinicki, A. J., & Scheck, C. L. (1991). Developing and testing a model of survivor responses to layoffs. *Journal of Vocational Behavior,* 38, 302-317.

De Bono, N. (2008). Presstran workers vote for reduced work week. *Sun Media.*

De Mause, K. P., Bergmann, T. J., & Vander-Heiden, P. A. (1997). Corporate downsizing: Separating myth from fact;. *Journal of Management Inquiry*, Vol. 6 Issue 2, p168-176, 9p.

De Meuse, K. P., Bergmann, T. J., Vanderheiden, P. A., & Roraff, C. E. (2004). *New Evidence Regarding Organizational Downsizing and a Firm's Financial Performance: A Long-term Analysis.,* . Journal of Managerial Issues.

DeFrank, R. S., & Ivancevich, J. M. (1986). Job loss: An individual level review and model. *Journal of Vocational Behavior*, 28, 1-20.

Dekker, I., & Barling, J. (1998). Personal and organizational predictors of workplace harassment of women by men. *Journal of Occupational Health Psychology*, 3 (1), 7-18.

Dekker, S. W., & Schaufelt, W. B. (1995). The effects of job insecurity on psychological health and withdrawal: A longitudinal study. *Australian Psychologist*, 30, 57-63.

Dertouzos, J. N., & Karoly, L. A. (1992). *Labor Market Responses to Employer Liability,* . The Rand Corporation.

Dewhurst, N. (2008, Dec). Before Offshoring Consider Homegrown

Options. *Industry Week*, pp. pg
    26-27.
Diamond, M. (1996, July). Kaiser
    Health Plan Sees Layoffs. *The
    Sun*.
DiMaggio, P., & Powell, W. (1983).
    The Iron Cage Revisited.
    Institutional Isomorphism .
Dougherty, D., & Bowman, E. (1995).
    The Effects of Organizational
    Downsizing on Product
    Innovation. . *California
    Management Review*, 37 (4): 28-
    44.
Dunn, L. F. (1979). Measuring the
    Value of Community. *Journal of
    Urban Economics*, 371-382.
Easterby-Smith, M., Thorpe, R., &
    Lowe, A. (1991). *Management
    research: an introduction*. Sage.
Ehrenberg, R. G., & Jakubson, G. H.
    (1989). Advance Notification of
    Plant Closings: Does IT Matter?
    . *Industrial Relations*, 60-71.
Elkin, T. (1998). *Momentous Shifts.*
    brandweek.
Encyclopedia.com. (2003).
    "Downsizing." . Dictionary of
    American History.
Engardio, P., Roberts, D., & Bremner,
    B. (2004, Dec 6). The China
    Price. *Business Week*, pp. 102-
    112.
Evans, M. A. (1995). Downsizing in

the U.S. Army: Common concerns
of survivors. *Journal of
Political and Military
Sociology*, 23, 271-287.

Fallows, J. (2012, Dec, Vol. 310
issue 5). Mr. China Comes to
America. *Atlantic Monthly*, pp.
54-66. .

Farr, J. L., & Ford, C. M. (1990).
*Individual innovation. In M. A.
West & J. L. Farr (Eds.),
Innovation and creativity at
work (pp. 63-80). Chichester,
UK: Wiley.* Chichester, UK:
Wiley.

Feldman, D. (1996). The nature,
antecedents, and consequences of
underemployment. *Journal of
Management*, 385-409.

Feldman, D. C., & Doerpinghaus, H. I.
(1992). Patterns of part-time
employment. Journal of
Vocational Behavior. *Journal of
Vocational Behavior*, 282-294.

Feldman, D. C., & Leana, C. R.
(1994). Better Practices in
Managing Layoffs. *Human Resource
Management* , 239-260.

Feldman, D. C., & Turnley, W. H.
(1995). Underemployment among
recent business college
graduates. *Journal of
Organizational Behavior*, 691-
706.

Feldman, D. C., Leana, C. R., & Bolino, M. C. (2002). Underemployment and Relative Deprivation among re-employed executives. *Journal of Occupational & Organizational Psychology*, Dec Vol. 75 Issue 4, p453, 19p.

Feldman, D. C., Leana, C. R., & Turnley, W. H. (1997). *A relative deprivation approach to understanding underemployment.* Wiley.

Ference, T. P., Stoner, J. A., & Warren, E. K. (1977). Ference, T. P., J. A. F. Stoner, and Managing the Career Plateau. *Academy of Management Review*, 602-612.

Ferris, G. R., Schellenberg, D. A., & Zammuto, R. F. (1984). Human Resource Management Strategies in Declining Industries. *Human Resource Management*, 381-394.

Fisher, S. R., & White, M. A. (2000). Downsizing in a Learning Organization: Are There Hidden Costs? . *Academy of Management Review*, Jan, Vol. 25 Issue 1.

Fishman, C. (2006). *The Wal-Mart Effect: How the World's Most Powerful Company Really Works--and HowIt's Transforming the American Economy.* Penguin Press.

Flanagan, J. C. (1954). Flanagan, J.
    C. (1954) The critical incident
    technique. . *Psychological
    Bulletin*, 51, 327-358.
Florian, E. (2001). *LAYOFF COUNT*.
    Fortune.
Folger, R., & Baron, R. A. (1996).
    *Violence and hostility at work:
    A model of reactions to
    perceived injustice. In G. R.
    van den Bos & E. Q. Bulatao
    (Eds.), Violence on the job:
    Identifying risks and developing
    solutions (pp. 51-85). .
    Washington, DC: : American
    Psychological Association Press.
Folger, R., & Skarlicki, D. P.
    (1998). When tough times make
    tough bosses: Managerial
    distancing as a function of
    layoff blame. *Academy of
    Management Journal*, 79-87.
Folkman, S., & Lazarus, R. S. (1980).
    An Analysis of Coping in a
    Middle-Aged Community Sample.
    *Journal of Health and Social
    Behavior*, 219-239.
Ford, J. D. (1980). The
    Administrative Component in
    Growing and Declining
    Organizations: A Longitudinal
    Analysis. *Academy of Management
    Journal*, 615-630.
Frank, R. (2014). *Luxury CEO: The*

poor should stop whining. CNN.

Friedman, M. (1971). *Government Revenue from Inflation.* Journal of Political Economy.

Frone, M. R., Russell, M., & Cooper, M. L. (1965). Job stressors, job involvement and employee health: A test of identity theory. *Journal of Occupational and Organizational Psychology*, 68, 1—11.

Fryer, D., & Payne, R. (1986). *Being unemployed: A review of the literature on the psychological experience of unemployment. In C. L. Cooper & Robertson eBds.), International review of Industrial and organizational psychology (pp. 23' pg-278). New.* John Wiley.

Galagan, P. (2010). *The Biggest Losers: The Perils of Extreme Downsizing.* www.td.com.

Galina Davidoff, G., & Neufer, N. (2002). Survey - DecisionQuest/Minority corporate Counsel Association. *DecisionQuest*.

Gallagher, L. J., Uccello, C. E., Pierce, A. B., & Reidy, E. B. (1999). *State general assistance programs, 1998.* Washington, DC: : Urban Institute.

Gandolfi, F. (2006). *Corporate*

downsizing demystified: a
scholarly analysis of a business
phenomenon. ICFAI University
Press, Hyderabad, India.

Gandolfi, F. (2008). *HR Strategies
That Can Take The Sting Out Of
Downsizing- Related Layoffs.*
Business Journal.

Gandolfi, F. (2008a). HR Strategies
That Can Take The Sting Out of
Downsizing-Related Layoffs. *IVEY
Business Journal.*

Gandolfi, F., & Oster, G. (2009).
*Innovating in an era of
Downsizing.* IVEY Journal.

Gardner, J. M. (1995, April). Worker
Displacement: a Decade of
Change. *Monthly Labor Review.*

Gee, E. P. (2000). *Leaner is Greener.*
Journal of Healthcare Management
.

George, J. (2004). Cutting costs:
should personnel be the first to
go? *Employment Practices
Solution.*

Gertz, D., & Baptista, J. (1995).
*Grow to Be Great: Breaking the
Downsizing Cycle.* Simon and
Schuster.

Glaser, B. G., & Strauss, A. L.
(1967). *The Discovery of
Grounded Theory: Strategies for
Qualitative Research.* Aldine
Pub.

Glynn, M. (2002). *Fifty in Buffalo,
    N.Y. Fear For Jobs in Downsizing
    at American Airlines* . Knight
    Ridder.

Godfrey, C. (1994). Downsizing:
    Coping with Personal Pain.
    Nursing Management , 25 (10):
    90-93.

Govreau, J. (2008). *Chrysler
    announces mandatory two- week
    shutdown of all plans in July
    2008,*. Dow Jones.

Greenberg, E. (1989). The Latest AMA
    Survey on Downsizing. *Personnel*,
    66 (10), October, 38-44. .

Greenberg, J. (1990). *Looking fair
    vs. being fair: Managing
    impressions of organizational
    justice. In B. M. Staw & L. L.
    Cummings (Eds.), Research in
    Organizational Behavior (Vol.
    12, pp. 111-157).* . Greenwich,
    CT:: JAI Press.

Greenberg. J., &. C. (2005). *Handbook
    of organizational justice.*
    Mahwah, NJ:: Lawrence Erlbaum.

Greenhalgh, L., & Lawrence, A. T.
    (1988). Determinants of Work
    Force Reduction Strategies in
    Declining Organizations. *Academy
    of Management Review*, 241-254.

Greenhalgh, L., & Rosenblatt, Z.
    (1984). Job insecurity: Toward
    conceptual clarity. *Academy of*

Managerial Review, 9, 438-448.

Greenhalgh, L., McKersie, R. B., & Gilkey, R. W. (1986). Rebalancing the Workforce at IBM: A Case Study of Redeployment and Revitalization. *Organizational Dynamics*, 30-47.

Greenhouse, S. (2015, June 8). How Walmart Persuades Its Workers Not to Unionize. *The Atlantic*.

Greising, D. (1998, January 12). It's the Best of Times--or Is It? *Business Week*, p. 36.

Gupta, N., & Beehr, T. A. (1979). Job stress and employee behaviors. . *Organizational behavior and Human Performance,*, 23, 373-387.

Hagen, J. (1999). Public welfare and human services: New directions under TANF? *Families in Society*, 78-90.

Halter, A. (1989). Welfare reform: One state's alternative. *Journal of Sociology and Social Welfare*, 151-162.

Halter, A. (1992). Homeless in Philadelphia: A qualitative study of the impact of state welfare reform on individuals. *Journal of Sociology and Social Welfare*, 7-20.

Hambrick, D. C. (1983). Turnaround Strategies for Mature Industrial-Product Business

Units. *Academy of Management Journal*, 231-248.

Hambrick, D. C., & D'Aveni, R. A. (1988). Large Corporate Failures as Downward Spirals. *Administrative Science Quarterly*, 1-23.

Hamel, G., & Prahalad, C. (1994). *Competing for the Future.* Harvard Business School Press.

Handy, C. (2002). What's a Business For? . *Harvard Business Review*, 80(12) pg. 49.

Hanisch, K. A. (1999). Job loss unemployment research from 1994 to 1998: A review and recommendations for research and intervention. *Journal of Vocational Behavior.*, 55, 188-220.

Hannan, M., & Freeman, J. (1977). *The Population Ecology of Organizations.* American Journal of Sociology.

Harari, O. (1993). Layoffs: An Internal Debate. *Management Review,*.

Harrigan, K. R. (1980). *Strategies for Declining Businesses.* Lexington, MA: : Lexington Books. .

Harrison, B., & Bluestone, B. (1988). *The Great U-turn: Corporate Restructuring and the Polarizing of America.* New York: : Basic Books.

Hartley, J., & Fryer, D. (1987). *The psychology of unemployment: A critical appraisal. In G. Stephenson & J. Davis (Eds.), Progress in applied social psychology.* London: Wiley.

Hays, L. (1994, April 28). IBM Aide Quits Under Pressure, Executives Say. *The Wall Street Journal,*.

Hazelwood School District v. United States, 4. U. (n.d.). Legal.

Hebron, R. (2006). Shortage of workers in China. *Economic Freedom and Growth.*

Hecksher, C. (1988). *The New Industrial Relations.* New York: Basic Books.

Heenan, D. A. (1989). *The downside of downsizing.* The Journal of Business Strategy.

Heffes, E. M. (2004). Heffes, Ellen M (2004) Offshoring: and the Winner is: . *Financial Executive* , Vol. 20 no 6 pg. 31-34.

Hendrix, W., T., R., Miller, J., & Summers, T. (1998). Effects of procedural and distributive justice on factor predictive or turnover. *Journal of Social Behavior and Personality*, 611-633.

Henkotf, R. (1990). *Cost Cutting: How*

to Do it Right. Fortune.

Hershey, R. (1972). Effects of Anticipated Job Loss on Employee Behavior. *Journal of Applied Psychology*, 273-275.

Heskett, J. L. (1997). *The Service Profit Chain.* Harvard Free Press.

Hickok, T. (1995). *The impact of work force reductions on those who remain: A study of civilian workers at two Department of Defense bases.* Unpublished doctoral dissertation - University of Southern California.

Hickok, T. A. (1997). Downsizing and Organizational Culture. *Public Administration and Management Journal.* .

Hironimus-Wendt, R. J., & Spannaus, F. (2007). The Social Costs of Worker Displacement. *Social Policy;* .

Hirsch, P. (1987). *Pack Your Own Parachute.* Reading, MA: .: Addison-Wesley.

Hitt, M., Freeman, R., & And Harrison, J. (2001). *Handbook of Strategic Management.* . Blackwell.

Hofstade, G. (1980). *Culture's Consequences.* Sage.

Hollinger, R. C. (1986). Acts against

the workplace: Social bonding and employee deviance. *Deviant Behavior*, 7(1), 53-75.

Hollinger, R. C., & Clark, J. P. (1983). *Theft by employees.* Lexington, MA: Lexington Books.

Holm, S., & Hovland, J. (1999). Waiting for the other shoe to drop: Help for the job-insecure employee. *Journal of Employment Counseling*, 36, 156-166.

Hopkins, S. M., & Weathington, B. L. (2006). The Relationships Between Justice Perceptions, Trust, and Employee Attitudes in a downsized Organization. *Journal of Psychology.* , Sep, Vol. 140 Issue 5, p477-498. 22p.

Houston, P. (1992). Surviving the survivor, . *Working Woman Magazine.*

Hudson, T. (1997). *Bye, Bye Big Boards: Bogged Down by Too Many Trustees, Health Systems Streamline to Set Clearer Goals and Speed Up Decisions .* Hospitals & Health Networks.

Humphrys, P., & O'Brien, G. E. (1986). Humphrys, P., & O'Brien, G. E. (1986) The relationship between skill utilization, professional orientation and job satisfaction for pharmacists. *Journal of Occupational*

Psychology, 315-326.

International Monetary Fund. (2014).
World Economic Outlook. U.S.
Census Bureau.

Ironson, G. (1992). *Work Job Stress
and Health, in Work Families and
Organizations*. San Francisco:
Jossey-Bass Publishers.

Jahoda, M. (1982). *Employment and
unemployment: A social
psychological analysis.* .
Cambridge University Press.

Jensen, P., & Svarer, M. (2003).
*Short- and long- term
unemployment: How do temporary
layoffs affect this distinction?*
. Empirical Economics.

Jex, S. M. (1998). *Stress and job
performance: Theory, research,
and implications for managerial
practice.* . Thousand Oaks, CA:
Sage Publications.

Johnson, D. (1997). *Paying for the
(Alleged) Sins of Columbia.
Health Care*. Strategic
Management .

Jubak, J. (2007). *Letting the World
Pick our Pockets*. moneycentral.

Kanter, R. M. (1977). *Men and Women
of the Corporation*. New York:
Basic Books.

Karesek, R. (1979). *Job Demands, Job
Decision Latitude, and Mental
Strain: Implications for Job*

Redesign. Sage Publishing for
Cornell University.

Kay, J. (2015). *Other People's Money.*
Public Affairs.

Kerr, S. (1975). On the Folly of
Rewarding A While Hoping for B.
Academy of Management Journal.

Kets de Vries, M. F., & Balazs, K.
(1997). *The downside of
downsizing.* Human Relations.

Khanna, S., & New, R. (2008). An HR
Planning Model for Outsourcing.
. *Human Resource Planning,*
Volume 4, 37-42.

Kilpatrick, A. (1988). *Humanizing the
Downsizing Process in Hospitals
and Other Health Care
Organizations.* . Journal of
Health and Human Resources
Administration .

Kimberly, J. R., & Miles, R. H.
(1980). *The Organizational Life
Cycle.* San Francisco:: Jossey-
Bass.

Kinicki, A., Bracker, J., Kreitner,
R., Lockwood, C., & Lemak, D.
(1987). Socially Responsible
Plant Closings. *Personnel
Administrator,* 116-128.

Kivimaki, M., Vahtera, J., Pentti, &
Ferrie, J. (2000). *Factors
Underlying the Effect of
Organizational Downsizing on
Health of Employees.* British

Medical Journal - Longitudinal
Cohort Study.

Kobasa, S. C. (1979). Stressful Life
Events, Personality, and Health:
An Inquiry into Hardiness.
*Journal of Personality and
Social Psychology*, 1-11.

Koenders, Kathryn; Rogerson, Richard.
(2005). *Organizational Dynamics
Over the Business Cycle: A View
on Jobless Recoveries*. Federal
Reserve Bank of St Lewis.

Konovsky, M. A., & Folger, R. (1991).
The effects of procedures,
social accounts, and benefits
level on victims' layoff
reactions. *Journal of Applied
Social Psychology*, 630-650.

Konovsky, M., & Brockner, J. (1993).
*Managing victim and survivor
layoff reactions: A procedural
justice perspective. In R.
Cropanzano (Ed.), Justice in the
workplace: A procedural justice
perspective.* Hillsdale, NJ:
Lawrence Erlbaum.

Kovach, S. (2014). *Legendary Silicon
Valley VC Says Criticism Of The
Super-Rich Is Like Nazis Going
After The Jews.* Business
Insider.

Kozlowski, S., Chao, G., Smith, E., &
Hedlund, J. (1993).
Organizational downsizing:

Strategies, interventions, and
research implications.
*International review of
industrial and organizational
psychology.*

Kozlowski, W., Chao, J., Smith, E.
M., & Hedlimd, J. (1993).
Organizational downsizing:
Strategies, interventions, and
research implications. In C. L.
Cooper & I. T. Robertson (eds,).
*International review of
industrial and organizational
psychology.*

Kram, K. (1985). *Mentoring at Work.*
Glenview, IL:: Scott Foresman.

Krausz, M., Yaakobovitz., N., &
Caspi, T. (1999). Evaluation of
coworker turnover outcomes and
its impact on the Intention to
leave of the remaining
employees. *Journal of Business
and Psychology.*

Krietner, R. (2004). *Management.*
houghton-Miflin.

Kubler-Ross, E. (1969). *On death and
dying.* New York:: MacMillan.

Kuhnert, K. (1989). The latent and
manifest consequences of work.
The Journal of Psychology, 417-
427.

Kuhnert, K. W., Sims, R. R., & Lacey,
M. A. (1989). The relationship
between job security and

employee health. . *Group and Organization Studies*, 14, 399-410.

Kuttner, R. (1994, August 29). Where have all the good jobs gone? *Business Week*.

Landsbergis, P. A., Cahill, J., & Schnall, P. (1999). The impact of lean production and related new systems of work organization on worker health. . *Journal of Occupational Health Psychology*, 4, 108-130.

Langley, M. (1984). Many Middle Managers Fight Back as More Firms Trim Their Work Forces. *Wall street Journal*.

Lasch, C. (1979). *The Culture of Narcissism*. W.W. Norton.

Lawler, E. E. (1973). *Motivation in work organizations*. Monterey, CA: Brooks/Cole.

Leana, C. R., & FeIdman, C. (1994). The psychology of job loss. *Research in Personnel and Human Resources Management*, 12, 271-302.

Leana, C. R., & Feldman, D. C. (1992). *Leana, C. R., & Feldman, D. C. (1992). Coping with job loss: How individuals, organizations, and communities respond to layoffs.* Macmillan/Lexington Books.

Leana, C. R., & Feldman, D. C.
    (1995). Finding new jobs after a
    plant closing: Antecedents and
    outcomes of the occurrence and
    quality of reemployment. *Human
    Relations*, 1381-1401.

Leana, C. R., & Ivancevich, J.
    (1987). Addressing the Problem
    of Involuntary Job Loss:
    Institutional Interventions and
    a Research Agenda. *Academy of
    Management Review*, 301-312.

Leatt, P., Baker, G., Halverson, P.,
    & Aird, C. (1997). *Downsizing,
    Re-engineering, and
    Restructuring: Long-term
    Implications for Healthcare
    Organizations*. Frontiers of
    Health Services Management.

LeBlanc v. Great American Insurance
    Company, 6. F. (1993). LeBlanc
    v. Great American Insurance
    Company, 6 F.3d 836, 847, 1st
    Cir.

Lee, S., & Alexander, J. (1999).
    Managing Hospitals in Turbulent
    Times: Do Organizational Changes
    Improve Hospital Survival? .
    Health Services Research, 34
    (4): 923-46.

Lewin, J. E., & Johnston, W. J.
    (2000). *Lewin, J. E., &
    Johnston, W. J. (2000). The
    impact of downsizing and*

restructuring on organizational
competitiveness. Competitiveness
Review.

Lewis, J. D., & Weigert, A. (1985).
Trust as a social reality.
Social Forces, 967-985.

Liem., R., & Liem, J. H. (1988).
Psychological effects of
unemployment on workers and
their families. *Journal of
Social Issues*, 87-105.

Lim, V. K. (1996). Job insecurity and
its outcomes: Moderating effects
of work-based and nonworking-
based social support. *Human
Relations*, 49, 171- 194.

Lind, E. A. (2001). *Fairness
heuristic theory: Justice
Judgments as pivotal cognitions
in organizational relations. In
J. Greenberg & R. Cropanzano
(Eds.), Advances in
organizational justice (pp. 56-
88).* Stanford, CA: : Stanford
University Press.

Lipsky, M. (1966). *The Quest for
Peace - The Story of the Nobel
Awards.* Barnes & Co.

Locke, E. A. (1976). *The nature and
causes of job satisfaction. In
M. D. Dunnette (Ed.), Handbook
of industrial and organizational
psychology (pp. 1297-1350).*
Chicago: Rand-McNally.

Lodahl, T., & Kejner, M. (1965). The
     definition and measurement of
     job involvement. *Journal of
     Applied Psychology*, 49, 24-33.
Lohr, S. (1996). Downsizing: How it
     feels to be fired. *The New York
     Times*.
London, M. (1988). Organizational
     Support for Employees' Career
     Motivation: A Guide to Human
     Resource Strategies in Changing
     Business Conditions. *Human
     Resource Planning*, 23-32.
Loomba, R. P. (1987). A Study of the
     Reemployment and Unemployment
     Experience of.
Lorange, P., & Nelson, R. T. (1987).
     How to Recognize and Avoid
     Organizational Decline. *Sloan
     Management Review* , 41-48.
Love, E. G., & Nohria, N. (2005).
     Reducing Slack: the performance
     consequences of downsizing by
     large industrial firms.
     Strategic Management Journal .
Lublin, J. (2007). *Employers see
     value in helping those laid off.*
     The Wall Street Journal.
Lublin, J. S. (1991, July 9).
     Executives Find Unemployment
     Takes a Heavier Toll the Second
     Time Around. *Wall Street Journal*
     .
Luthans, B. C., & M., S. S. (1999).

The impact of downsizing on
workplace attitudes. *Group and
Organization Management.*, 24,
46-70.

Luthans, B., & Sommer, S. (1999). *The
impact of downsizing on
workplace attitudes*. Group and
Organization Management.

Madrick, J. (1995). Corporate surveys
can't find a productivity
revolution either. *Challenge*,
38, 31-44.

Makawatsakul, N., & Kleiner, B.
(2003). The effect of downsizing
on morale and attrition.
Management Research News, Vol.
26, No. 2, pp. 52-62.

Maniscalco, M. (2004). *Manufacturing
in China, The True Costs May
Surprise You.* eworksglobal.

Markham, S. E., & McKee, G. H.
(1991). Declining Organizational
Size and Increasing Unemployment
Rates: Predicting Employee
Absenteeism from Within- and
Between-Plant Perspectives.
Academy of Management Journal ,
952-965.

Martin, J. (1991). Relative
deprivation: A theory of
distributive injustice for an
era of shrinking resources.
*Research in organizational
behavior*, Vol. 3, pp. 53-107.

Mathews, V., & Duran., C. (1999).
    *Market Memo: Some Downsizing
    Approaches More Effective than
    Others.* Health Care Strategic
    Management.

Maxon, T. (2008). *American Airlines
    imposes hiring freeze on
    management and support staff.*
    The Dallas Morning News.

McGill, A. L. (1989). Context effects
    in judgments of causation.
    *Journal of Personality and
    Social Psychology*, 189-200.

McGrath, J. (1982, pg 79).
    *Dilemmatics: The study of
    research choices and dilemmas.
    In J. McGrath (Ed.), Judgment
    calls in research.* Sage
    Publications.

McKinley, W., Sanchez, C., & Schick,
    A. (1995). *Organizational
    Downsizing: Constraining,
    Cloning,.* Learning. Academy of
    Management Executive.

McKinley, W., Zhao, R., & Garrett, K.
    (2000). *A Sociocognitive
    Interpretation of Organizational
    Downsizing. .* Academy of
    Management Review.

Merton, R. K. (1936). The
    Unanticipated Consequences of
    Purposive Social Action.
    American Sociological Review .

Meyer, J. P., Allen, N. J., &

Topolnytsky, L. (1998). Commitment in a changing world of work. *Canadian Psychology*, 39, 82-93.

Meyer, J., & N., A. (1991). A three-component conceptualization of organizational commitment. *Human Resource Management Review*, 61-89.

Mick, S., & Wise, C. (1996). Downsizing and Financial Performance in Rural Hospitals. *Health Care Management Review*, 21 (2): 16-25. .

Miller, D., & Friesen, P. (1983). *Successful and Unsuccessful Phases of the Corporate.* Organizational .

Mishel, L., & Bernstein, J. (1994). *The State of Working America, 1994-95.* Economic Policy Institute,.

Mishra, A. K., & Spreitzer, G. M. (1998). Explaining how survivors respond to downsizing: The roles of trust, empowerment, justice, and work redesign. *Academy of Management Review*, 23, 567-588.

Missirian, A. K. (1982). *The Corporate Connection: Why Executive Women Need Mentors to Reach the Top.* Englewood Cliffs, NJ:: Prentice-Hall.

Mone, M. A. (1994). Relationships

between self- concepts,
aspirations, emotional responses
and intent to leave downsizing
organizations. *Human Resource
Management*, 33, 281-298.

Mone, M. A. (1994). Relationships
Between Self-Concepts,
Aspirations, Emotional
Responses, and Intent to Leave a
Downsizing Organization. *Human
Resource Management*, 33: 281-
298.

Mone, M. A. (1997). How we got along
after the downsizing: Post-
downsizing trust as a double-
edged sword. *Public
Administration Quarterly,* ,
Fall, Vol. 21 Issue 3, p309,
28p.

Mone, M. A., & V., B. (1996). A post-
modem Dr. Strangelove: Or, how
we got along after the
downsizing. In S. M. Sommer The
role of trust in understanding
the corporate lace in
cooperation and competition.

Moore, K. A. (2001). *Hospital
Restructuring: Impact on Nurses
Mediated by Social Support and a
Perception of Challenge.* Journal
of Health and Health Services
Administration .

Moore, T. (1994). *Rightsizing: Living
with the New Reality.* Healthcare

Financial Management.

Moorman, R. H. (1991). Relationship
between organizational justice
and organizational citizenship
behaviors: Do fairness
perceptions influence employee
citizenship? , . *Journal of
Applied Psychology*, 76, 845-855.

Morris, J. R., Cascio, W. F., &
Young, C. E. (1999). Downsizing
after all these years: Questions
and answers about who did it,
how many did it, and who
benefited from it.
Organizational Dynamics, 27, 78-
87.

Morrow, L. (1993, March 29). The
Temping of America. *Time*, pp.
40-47.

Morss, R. (2008). Creative layoff
policy and alternatives to
layoffs. *Salary.com, Inc.*

Murphy, M., & Murphy, E. (1996).
Cutting Healthcare Costs Through
Work Force Reductions.
Healthcare Financial Management
.

Murray, V. V., & Jick, T. D. (1985).
Taking Stock of Organizational
Decline Management: Some Issues
and Illustrations from an
Empirical Study. *Journal of
Management*, 111-123.

National Bureau of Economic Research.

(2008). *Determination of the December 2007 Peak in Economic Activity.* NBER.

Neal, D. (1995). Industry-Specific Human Capital: Evidence from Displaced Workers. *Journal of Labor Economics*, 13(4): 653-77.
.

Neuman, J. H., & Baron, R. A. (1997). *Aggression in the workplace. In R. A. Giaclone & J. Greenberg (Eds.), Antisocial behavior in organizations.* Thousand Oaks, CA: Sage.

Newman, J. M., & Krzystofiak, F. J. (1993). Changes in employee attitudes after an acquisition. *Group and Organization Management.*

Newman, K. S. (1988). *Falling from Grace: The Experience of Downward Mobility in the American Middle Class.* New York: : Vintage Books.

Nicholson, N., & West, M. A. (1988). *Managerial job change: Men and women in transition.* Cambridge University Press.

Noer, D. M. (1990). Layoff survivor sickness: A new challenge for supervisors. *Supervisory Management.*

Noer, D. M. (1993). *Healing the wounds: Overcoming the trauma of*

*layoffs and revitalizing
downsized organizations.* Jossey-
Bass.

Noer, D. M. (1998). Layoff survivor
sickness: What it is and what to
do about it. In M. K. Groing, J.
D. Kraft, & J. C. Quick (Eds.),
The new organizational reality:
Downsizing, restructuring and
revitalization. . *American
Psychological A.*

Nohria, N., & Beer, M. (2000).
Cracking the Code of Change.
Harvard business Review.

Noor, J. (2013). Australia Has $16
Minimum Wage and Is the Only
Rich Country to Dodge the Global
Recession. *The Real News
Network.*

Nordhaus-Bike, A. (1997). *Cutting
with Kindness.* . Hospitals &
Health Networks.

Nowak, T. C., & Snyder, K. A. (1983).
Women's Struggle to Survive a
Plant Shutdown . *Journal of
Intergroup Relations*, 25-44.

Nystrom, P. C., & Starbuck, W. H.
(1984). To Avoid Organizational
Crises, Unlearn. *Organizational
Dynamics*, 53-65.

O'Leary-Kelly, A. M., Griffin, R. W.,
& Glew, D. J. (1996).
Organization-motivated
aggression: A research

framework. *Academy of Management Review*, 21, 225-253.

O'Brien, G. E., & Feather, N. T. (1990). The relative effects of unemployment and quality of employment on the affect, work values, and personal control of adolescents. *Journal of Occupational Psychology*, 63, 151-165.

Olson, J., & Hafer, C. L. (1996). *Affect, motivation, and cognition in relative deprivation research. In R. M. Sorrentino & E. T. Higgins (Eds.), Handbook of motivation and cognition (Vol. 3, pp. 85-117).* . New York:: Guilford Press.

Organ, D. W. (1988). *Organizational Citizenship Behavior: The "Good Soldier" Syndrome.* Lexington, MA:: Lexington Books.

Pearce, J. (1993). Toward an Organizational Behavior of Contract Laborers: Their Psychological Involvement and Effects on Employee Coworkers. *Academy of Management Journal*, 1082-1096.

Pech, R. J. (2001). Termites, group behaviour, and the loss of innovation: Conformity rules!, . *Journal of Managerial*

Psychology,, 16, 559-574.

Perry, L. T. (1986). Least-Cost Alternatives to Layoffs in Declining Industries. *Organizational Dynamics*, 48-61.

Pinsonneault, A., & Kraemer, K. L. (2002). *Exploring the Role of Information Technology in Organizational Downsizing: A Tale of Two American Cities.* Journal of the Institute of Management Sciences.

Probst, T. M. (2002). Layoffs and tradeoffs: Production, quality, and safety demands under the threat of job loss. *Journal of Occupational Health Psychology*, 7, 211- 220.

Probst, T. M. (2003). Development and validation of the job security index and the job security satisfaction scale: A classical test theory and IRT approach. *Journal of Occupational and Organizational Psychology*, 76, 451-467.

Probst, T. M., & Brubaker, T. L. (2001). The effects of job insecurity on employee safety outcomes: Cross-sectional and longitudinal explorations. . *Journal of Occupational Health Psychology*, 6, 139-159.

Probst, T. M., Stewart, S. M., Gruys,

M. L., & Tierney, B. W. (2007).
Productivity, counter
Productivity and Creativity: The
ups and downs of insecurity.
*Journal of Occupational &
Organizational Psychology*, Sep,
Vol. 80 Issue 3, p479-497.

Puplava, J. J. (2005). *The Core Rate.*
Financial Sense.

Raber, M. J., Hawkins, M. J., &
Hawkins, W. E. (1995).
Organizational and employee
responses to surviving the
downsizing. *Employee Assistance
Quarterly*, 10, 1-11.

Rand, A. (1947). *Atlas shrugged.*
Penguin.

Reeves v. Sanderson Plumbing
Products, I. 5. (2000). Reeves
v. Sanderson Plumbing Products,
Inc., 530 U.S. 133.

Reichheld, F. (2006). *The Ultimate
Question: Driving Good Profits
and True Growth.* Harvard
Business School Press.

Richtnér, A., & Ahlström, P. (2006).
Organizational Downsizing and
Innovation. *working paper-
http://swoba.hhs.se/.*

Roberts, P. C. (2005, September). One
Foot in the Third World. *The
Ecologist,,* p. Vol 35 p 17.

Robinson, S. L. (1996). Trust and
breach of the psychological

contract. *Administrative Science Quarterly*, 574-599.

Robinson, S. L., & Bennett, R. J. (1995). A typology of deviant workplace behaviors: A multidimensional scaling study. *Academy of Management Journal, ,* 38, 555-572. .

Robinson, S. L., Kraatz, M. S., & & Rousseau, D. M. (1994). Changing obligations and the psychological contract: A longitudinal study. *Academy of Management Journal*, M, 137-152.

Rondeau, K. V., & Wagar, T. (2001). Downsizing and Organizational Restructuring: Differentiating their Impact on Hospital Performance. *Academy of Management Annual Meeting, Health Care Management Division,*.

Rose, F. (1994). Job-Cutting Medicine Fails to Remedy Productivity Ills at Many Companies. *The Wall Street Journal*.

Rosenstein, A. H. (2000). A System wide Approach to Cost Reduction. . *Health Forum Journal* , 43 (6): 48-52.

Roskies, E., & Louis-Guerin, C. (1990). Job insecurity in managers: Antecedents and consequences. . *Journal of*

Organizational Behavior, 11,
  345-359.
Roth, W. (1993). The dangerous ploy
  of downsizing. *The Free Library*.
Rousseau, D. M. (1990). New hire
  perceptions of their own and
  their employer's obligations: A
  study of psychological
  contracts. *Journal of
  Organizational Behavior*, 11,
  389-400.
Rousseau, D. M., & Wade-Benzoni, K.
  (1995). *Changing individual-
  organizational attachments: A
  two-way street. In A. Howard
  (Ed.), The changing nature of
  work*. San Francisco: Jossey-
  Bass.
Rousseau, D. M., Sitkin, S. B., Burt,
  R. S., & Camerer, C. (1998). Not
  so difficult after all: A cross-
  discipline view of trust.
  Academy of Management Review,
  393-404.
Rubach, L. (1995). Downsizing: How
  quality is affected as companies
  shrink. *Quality Progress,*, 28,
  23-25.
Ruhm, C. J., & Sum, A. (1988). Job
  stopping: The changing
  employment patterns of older
  workers. *Industrial Relations
  Research Association Meetings*
  (pp. pp. 21-28). Industrial

Relations Research Association.

Sanders, G. S., & Baron, R. S. (1975). The motivating effects of distraction on task performance. *Journal of Personality and Social Psychology, , 32,* 956–963.

Schein, E. H. (1990). Career stress in changing times: Some final observations. *Prevention in Human Services,* 8, 251–261.

Schuler, R. S., & Jackson, S. E. (1987). Organizational Strategy and Organizational Level as Determinants of Human Resource Management Practices. *Human Resource Planning,* 125–141.

Schuman, M., Woo, L., & Overland, M. (2008, Sept 29). Can China Compete? *Time International,* pp. Vol. 172 Issue 13, p45.

Schumpeter, J. A. (1942). *Capitalism, Socialism and Democracy.* Harper and Row.

Schumpeter, J. A. (1950). *Capitalism, Socialism, and Democracy: Third Edition.* Harper & Brothers.

Schwartz, K. D. (2005). A Lawyer's Perspective on Planning a Reduction in Force, , . *Economic Perspectives. 2nd Quarter,* Vol. 29 Issue 2, p94–107. 14P.

Schweiger, D. M., lvancevich, J. M., & Power, F. R. (1987). Executive

Actions for Managing Human
Resources Before and After
Acquisitions. *Academy of
Management Executive*, 127-138.

Scott, R., & Ratner, D. (2010).
NAFTA's Cautionary Tale. EPI
issue brief, July 20.

Sethi, S. P. (1975). Dimensions of
Corporate Social Performance: An
Analytical Frame work.
California Management Review ,
55-64.

Seybold, P. (2006). *Outside
Innovation: How Your Customers
Will Co- Design Your Company's
Future* . Harper Collins.

Shah, P. P. (2000). Network
Destruction: The Structural
Implications of Downsizing.
Academy of Management Journal,
Feb, Vol. 43 Issue 1, p101.

Shahani, C., Dipboye, R. L., &
Phillips, A. P. (1990). Global
Self-Esteem as a Correlate of
Work- Related Attitudes: A
Question of Dimensionality.
Journal of Personality, 276-
288.

Shanteau, J., & Dino, G. A. (1993).
*Environmental stressor effects
on creativity and decision
making. In O. Svenson & A. J.
Maule (Eds.), Time pressure and
stress in human judgment and*

decision making (pp. 293-308).
New york: Plenum Press.

Sherer, J. L. (1997). *The Human Side of Change: Managing Employee Morale and Expectations.* Healthcare Executive.

Shore, B. (1996). *The legacy of downsizing: putting the pieces back together.* Clarendon Press.

Sill, B. R. (2016). *Government Economics Gone Wild.* Pendragon-Createspace.

Sill, B. R. (2016). *Inequality - Must there be Blood in the Streets!* Pendragon-Creatspace.

Sill, B. R. (2016). *Inflation - Worse than Vampires, Zombies or the Plague!* Pendragon-Createspace.

Simonton, B. K. (1999). *Creativity from a historiometric perspective. In R. J. Sternberg (Ed.), Handbook of Creativity (pp. 116-136).* Cambridge, England: Cambridge University Press.

Skarlicki, D. P., & Folger, R. (1997). Retaliation in the workplace: The roles of distributive, procedural, and interactional justice. *Journal of Applied Psychology*, 434-443.

Skarlicki, D. P., Barclay, L. J., & Pugh, D. S. (2008). When explanations for layoffs are not enough: Employer's integrity as a moderator of the relationship between informational justice and retaliation. *Journal of Occupational & Organi.*

Sklar, H. (2004). *Outsource CEOs, not workers.* The Record (Bergen County, NJ).

Small, S. A., & Riley, D. (1990). Toward a multidimensional assessment of work spillover into family life. *Journal of Marriage and Family,,* 52, 51-61.
 .

Smith, A. (1776). *Wealth of Nations.* William Strahan, Thomas Cadell.

Soderquist, D. (2005). *The Wal-Mart Way: The Inside Story of the Success of the World's Largest Company* . Thomas Nelson.

Solman, P. (2013). *How Much Do You Need to Survive: An Interactive Guide to the Living Wage.* PBS.

Somers, M. (1995). Organizational commitment, turnover, and absenteeism: An examination of direct and interaction effects. *Journal of Organizational Behavior*, 49-58.

Spreitzer, G., & Mishra, A. (2002). To slay or to go: Voluntary survivor turnover following an organizational downsizing. *Journal of Organizational*

Behavior., 707-729.

Stafford, D. (2008, December). 10 million job hunters for 3 million jobs. *Kansas City Star.*

Starbuck, W. H., Greve, A., & Hedberg, B. L. (1978). Responding to Crisis . *Journal of Business Administration*, 111-137.

Staw, B. M., L. E. Sandelands, L. E., & Dutton, J. E. (1981). Threat-Rigidity Effects in Organizational Behavior: A Multilevel Analysis. *Administrative Science Quarterly*, 26: 501-524.

Staw, B. M., Sandelands, L. E., & Dutton, J. E. (1981). Threat-rigidity effects in organizational behavior: A multilevel analysis. *Administrative Science Quarterly*, 501-524.

Stevens, A. H. (1997). Persistent Effects of Job Displacement: The Importance of Multiple Job Losses. *Journal of Labor Economics*, 165-188.

Stewart, T. A. (1989, November). New ways to exercise power. pp. 52-66.

Stinchcombe, A. L. (1965). *Social Structure and Organizations. Pp. 142-193 in Handbook of*

Organizations, edited by J. G. March. . Chicago: : Rand McNally.

Stouffer, S. A., Suchman, E. A., DeVinney, L. C., & Williams, R. M. (1949). *The American soldier: Adjustments during army life (Vol. 1).* . Princeton, NJ: : Princeton University Press.

Sutton, R. I., & Callahan, A. L. (1987). The Stigma of Bankruptcy: Spoiled Organizational Image and Its Management. *Academy of Management Journal*, 30: 405-436.

Sverke, M., Hellgren, J., & Naswall, K. (2002). No security: A review and meta-analysis of job insecurity and its consequences. *Journal of Occupational Health Psychology,*, 7, 242-264.

Sweeney, P. D., McFarlin, D. B., & Inderrieden, E. J. (1990). Using relative deprivation theory to explain satisfaction with income and pay level: A multi study examination. *Academy of Management Journal*, 423-436.

Swinburne, P. (1981). The psychological impact of unemployment on managers and professional staff. *Journal of Occupational Psychology*, 54, 47-64.

Tangri, R. (2003). *Stress Costs, Stress Cures.* Trafford Publishing, .

Task, A. (2014). *Whining 1%-ers are "wrong on moral and policy grounds": Steven Rattner.* Yahoo Daily Ticker.

Thorpe, R., & Smith, M. E. (1991). *Management Research.* Sage.

Tichy, N. M., & Sherman, S. (1994). *Control Your Own Destiny or Someone Else Will.* Harper Business.

Tilly, C. (1991). Reasons for the Continuing Growth of Part-Time Employment. *Monthly Labor Review,* 10-18.

Tombaugh, J. R., & White, L. P. (1990). Downsizing: An empirical assessment of survivors' perceptions in a post layoff environment. *Organization Development Journal,* Summer, 32-43.

Topel, R. (1991). Specific Capital, Mobility and Wages: Wages Rise with Job Seniority. ,. *Journal of Political Economy,* 99(1): 145-76.

Turner v. North American Rubber, I. 9. (1992). Legal.

Tushman, M. L., & Newman, W. H. (1986). Convergence and Upheaval: Managing the Unsteady

Pace of Organizational Evolution. *California Management Review*, 29-44.

Tyler, T. R., Casper, J. D., & Fisher, B. (1989). Maintaining allegiance toward political authorities: The role of prior attitudes and the use of fair procedures. *American Journal of Political Science*, 629-652.

U.S. Department of Labor. Bureau of Labor Statistics. (2009). *Job Openings and Labor Turnover Survey. January,* . U.S. government.

U.S. Department of Labor. Bureau of Labor Statistics. (2011). *Data on the unemployment rates.* Government Printing Office.

Uchitelle, L. (2006). *The disposable American: Layoffs and their consequences*. New York: Random House.

Ullah, P. (1987). *Unemployed Black Youths in a Northern City. Pp. 110-147 in Unemployed People, edited by D. Fryer and P. Ullah.* Milton Keynes, UK: Open University Press.

Vaherta, J. (2004). Downsizing and Heart Disease. *British Medical Journal*, March 26; 328: 555-558.

Van den Bos, K., Vermunt, R., & Wilke, H. A. (1997). Procedural

and distributive justice: What
is fair depends more on what
comes first than on what comes
next. *Journal of Personality and
Social Psychology*, 95-104.

Vernon, L. (2003). The downsizing
dilemma; a manager's toolkit for
avoiding layoffs. *Society for
Human Resources Management
(SHRM)*.

Vlasic, B. (2008). *Ford is pushing
buyouts to workers*. New York
Times.

Vollmann, T., & Brazas, M. (1993).
Downsizing. *European Management
Journal*.

Wagar, T. H. (2001). Consequences of
Work Force Reduction: Some
Employer and Union Evidence.
Journal of Labor Research, 32
(4): 851-62. .

Walker, R. (1985). *Applied
qualitative research*. Gower.

Walston, S. L., Urden, L. D., &
Sullivan, P. (2001). Hospital Re
engineering: An Evolving
Management Innovation: History,
Current Status and Future
Direction. *Journal of Health and
Health Services Administration*.

Walther, j. (2009). *The U. S.
Congress is too darn BIG!*
truefacts.

Warr, P., Jackson, P., & Banks, M.

(1988). Unemployment and Mental
    Health. *Journal of Social
    Issues*, 47-68.
Weil, N. (2005, Dec 5). Slowing the
    boat to China. *Infoworld*, pp.
    Vol 27 Issue 49, pg. 18.
Weitzel, W., & Jonsson, E. (1989).
    Decline in Organizations: A
    Literature Integration and
    Extension. *Administrative
    Science Quarterly*, 91-109.
Westman, M., Etzion, D., & Danon, E.
    (2001). Job insecurity and
    crossover of burnout in married
    couples. *Journal of
    Organizational Behavior*, 22,
    467-481. .
Whetten, D. A. (1980). Organizational
    Decline: A Neglected Topic in
    Organizational Science . *Academy
    of Management Review*, 577-588.
Widmaier, W. (2013). Obama's pledge
    to raise the minimum wage is
    good policy. *The Conversation*.
Wiersema, F. (2002). *Who's Winning
    and How, in the Battle for
    Customers*. Simon & Schuster.
Wilkinson, C. (1998). *Violence in the
    workplace: Preventing, assessing
    and managing threats at work*.
    Rothstein Associates.
Wilson, S. M., Larson, J. H., &
    Stone, K. L. (1993). Stress
    among job insecure workers and

their spouses. *Family Relations*,
42, 74-80. .

Winefield, A. H. (2002).
Unemployment, Underemployment,
Occupational Stress and
Psychological Well-Being.
*Australian Journal of
Management,,* Special Issue, Vol.
27, p137, 12p .

Winefield, A., & Tiggemann, M.
(1990). Employment status and
psychological well-being: A
longitudinal study. *Journal of
Applied Psychology,,* 455-459.

Winefield, A., Winefield, H., &
Tiggemann, M. G. (1991). A
longitudinal study of the
psychological effects of
unemployment and unsatisfactory
employment on young adults.
Journal of Applied Psychology,
424-431. .

Wise, G. (1992). *Inventor and
corporations in the maturing
electrical industry. In R. J.
Weber & D. W. Perkins (Eds.),
Inventive minds: Creativity in
technology (pp. 291-310).*
Oxford, England: : Oxford
University Press.

Woodard, B., Fottler, M., &
Kilpatrick, A. (1999).
Transformation of an Academic
Medical Center: Lessons Learned

from Restructuring to
Downsizing. *Health Care
Management Review*.

Zhi Boon, u. (2007). Job openings,
hires, and turnover decrease in
2007. *Monthly Labor Review*, 14-
23.

Zieminski, N. (2008). *Workers less
willing to move or switch jobs*.
Reuters.

Zvonkovic, A. M. (1988).
Underemployment: Individual and
marital adjustment to income
loss . *Lifestyles: Family and
Economic Issues*, 161-178.

www.ingramcontent.com/pod-product-compliance
Lightning Source LLC
Chambersburg PA
CBHW060321200326
41519CB00011BA/1801